ESSAYS IN LAW AND SOCIETY

routledge direct editions

ESSAYS IN LAW AND SOCIETY

EDITED BY ZENON BANKOWSKI
AND GEOFF MUNGHAM

ROUTLEDGE DIRECT EDITIONS

ROUTLEDGE & KEGAN PAUL
LONDON, BOSTON AND HENLEY

First published in 1980
by Routledge & Kegan Paul Ltd
39 Store Street,
London WC1E 7DD,
9 Park Street,
Boston, Mass. 02108, USA and
Broadway House,
Newtown Road,
Henley-on-Thames,
Oxon RG9 1EN
Printed in Great Britain by
Thomson Litho Ltd
East Kilbride, Scotland

British Library Cataloguing in Publication Data
Essays in law and society.
1. Law - England
2. Sociological jurisprudence
I. Bankowski, Zenon
II. Mungham, Geoff
340.1'15'0942 KD660 80-41030

ISBN 0 7100 0489 3

CONTENTS

CONTRIBUTORS

Zenon Bankowski LLB	Lecturer in Jurisprudence, University of Edinburgh; co-author (with G. Mungham) of 'Images of Law' (Routledge & Kegan Paul, 1976); author of articles on legal education, legal services, the jury, political trials and anarchism
Geoff Mungham BA, BLitt.	Lecturer in Sociology, Cardiff University; co-author (with Z. Bankowski) of 'Images of Law' (Routledge & Kegan Paul, 1976) and co-editor (with G. Pearson) of 'Working Class Youth Culture' (Routledge & Kegan Paul, 1976); author of articles on the legal profession, legal education, lay advocacy, the jury and political trials
David Dixon BA	Lecturer in Law, Faculty of Law, University of East Anglia
Rhian Ellis BSc	Research Fellow, Department of Education, Cardiff University
Phil Fennell LLB	Lecturer in Law, Faculty of Law, Cardiff University
Tom Keenoy BA, DPhil	Lecturer in Industrial Relations and Management Studies, Cardiff University
Colin May BA, BPhil	Tutorial Fellow, Department of Sociology, Cardiff University
Rose Pearson BA, BSc	Lecturer in Social Science, Polytechnic of Wales
Mike Stephens BSc	Lecturer in Sociology, School of Social Work, Leicester University

Howard Williamson BSc	Research Officer, Department of Social and Administrative Studies, Oxford University
Peter Young BA, MA	Lecturer in Criminology, University of Edinburgh

INTRODUCTION AND OVERVIEW

Zenon Bankowski and
Geoff Mungham

The papers in this collection represent a wide range of theoretical and empirical materials. While the essays are not worked out in relation to any single theme - save an obvious shared interest in the interrelationship between law and other social forms - between them they put on display a spectrum of original work in the area of the sociology of law in this country.

We would not be the first to draw attention to the rapid expansion of this discipline, and in any case the signs of its growing presence are everywhere tangible enough. Thus the last five years have witnessed, in Britain, the convergence of two new journals in the area, several important texts, as well as the consolidation of a number of centres of 'socio-legal' research under the general auspices of the Law and Social Sciences Committee of the SSRC. (1)

Not surprisingly, there are questions and arguments as to how the sociology of law should be 'constituted', and disputes about an appropriate theory, method and focus for the discpline. There has been a concern to establish definitions, boundaries and key issues and from some quarters strong advocacy of specific modes of inquiry and investigation. (2)

The authors in this book are not unmindful of these controversies, but each has settled for his or her own way of resolving them. Significantly, many of our contributors are young scholars and their work provides an important introduction to some of the contemporary work being done by those who represent, as it were, the 'newest generation' in the field. None of the essays has previously been published and some are the offshoots of research still in progress (especially those by Dixon, Ellis, Pearson and Williamson).

The essays are grouped into two sections, one treating with 'Legal Culture, the Legal Profession and the Process of Trial', the other taking up broader issues in the relationship between 'Social Order and the Law'. Although the papers are apparently disparate (in the sense they are not the work of any 'collective'), there are certain convergences and themes in common. This point becomes clearer if we offer a brief guide to the principal aspects of each essay.

In Part I, Fennell's paper offers an analysis of attempts by the Council of the Law Society to manage a series of cases which beset the solicitor's profession in the period 1960-76, principally those turning upon public criticism of solicitors. Fennell examines the ways in which criticism has been deflected or denied by leaders of the profession and discusses the consequences of these strategies of retaliation for the occupational ideology and internal cohesion of the solicitor's profession. In a different vein, May deals with another aspect of what might be regarded as crisis management involving lawyers. May's concern is with plea-bargaining and other forms of out-of-court settlement, and how the judicial authorities have traditionally worked to deny the claim that 'negotiated justice' is necessarily antithetical to due process or the legitimacy of the English criminal justice system. Like Fennell, May deals with the response of one segment of the leadership of the legal profession to criticism of and inquiry into the workings and deliberation of legal institutions and practices.

Williamson deals directly with the trial process, in this instance the role of the solicitor in juvenile court proceedings. He seeks to explain the increasing presence of solicitors in juvenile courts, the strategies favoured by them in what are commonly held to be 'welfare-oriented' forums and the implications of their role in juvenile justice for both their clients and the court. A radically different dimension of the process is taken up by Bankowski and Mungham in their discussion of the 'political trial'. Their paper examines several views on what constitutes a 'political trial', but concentrates mainly on what happens when defendants take their politics into the courtroom. We examine in detail how some specific trial activities are made political, attempting to do this through the study of different litigation tactics where the defence is part of a wider political struggle. The paper's empirical focus is on political trials in contemporary Wales, worked out through the study of the controversial Welsh language issue and Welsh nationalism and how the British state attempted (and, indeed, is still attempting) to defuse these phenomena. The trials they discuss represent only one point of conflict and confrontation between Welsh nationalist groups and the British state. As such these courtroom struggles have obvious, though complex, links with other, wider political developments within Welsh society.

The essays in Part II raise, between them, complex issues of theory, practice and policy. Pearson, for instance, seeks to define some of the key characteristics of the lay magistracy and to look at the long-term implications of increased working-class involvement on the Bench. The core of her argument is that the process whereby key members of the working class are co-opted and incorporated into the legal order will continue to act as a source of stability for the state (by helping to legitimate existing legal structures) unless greater working-class participation, rather than less, is demanded. Pearson justifies this thesis with the claim that the only 'appropriate strategy' for those who wish to democratize the Bench is to demand that questions concerning the structure and process of the magistracy should be publicly debated.

The links between law and social order are explored in Williamson's paper through the study of the workings of a police force in a particular neighbourhood, a community which has developed a widespread reputation for being a 'problem' area with high rates of vandalism, delinquency and other illegal activity. Williamson demonstrates those structural and empirical factors which help determine the police's view of the community and the community's view of the police and police powers. In particular his paper examines that police behaviour which is of dubious legality. Williamson makes the point that, in this working-class community at least, resentment of the police is intensified not as a result of any unlawful police behaviour in itself, but rather as a result of the way in which it is applied. As such, Williamson's essay is an important contribution to the corpus of 'police-community' studies in the British context.

Young's essay engages with the 'law and order' problem by attempting to lay the basis from which a sociology of penal control could be constructed. Young's object is to relate styles of penal control, and the ideologies of punishment and treatment, to the organization of power and of social life in general. In exploring penal control, Young draws substantially from the work of Gurvitch. And, following him, Young insists that the sociological rationale for studying penal control is that it allows an analysis in concrete and theoretical terms of the very nature of social life, of what Gurvitch called 'sociality'. In this way it becomes possible to illustrate the linkages between forms of incarceration and secondary control with broader consideration on the nature of social order itself.

The concept of 'community' has already been (critically) involved in different ways by certain contributors (cf. Fennell, Williamson, Pearson); and Stephens, in his essay, adds a further dimension to the discussion in his work on 'neighbourhood' or 'community' law centres. Current negotiations between the Lord Chancellor's Advisory Committee, the Law Centre Working Group and others are moving towards more detailed discussions of the future operational structure and practices of neighbourhood law centres. Though styles of operation vary quite considerably among law centres at the moment, Stephens identifies four main types of operation which appear to constitute the viable options for future practice. Stephens's essay considers these options and outlines their various advantages and disadvantages; and perhaps most significantly, he examines the nature and extent of community control which characterize the respective four principal styles of operation. Stephens argues that many of the writings from individual law centres and the Law Centres Working Group provide good examples of what they appear to mean by the concept of community control. However, there is no common nor adequate definition of the concept, and it is often - says Stephens - merely equated with a particular law centre's ability to identify local community needs, and to adopt a flexible response to them. On many occasions, the concept is used as if it were a divine command or a touchstone. These loose definitions beg the question of who decides what constitute local needs, and who decides to steer the operations of a particular law centre in one direction rather than another. In short, the law centre movement as a whole has, according to Stephens, failed to face squarely the potential and actual problems inherent in its own notions and practices of professionalism. It has ignored too the historical influences in Britain upon the formation of law centres, the nature of the legal profession and its training so far as large-scale recruitment of law centre lawyers is concerned, and the haphazard and often unsatisfactory nature of the structure of law centres' management committees. These matters are neglected to the detriment of the emergence of radical law centres of the community resource variety. What Stephens is tracing are the inherent tensions between the professional concerns and activities of law centres on the one hand, and the publicly stated goal of the law centre movement to institute systems of community control on the other. In this respect, we find invoked the issues of professionalism, lay participation and control and the drift of public policy in the area of legal service provision.

The paper by Ellis deals with the phenomenon of 'battered women'. There has been a steady widening of interest in, and much debate on, the nature and genesis of this problem. Part of her paper focuses on the effects of the law and its attendant institutions upon the social circumstances of the battered woman. The issues traditionally addressed have included the efficacy of legal remedies available to women who have been battered and proposals and suggestions for legal reform. These concerns form part of Ellis's paper, but they are presented in a context which attempts also to study the assumptions of reformers, legislators and resisters alike, as well as trying to gauge the measure of specific pieces of legislation. Dixon's essay is an important historical study of pressure groups and their influence on legislation and public policy. The empirical focus are those groups opposed to gambling in Britain from the 1890s to the present. Dixon's main concern is to incorporate the analysis of pressure group activity into a wider theoretical perspective on the nature of law creation and the legislative process. His paper is about a pressure group in crisis because of changes in its environment and the group's attempt to resolve that crisis by lobbying for the reconstitution of legal and social policy around a new definition of the situation as promoted by it. Not the least value of Dixon's paper is that it permits us to read the recent Report of the Royal Commission on Gambling (The Rothschild Report) in new and insightful ways. For this alone, the paper stands as an interesting contribution to our understanding of social changes in the reconstitution of the relationship between work and leisure and of the accompanying morality.

The final paper in the collection is Keenoy's discussion of aspects of industrial relations and the law. Two fairly recent developments in the field of industrial relations are (i) an increase in the extent to which terms and conditions of employment are now governed by legal statute, and (ii) the more or less stable institution of incomes policy as a basic or major parameter to increases in wages and salaries. Keenoy argues that these two features can also be seen as critical elements in the emergence of the idea of the 'corporate state' (Winkler, 1975). They would certainly be central to the stability of any economy which was identified as corporatist in character. Keenoy's paper seeks to cover two issues which emerge out of the contemporary debate about industrial relations and corporatism.

First, he advances the claim that the development of corporatism has been a consistent theme in industrial relations since the publication of the Webbs' 'Industrial Democracy' in 1898. The acrimonious academic and political dispute between the Fabians (led by the Webbs) and the Guild Socialists (led by G.D.H. Cole) about the role and function of trade unions in society was, in essence, a debate about corporatism. The Webbs' predictions concerning trade unions' favouring 'legal enactment' as a mode of job regulation are reflected in the running debate about the role of law in industrial relations, and become particularly significant in the arguments surrounding the Donovan Report, 'In Place of Strife', the 1971 Industrial Relations Act, as well as the more recent Employment Protection Act and the Trade Union and Labour Relations Act. In his analysis he highlights the affinity between the Webbs' collectivist proposals and the dominant themes in the current corporatist theses.

Second, Keenoy argues that the role of law in industrial relations can best be understood in terms of a socio-legal perspective; viz., that the increasing amount and scope of 'legal enactment' in industrial relations must be viewed as the end product of a complex process of increasing centralization/rationalisation. Order in industrial relations has, since the emergence of trade unions as significant institutions, always relied upon some form of law; and, theoretically, it is no accident that the proponents of and commentators on collective bargaining have considered it as a process which establishes 'industrial jurisprudence'. Keenoy goes on to say that, given such a perspective, it becomes unrealistic to view the creation of legal statute in employment relations as a particularly dramatic change in the nature of industrial relations. What Keenoy has succeeded in doing is adding an important new dimension to contemporary discussions of the nature of 'corporatism' in British society.

Taken together, the problems the authors explore are manifold and are analysed, as we indicated earlier, from a variety of theoretical and methodological perspectives. Their particular merits are for the reader to judge, but the collection is offered as one contribution towards the developing sociology of law in this country.

NOTES

1 We have in mind the 'British Journal of Law and Society', the 'International Journal of the Sociology of Law', books by Carlen (1976), Grace and Wilkinson (1978) and Hunt (1979) among others, the Centre for Socio-Legal Research at Oxford University, as well as the socio-legal 'outposts' at the Universities of Cardiff, Edinburgh, Kent and Warwick.

2 See especially Hunt (1979), particularly chapters 1 and 6.

BIBLIOGRAPHY

CARLEN, P. (1976), ed., 'The Sociology of Law', Sociological Review Monograph no. 23, Keele University.

GRACE, C. and WILKINSON, P. (1978), 'Sociological Inquiry and Legal Phenomena', Collier-Macmillan, London.

HUNT, A. (1979), 'The Sociological Movement in Law', Macmillan, London.

WINKLER, J.T. (1975), Law, Society and Economy: The Industry Act 1975 in Context, 'British Journal of Law and Society', vol. 2.

Part I

LEGAL CULTURE, THE LEGAL PROFESSION AND THE PROCESS OF THE TRIAL

Chapter 1

SOLICITORS, THEIR MARKETS AND THEIR 'IGNORANT PUBLIC': THE CRISIS OF THE PROFESSIONAL IDEAL

Phil Fennell

INTRODUCTION

This chapter concerns attempts by the Council of the Law Society to manage a series of crises which have beset the solicitors' profession in the period 1960-76. The focus of the argument is upon the way in which the Law Society has attempted to pursue three separate but interrelated goals in the last twenty years. These three goals have been: the enhancement of public image; the maintenance of self-image; and the preservation of solicitors' markets. The Law Society is the professional body of the solicitors' profession. It is controlled in matters of policy by the Council. Members of the Council are elected from the local law societies. In practice it tends to be the most prosperous members of the local societies who become members of the Council, since only they are likely to be in a position to spare the necessary time. The Council also tends to draw its largest block of members from London rather than the provinces: in 1976 approximately 45 per cent of Council members gave London addresses.

One of the major aims of this chapter will be to explain the apparent contradiction in the ideology of the solicitors' profession between the over-emphasis on altruism in the pronouncements of the Council to official bodies who investigate the affairs of the profession on the one hand, and the concern of the Law Society with the maintenance of solicitors' markets so manifest in the pages of the 'Law Society's Gazette' on the other. Hadfield (1975, p. 98) has suggested that two images of the legal profession, the altruistic model and the self-interest model, are separately held by different sections of the profession:

> It is hypothesised that the self-interest model will be espoused by small, possibly unorganised subgroups (or individuals) within the profession itself who are dissatisfied with the operation and effect of the existing rules, whereas the Altruistic model will be espoused by the Law Society itself.

I will argue that this is not the case; rather that, while the Council of the Law Society is keen to present a public image of altruism, it is equally concerned to project itself to solicitors as an efficient market regulator and protector of their financial interests.

In their evidence to the Monopolies Commission in relation to restrictions on advertising, the Council was at pains to emphasise the distinction between professional practice and commerce. They did so in the following terms (Monopolies and Mergers Commission 1976, para. 74):

> A professional man (sic) was expected to observe certain obligations which arose out of the trust reposed in him. Certain common commercial practices were incompatible with the rendering of professional services, and from these practices the professional man was required to abstain. In particular, while professional men competed in reputation for ability, they did not compete by way of advertisement, price-cutting and other methods familiar and unobjectionable in the business world.

While the Council remained implacably opposed to individual advertising, there was acceptance by them of a 'need' on the part of the general public for more information about the availability of services which solicitors could provide. This 'need' could be fulfilled by collective advertising, the Council felt, an activity in which they had been engaged for some time.

We begin by considering the way in which the legal profession perceives its relation to the state. Second, we look at the background against which concern over the profession's image emerged. Next, we examine developments in the period 1963-72 throughout the conveyancing controversy, and the Council's increasing concern with the problem of expanding professional recruitment and the maintenance and expansion of solicitors' markets during this period. Finally, we discuss attempts by the Law Society to secure control over the development of law centres.

Two interwoven themes permeate the legal professional journals over the past two decades, and since these will repeatedly surface in the argument it is useful to refer to them now. The first is that of 'the ignorant public', which has latterly been supplemented with other notions of 'media' conspiracies, 'subversives' and 'political strangleholds on the profession'. In the course of the argument it will become clear that, with one exception, concern over 'professional image' and 'public ignorance' has coincided with periods when the Council perceived threats to the economic prosperity of the profession. The second theme is that of the need to maintain 'the independence of the legal profession' from state intervention in its affairs. This is spoken of at those times when the autonomy of the Society over solicitors' affairs is threatened with interference by state regulation or lay involvement.

RELATIONS WITH THE STATE AND THE PUBLIC

Rueschemeyer (1973, p. 13) has pointed to the prominence in professional ideologies of the 'bargain theory' of profession, according to which:

> Professions strike a bargain with Society in which trust, autonomy from lay control, protection from lay competition, substantial remuneration and high status are exchanged for individual and collective self-control, designed to protect the interests of both clients and the public at large.

Rueschemeyer takes pains to emphasise the stylised nature of 'bargain' theory, in that it over-emphasises the service orientation and under-emphasises the use of outside regulatory bodies in the enterprise of controlling the profession. He also points out that the terms of the bargain theory in most modern societies are not so alien from major tenets and aspirations of the middle and upper middle strata in general (Rueschemeyer, 1973, p. 18).

The major plank of professional self-image is that of autonomy from lay or state control; and, as will become evident, the activities of the Council throughout the last twenty years have been aimed primarily at maintaining this autonomy. There were two organizational developments within the Law Society during that period which are of immediate concern, and we must leap ahead to deal with them.

The first was the gradual development of a fully fledged public relations machinery for the profession. This began relatively humbly in 1956 with the establishment of a public relations department, which grew slowly over the next eight years to boast a staff of 'one solicitor, two girls and an unadmitted man' (Lund, 1964a, p. 464). By 1964 the profession was consulting outside public relations experts to deal with the conveyancing question, and in 1971 a standing committee of the Council was established to deal with professional and public relations. This involvement with collective public relations reached its apotheosis in the period since the last Monopolies Commission report, with the extensive appearance in the press of the 'Whatsisname' advertising campaign. The 'Whatsisname' campaign was aimed mainly at the house purchaser or the small investor, and highlighted, through a number of nightmarish cartoon vignettes, the perils of investing in anything without seeing a solicitor first.

The second development was the establishment in 1966 of a Special Committee on the Future of the Profession, which was made into a standing committee of the Council in 1975. The Committee began with eight objectives:

(i) to select and train sufficient numbers of potential solicitors of due educational and moral standards to meet the public need for solicitors' services;

(ii) to provide continuing education for solicitors to help them to meet need;

(iii) to ensure a satisfactory level of remuneration;

(iv) to extend the scope of solicitors' services to the community;

(v) to promote and maintain high professional standards and maintain the public reputation of solicitors;

(vi) to provide for the organization of the profession and to promote professional cohesion and a pride in their profession among solicitors;

(vii) to keep the law and its practice under review;

(viii) to maintain contacts with the Bar in order to promote the professional ideal.

These two developments can be seen as part of an increasing concern on the part of the Council to establish some sort of regulation of solicitors' markets, to ensure remuneration levels, to project new areas of 'need', to attempt to ensure that these new areas and pre-existing areas were not invaded by other professions or by 'the unqualified man', and to attempt some form of regulation of entry so that the growth of the profession did not outstrip the amount of work available. It is with the emergence and the activities of these two bodies that we shall be most concerned, together with the responses they initiated to various crises which beset their profession throughout the 1960s and 1970s.

THE EMERGENCE OF CONCERN WITH IMAGE

Before the 1960s, the last real crisis of public relations for the profession had occurred in 1938 with the scandal over solicitors' defalcations, an affair which occasioned over 100 parliamentary questions in 1938 alone. The profession was required to put its house in order on that occasion and did so with the introduction of changes in the standard required for entry into the profession, the passage of the solicitors' accounts rules and the accountants' certificate rules, and through the establishment of the compensation fund for the victims of any future transgressors.

In the decade 1945-55, the major triumph for the Law Society was the securing of exclusive control over the administration of the new Legal Aid and Advice Scheme, introduced after the recommendations of the Rushcliffe Committee. The attitude towards the profession at that time is exemplified by that of Sir George Haynes, a member of the Rushcliffe Committee, who was later to remark in a speech to the Law Society in 1973 that it had rapidly become clear to him 'that the administration of the scheme did not call for any lay participation since the administrative committees would be solely concerned with legal discussions requiring professional expertise and knowledge' (Haynes, 1973, p. 254).

As a result of this period of relative success, during which attitudes towards the profession in high places closely resembled those held by Sir George, agonising over the image and status of the profession is notably absent from the pages of the official organ of the Law Society, the 'Gazette'. The only exception to this was the odd crie de coeur about the lowly status of solicitors by comparison with the public esteem accorded to their brethren at the Bar. However, in 1960 the Law Society and most of its members became preoccupied with the public image of the profession. The occasion was the televising by the BBC of a documentary entitled 'The Lawyers', which portrayed both branches of the legal profession in a very favourable light. In 1964 Sir Thomas Lund recalled with pride the part played by the Law Society in persuading the BBC 'to produce it in order to show how solicitors work and that a great deal of thought is put into the work that they do for their clients' (Lund, 1964a, p. 464). The 'Gazette' and the 'Solicitors Journal' are filled with glowing references to 'The Lawyers' throughout 1960-1, the major cause for gratification appearing to be that an estimated 10 million had watched the programme. By July 1961 its popularity was still such that a special showing was arranged in the Metropole Hotel, Brighton, for the National Conference of the Law Society. By now, the question of public image was interpreted, as the presidential address for that year testifies, as 'the public relations problem'. Despite this reference to public relations as a problem, however, the President was pleased to report that the legal profession still enjoyed pride of place in the community. He saw a connection between the need to work hard at public relations and the need to regain lost market positions.

The President's address contained the following plea for vigilance: (1)

> I do not tire of stressing what has not passed unnoticed by the profession but seems to have been accepted almost grudgingly, that over the last 50 years we have lost a good deal of work to other professions, which, to put it bluntly, have beaten us at our own game!

These themes had found constant expression in the writings of Council members in the 'Gazette' in 1960. For example one (Roberts, 1960, p. 433) related that somewhere or other on his peregrinations it

> had struck him with some force that if the good fairy ... could grant only one wish for the profession, this could be that solicitors should have their deserved place in the respect and attention of the public. I know of no other factor which could provide greater satisfaction.

Another was more hard-headed, referring to the Council's record in planning for the future, as evidenced by the fact that they had secured for the profession the administration of the legal aid scheme. However, 'the profession should not be complacent', since 'the trend of legislation is such that traditional forms of work are likely to diminish in the future, and new and artificial work will arise' (Rowe, 1960, p. 479).

Also in 1960 the President of the Law Society urged that the Society should undertake an institutional advertising campaign on behalf of the profession, while letters bemoaned the fact that the citizenry regarded solicitors as 'legally skilled businessmen' rather than 'professional advisers and friends', and 'that we do not seem, once we have been admitted, to regard ourselves as highly as members of other professions'. (2) Indeed, from 1960 on we might be forgiven for mistaking the Council of the Law Society for Pynchon's true paranoiac 'for whom all is organized in spheres joyful or threatening about the central pulse of himself' (Pynchon, 1974, p. 97).

THE 'ATTACK' ON CONVEYANCING REMUNERATION 1963-72

Kirk reports that the profession 'came under heavy fire on account of its policy in relation to costs and the level of conveyancing charges during the 1960s and early 1970s. It did not have many friends' (Kirk, 1977, pp. 145-6). Conveyancing has always provided the largest single source of revenue for the profession. Remuneration had been subject to regulation by a system of scale fees since the passage of the Solicitors Remuneration Order 1883. The rate of remuneration was kept under review by the statutory committee dealing with non-contentious business. The statutory committee included members of the Law Society, and so could be relied upon not to fix rates at a level that would be regarded by the profession as niggardly. In fact, Kirk goes so far as to say that the order 'became the guarantee of the profession's prosperity until 1972' (Kirk, 1977, p. 145).

By the end of 1963 the profession had already come under attack in the media over the issue of conveyancing remuneration. The 'Sunday Times' ran an article in December with heavy criticism of conveyancing charges. By February 1964 Mr C.P.G. Chavasse, a frequent contributor to the 'Gazette' and the 'New Law Journal' on the subject of conveyancing rates, was calling upon the Council (Chavasse, 1964, p. 93)

> on our behalf to cut through the irrelevant arguments which are so often made, and make the point - which incidentally has nothing to do with politics - that in the present system of English conveyancing, lawyers continue to provide a necessary and responsible service for which they deserve to be paid a proper fee.

In June, the 'Gazette' editorial referred to the recent public controversy over conveyancing, to 'the prevailing mood of disquiet' and, most important, to the fact that the Council had sought the advice of a leading firm of public relations consultants who had stated that the Society was 'doing a great deal of good work'. This was a new departure, in that it was the first time that the profession had hired public relations experts in order to defend its markets against public criticism, and possible state intervention. The Council was well supported in this. Mr Vernon Williams of Cardiff alerted the Council, through the correspondence columns of the 'Gazette', to the fact that 'the present situation calls for a man of the very highest calibre ... such a man is needed to put the profession's case fairly and squarely before the very largely ignorant public'. (3)

Suddenly, public relations had become an extremely hot topic. At the Southern Regional Conference of the Law Society Sir Thomas Lund, the Society secretary, issued a call to arms on the public relations front. He informed the assembly that the Council had authorized him to 'obtain the services of an entirely independent and very well-known firm of public relations consultants, and they are now advising us directly on the problems of conveyancing practice and procedure and conveyancing costs' (Lund, 1964a, p. 464). This is an interesting development since it represents a departure for the normal ideal of the profession, which is that no one outside its ranks should be accredited with any competence to pronounce upon matters about which only solicitors are knowledgeable. The rank and file were exhorted to be mindful of the importance of the membership of clubs for improving public relations - 'the golf club, the sailing club, and so on' (though the importance of membership of clubs and societies for the cultivation and maintenance of client networks was likely to have been old hat to his audience). Sir Thomas concluded that it was not sufficient to be 'a good lawyer' (Lund, 1964a, p. 468), but 'it was absolutely vital to be a good fellow and friend if our public relations are to be of the best'.

By the time the National Conference had come round, Sir Thomas's attitudes had become markedly more acerbic (Lund, 1964b, p. 827):

> The public will cheerfully buy washing machines and other consumer goods on the 'never-never' system, but - and whether this is a symptom of the welfare state I know not - they are reluctant

to pay for services, however beneficial those services may be. Therefore it is all the more important that our public relations campaign should explain how beneficial our services really are.

The significance of 1964, then, is that it marked the beginning of the Law Society involvement with the technology of public relations as a means of protecting the profession's traditional areas of business. The next five years were to impress upon the Council that their conveyancing business was not as secure as they might have hoped. The public criticism of conveyancing charges continued unabated from 1964 to 1967. In February 1967 the question of solicitors' renumeration was referred to the Prices and Incomes Board (PIB). The Law Society, after expressions of disgruntlement that professional men should be treated as on a par with those involved in trade, prepared a memorandum which would put before the PIB 'Facts which it is hoped will remind the Board of the well-known words of Adam Smith regarding doctors and lawyers: "Their reward must be such therefore as may give them that rank in society which so important a trust requires."' (4)

It had been in the midst of this climate of unrest about conveyancing that the Committee on the Future of the Profession had been established in 1966. In 1967 its work began to bear fruit. The first chairman of the committee was K.O.G. Huntley who, with masterly circumlocution, outlined the need for the committee (1967, p. 715):

> The costs of conveyancing, which, at any rate, in some respects, having regard to the work we do, are too low, are substantially under attack, mainly, I think, because of a political view.... When land registration takes place up and down the country as it will, ... our gross receipts will shrink, and therefore, unless we become more efficient and work with reduced staff, or exercise our work in other spheres than we use now, our earnings must shrink.... We must concentrate more on seeing that the profession is more properly equipped to deal with taxation and like matters, and by public relations make all aware of that skill. As we sell something so we must make the public aware of us and what we sell.

How starkly this language of the market place contrasts with the later pronouncements of the Council before the Monopolies Commission! Obviously the Council were of the opinion that total reliance on conveyancing would provide an extremely parlous economic base for the profession, and envisaged the necessity to expand, particularly in the areas of taxation lost to the accounting profession.

The publication of the PIB report in February 1968 was met with dismay, the feeling being that there was 'nothing new', but such proposals as were now put seemed in one or two instances to have a 'faintly political flavour to them' and 'the whole thing was marked by a superficiality of approach'. (5) The report recommended that the remuneration for county court work should be raised, but that conveyancing remuneration should be cut. What was perceived as most ominous, however, was the information that there would be a standing reference to the PIB of solicitors' earnings. This would mean that the relative autonomy which the profession had enjoyed through the statutory committee system was likely to be replaced by what the Council saw as politically motivated state regulation. The statement issued by the Council on the PIB report makes this worry quite clear: (6)

> Decisions taken by the Board on economic or political grounds which are inapplicable to a learned profession may turn the Statutory Committee dealing with Solicitors' remuneration ...into mere legal ciphers so far as legal charges are concerned, leaving them the sole task of putting into legal form decisions taken by the P.I.B. from time to time.

Indeed, the theme of the 'political stranglehold on the profession' was particularly prevalent in writings in the 'Gazette', even as far back as the early 1960s. And it was a theme which was to be developed and amplified throughout the crises of the early 1970s.

At the same time as the profession was under 'political attack' in its prime area of business, there was also to emerge widespread concern over the increase in the numbers of practising solicitors. The publication of the PIB report in February 1968 coincided with the appearance of a Special Subcommittee of Young Members on the Future of the Profession, which pointed out that much of the work now done by legal executives ('unadmitted men') would in future be done by assistant solicitors. The advantage of having legal executives do the work was that, although they might command a higher salary than an assistant solicitor, an assistant solicitor might expect promotion to partnership level. In the climate of uncertainty surrounding conveyancing, this expansion could have presented an added problem. However, the Young Members sanguinely predicted that: (7)

> There will emerge a new class of assistant solicitors who will not aspire to partnership responsibilities and status, but who, by reason of the improvement in standards of education and the greater facilities for further education, have chosen to enter the profession as qualified 'men'.

The implication is that they would previously have 'entered the profession' as legal executives. Obviously, for these 'Nature's NCOs' (as one critic of the Young Members' attitudes was to dub them) the joys of the sodality of solicitorhood would be enough to satisfy their ambition. Obviously the Council was anxious to look at the problem of regulating the types of staff recruited to work in a solicitor's office as one way of tackling the problem of market recession, should it arise. Further evidence of this is supplied by an article in the 'Gazette' in which a Mr Montgomery-Campbell refers to 'the continuing concern felt by a great many solicitors at the profession's failure since the war to recruit unadmitted staff in sufficient numbers' (Montgomery-Campbell, 1968, p. 242). He went on to advocate the extension on a national basis of a scheme in existence in central London which placed emphasis upon 'recruitment of lower-stream grammar school pupils and 'A' stream secondary modern and comprehensive school pupils with the object of training entrants for lifelong service as conveyancing, probate, litigation costs and general clerks, who will as soon as possible be qualified as legal executives' (Montgomery-Campbell, 1968, p. 243). Obviously there was a strong desire not to go 'below' the upper streams of the grammar schools to recruit 'admitted men'.

The period 1968-72 is characterised by this continuing sense of vulnerability over conveyancing and manpower, with particular emphasis on the pros and cons of abolishing the scale fee. Certainly there was pressure from the Council for the retention of scale, but many members of the profession, including the Young Member' Subcommittee on the Future of the Profession, advocated its abolition since 'the perpetuation of scale fees serves to disguise the true economics of a solicitor's practice.' (8) In 1972, almost out of the blue, the scale fee was abolished. Kirk describes the development as an entirely welcome one (1977, p. 152):

> Abandonment of scale meant release from the statutory committee. It meant submission of Bills for taxation if the client so required; but it rarely was required.... At a stroke the profession which had been born in chains was free.

The protracted public controversy over conveyancing had left the Council with a number of lessons, even though the profession had eventually been almost totally freed from external control over their remuneration levels for conveyancing. It was now clear that the economic base of the profession was not impregnable. What emerged in the period between 1963 and 1972 was the development of an organizational structure within the National Law Society, rudimentary to begin with but later more sophisticated, to deal with the problem of ensuring that the profession as a whole had sufficient business to ensure its prosperity. This task was to be accomplished through public relations work and through attempts to gather information which would be of use in regulating the growth of the profession and its markets. The lessons learned in this period were to be used by the Council in attempting to combat a new threat which emerged in 1968. That threat was the spectre of the National Legal Service.

'MARCHING AS TO WAR'; THE NATIONAL LEGAL SERVICE

The attention of the Law Society was first drawn to the question of law centres in the President's inaugural address of 1968. Referring to the Society of Labour Lawyers proposals (later to be published as 'Justice for All'), the President saw significance in the fact that the Labour Lawyers 'favoured the setting up on the American plan of Neighbourhood law firms manned by fully paid, full-time lawyers' (Sargent, 1968, p. 654). 'Such a plan', he said, 'would be the thin end of the wedge. It would mean the loss of the independence of the profession and could lead to a total Nationalized Legal Service'. A Mr Ashworth, writing in the 'Gazette' in 1969 (1969, pp. 182-3), alerted the profession to the fact that:

> pilot schemes could be the thin edge of a very sharp wedge. The temptation to sound the cry of a free Legal Health Service would be irresistable and could well be a useful vote catcher for any politician. We could easily find ourselves becoming political pawns.

This, it will be remembered, came at a time when the profession already felt itself a victim of political machinations over the question of its remuneration.

In 1970 came the first Monopolies Commission Report on Professional Services, which as Hadfield (1975, p. 94) records, was met with profound disapproval by the Law Society. In 1971 Bennion advocated the formation of a Council of Consultant Professions to combat increasing attacks of the professional ideal, which he defined as (1971, p. 90):

> a brotherhood the members of which count upon each other. This rules out poaching of clients whether by undercutting or otherwise, and the obtaining of business by ruthless advertising. It fosters co-operation between members of a profession, the training of new entrants, and the helping hand for brothers who have fallen by the wayside.

These ideals were in peril, and Bennion went on (1971, p. 91) to refer to the

> overwhelming need for the individual practitioner to see the dangers that face him, to realise that there are powerful and widespread forces which would like to see an end to private practice as we know it and to resolve to take time and effort to deal with the matter before it is too late.

A number of important developments took place between 1970 and 1972. The first was the establishment of several law centres, the most famous of these being the North Kensington Neighbourhood Law Centre. These law centres were responsible to local management committees on matters of policy, while the lawyers working in them were subject to the ethical codes of the professions. Although the Law Society initially objected to the establishment of such centres on the grounds that they would be socially divisive and would lead to a loss of independence for the legal profession, in a memorandum in June 1969 the Council advocated the establishment of law centres controlled by the Law Society through the existing Legal Aid Scheme machinery. Provision was made in Part II of the Legal Aid (Advice and Assistance) Act 1972 for the establishment of Law Society controlled law centres in areas of need. By 1975 there were fifteen law centres financed from various sources including local authorities, Urban Aid Grants and private charities. However, by 1975 no money had been available to the Law Society to open their centres. As Zander observes (1976, p. 396),

> In other words, the development of law centres, in spite of the 1972 Act, was proceeding without the direct involvement of the Law Society. The Law Society could, however, exert some indirect control over events by its policy on the grants of waivers from the Solicitors Practice Rules required by every law centre.

Later on, as it became clear that the Labour Government had no inclination to implement Part II of the Act, the Law Society began to adopt a tougher attitude on waivers, tightening up their form and issuing them for one year only and revocable at will. They also ensured that centres would not be able to engage in any lucrative business. (9)

Throughout the 1970s the Law Society has repeatedly called on the government to implement Part II of the Act, but to no avail. One worry which seemed to trouble the Council was expressed most clearly by Seton Pollock, the Legal Aid Secretary of the Law Society. It was that 'the general profession and the innovators might tend to fall into "two camps" with a groundswell of mutual hostility threatening to divide them' (Pollock, 1973b, p. 1508). There was also some disappointment in 1973 that legal aid had not been extended to tribunals, work for which Pollock felt 'essentially lawyerly skills were required', but for which 'the profession, for economic reasons, has had little reason to develop the style of advocacy' (Pollock, 1973a, p. 1250).

However, the new areas of poverty law were not without ambivalence as far as Council members were concerned. David Napley (later a president of the Society) showed his scepticism in a review of 'Legal Problems and the Citizen', by Abel-Smith, Zander and Brooke (1973 (Napley, 1973, p. 1798):

> Some - more cynical than this reviewer - have said that the only clearly recognizable consequence which flowed from the taking of Western Civilization to the so-called backward areas was the appearance there of venereal disease.... I have still to be convinced that the millennium will not have arrived for the poorer sections of our society until we have brought to them the benefits of litigation.

However, Napley remained convinced that such benefits as could be brought to the lower orders would be amply provided by Citizens Advice Bureaux and the recently instigated legal advice green form scheme.

The question of legal aid for tribunals came up again in 1973, with the publication of the Annual Report on Legal Aid and Advice, which was the subject of editorial comment in the 'Gazette'. The editorial contested the view that a change in management would result in a 'relaxation of the present restrictions on legal aid', arguing it was 'Unrealistic to suppose that we can undo overnight the ravages which have resulted from the profession hitherto being barred out for economic reasons, from important areas of service'. (10)

Throughout 1973-4 the major topic continued to be 'the future of the profession', with Paul Leach, who was to become something of a soothsayer for the Law Society, contributing a series of articles on the subject of 'Law in a Changing Society'. In one of these he outlined the need for improvement in continuing education, since the reason that so much business had been lost to accountants in the early part of this century was that the profession had not been 'looking ahead'. Had it been looking ahead changes would have been introduced in the training of solicitors. The importance of this topic was underlined in the presidential address at Eastbourne that year, where the suggestion was that a per capita levy of £40 should be accepted by the profession. This levy would finance a system of legal education which would be controlled by the profession. That the autonomy of the profession over entry requirements and procedures was the goal of this enterprise was not in doubt, as the letters to the 'Gazette' testify. One writer believed that 'the main objective of which we must not lose sight, is simply for the solicitors' profession to be responsible for the education of its future members without interference from outside', (11) while another claimed that 'objections based on the expense to the individual practitioner came to nothing when set against this aim'. (12)

In spring 1974 there was a resurgence of interest in the question of legal aid for tribunals. In their submission to the Lord Chancellor's Advisory Committee on Legal Aid and Advice the Council advocated the extension of the 'green form scheme' to tribunals.

They also attempted both to defend themselves against the suggestion that 'lay' representatives were better than lawyers at tribunal work, and to secure the monopoly on paid involvement in the area: (13)

> Although there may be differing levels of skill amongst advocates, it remains clear, the Council argue, that the basic skills and habits of mind can only be gained through training and experience as a lawyer.... The Council emphasise that the lay services should still be utilised, but not so as to foster - at public expense - a new type of advocate designed to serve those of small means insufficiently trained in the law and freed from those requirements and disciplines designed to preserve the high professional standards of the legal profession.

In other words, the Council was anxious that if anyone was to be fostered at public expense it should be the solicitors' profession.

> There was also an expression of alarm from Leach (1974) at the large number of solicitors who will be seeking to become eligible for partnerships, and who will form a high proportion of the profession at a time when prospects in private practice are less certain than for many years.

The Council considered the question of numbers and narrowly defeated a motion that a detailed look should be taken at the raising of exam standards or the introduction of a prohibition on re-sitting failed subjects at a time.

In November 1974, the Law Society published its appendix to the Annual Report on Legal Aid and Advice. The Report called for the introduction of Law Society-controlled law centres, and dealt in detail with the question of control of the activities of law centres. Part II of the 1972 Act had been criticised because it ensured that control would be vested in the Law Society and the legal aid committees, and not in the local community. The Society saw a need to: (14)

> form local committees of laymen with local knowledge and social concern or responsibility, to join with representatives of the Local Law Society and members of the legal aid committees to determine how best the legal services provided could be brought to those needing them and to help in spreading the knowledge of the facilities available.

This policy of 'using the locals to bring the lawyers to the people' rather than involve them in matters of policy concerning the types of service provided, reflects the Council's concern 'to avoid partisanship on behalf of a sectional interest within the community, stirring up political and quasi-political confrontation far removed from ensuring equal access to the process(es) of the law'.

Such partisanship would, in the Council's view, result from control by the local community; whereas what was really desirable was that the lawyers should run the show, telling the community what it needed, with 'lay co-operation and participation'. Such an arrangement would ensure that it was the Law Society, through their representatives, who defined need, the public interest and the lawyer-client relationship.

Speaking in February 1975, Mr Singleton, then the president, felt that the question on everybody's lips at local Law Society meetings was 'What is the Law Society doing to get more work for the profession?' (Singleton, 1975a, p. 181). He pointed to the main problems of 'a general slowing down of business', and 'invasion by outsiders', and asked 'what positive action can the society take both to protect the present fields of work and to explore new avenues'. The foremost avenue to be explored was the publishing of 'the services which solicitors can offer'. The individual solicitor should 'be involved in affairs of every kind and at every level so that people will say "That man is a lawyer and he makes a lot of sense. He is the sort of person I will go to for advice on my own affairs"' (Singleton, 1975a, p. 181).

Singleton returned to this theme in June 1975, advocating the extension of solicitors' advice to 'small businessmen' (and, indeed, big businessmen) on the grounds that solicitors, 'very often jointly with other professional people can help those who want to help themselves and are prepared to make some sacrifices to do so' (Singleton, 1975b, p. 605).

However, the focus of the Council's attention was soon shifted away from small businessmen by the looming spectre of the 'National Legal Service'. Leach reported that the Future of the Profession Committee had reported to the Council on the subject, declaring that national legal services in other countries (Leach, 1975, p. 1219)

> present a forbidding picture which illustrates only too clearly the fact of the legal profession where the state is the master of all. He would be a bold man who could say that our society is entirely safe from peril. The power of Marxists and other anti-democratic groups within the unions and the Labour party itself shows that the danger may be nearer than many suppose.

In the same issue of the 'Gazette' Leach stressed the need to ensure that services were provided competently (1975, p. 1219) if the profession did not want some compulsory continuing education system to be introduced by the government.

Within the year, Leach had woven the threats to the autonomy of the profession into a full-blown political theory - the theory of etatism: 'Etatism is the movement by which the state removes all the props to a free society. It is done in the name of equality or some other label' (Leach, 1976, p. 26). Referring to the attendant limitations of freedom, he talked of the removal or limitation of 'the right to own property, or the right to buy education or medical care, or to amass wealth, or to let houses and evict tenants', and attacks on the independence of the legal profession; he went on to predict that the profession in the year ahead would be 'marching as to war'. The prescience of his prognosis was demonstrated by the announcement within the month of the appointment of a Royal Commission on Legal Services. Leach also promised that the 'problem of numbers' would be examined searchingly over the year ahead, since over 2,000 solicitors had been admitted in 1975.

The appointment of the Royal Commission really set the cat among the pigeons. The President saw it as the result of 'ill-informed, stupid criticism' (15) from the press and some academics. He chastised the critics for failing to realise that 'Unless you have a strong and independent legal profession, there is virtually no defence for the citizen against arbitrary state power'. (16) Others were less moderate in their castigations. One contributor to the 'Gazette' put the whole thing down to the neanderthal qualities of the critics (Barr, 1976, p. 234):

> A moment when shrill voices unite in common criticism of lawyers is one to seize and benefit from. Not because of the calibre of our critics or the lack of it. I wish I could earn a pound a year in my practice for every chip on some of their shoulders.

Also in 1976 the Law Society came under fire for refusing to grant 'waivers' to Hillingdon Law Centre, granting them exemption from the rules against advocating and the sharing of profits with non-lawyers. The Lord Chancellor's intervention secured the waivers for the Hillingdon centre. In May the Council issued a statement on the Hillingdon affair, from which they had emerged as the bêtes noires, inviting the Lord Chancellor to re-open discussion on the siting of law centres and stating that: (17)

> The Society regards it as vital that the same standards of conduct should apply to solicitors wherever they work and that the Society as the professional association, should retain the Statutory powers it already has to regulate this conduct.... The Law Society is in favour of Law Centres. Parliament has given the Society the power to set them up, but we have been refused government money to do so.

At the same time Napley, addressing the Guild of British Newspaper Editors (1976, p. 393), returned to the theme of Law Society autonomy when he expressed doubt as to whether the public

> understood the close connection that existed between bringing the nation down to a level of universal conformity and the imperative need to preserve an independent legal profession. In particular, the administration of legal aid should remain in the hands of the profession. In particular it was essential that lawyers should not become increasingly dependent upon state remuneration.

By July it was clear that the Law Society was not going to receive the money for Part II centres and that the Monopolies Commission had recommended the abolition of the rule against advertising. The controversy over the National Legal Service has continued unabated with the Law Society continuing to advocate the establishment of Part II (now s. 16 of the Legal Aid Act 1974) centres. The essential issue for the Council throughout this controversy has been how to secure control of the development of centres for the Law Society.

CONCLUSION

At the outset I posed the fundamental contradiction of the ideology of the Council of the Law Society, the contradiction between altruism and self-interest. These two conceptions of solicitors' motivations are not, as Hadfield suggests, exclusively held by conflicting groups within the profession. Elements of both are articulated by the Council of the Law Society simultaneously. The reason for this, I have argued, has been the Law Society Council's concern to project an image of itself as espousing ideals of altruism and ascetic public service in order to justify itself to the public and to various state investigatory bodies, while at the same time justifying itself to its own membership. To perform this latter task it had to reveal to the profession at large the extent to which the Society had been bending its best efforts towards the protection and maintenance of solicitors' markets, as well as the extent to which the question of regulating intake of both qualified and unqualified persons was being kept under review. These attempts at regulation took a number of forms.

First of all, the campaign to expand solicitors' markets through the use of collective advertising has been a theme of the last two decades. This trend reached its apotheosis with the drying of the ink on the Monopolies Commission Report and the introduction of the recent 'Whatsisname' cartoon advertisements. Second, there was the prohibition of advertising as a vehicle of individual competition within the market thus carved out. There are a number of possible explanations for this. In his study of the legal profession in the United States, Auerbach draws the conclusion that a prohibition on advertising (1976, p. 43)

> rewarded the lawyer whose law firm partners and social contacts made advertising unnecessary at the same time that it attributed inferior character and unethical behaviour to attorneys who could not afford to sit passively in their offices awaiting clients.

However, a statement of consequences, in the absence of corroborating evidence, does not explain intentions. Certainly a prohibition on advertising defends the market portion of those who have the necessary client-yielding networks established, and also protects the value of the important commodity of 'good will'. However, it is also true of the 1960s and 1970s that there was an increasing concern on the part of the Council to maintain their regulation of the affairs of the profession. Therefore it is possible that Council members, apart from their interest in maintaining their own, mainly prosperous, practices, saw an important need to sustain the sort of fraternal homogeneity which was a prerequisite of governability. It is also true to say that the Society seemed grateful to be able to use the rule against advertising as a sort of Fabian tactic in the law centres controversy.

The third area where increased regulation has not yet been attempted, but is likely, concerns entry into the profession. This is why there has been so much support for the retention by the profession of control over its own intake. The fourth area where the Law Society has attempted to maintain and expand market autonomy has been that of state-funded legal services. The dominating concern of the Council in the law centres debate has been to ensure that control of the development of law centres is vested in the Law Society. The goals to which this policy appears to be directed are the maintenance of private practitioner markets, the desire to avoid a National Legal Service, and also a wish to discourage the politicization of the legal services provided for the poor.

In the period 1960-76, then, we have witnessed the development of an ideological framework within which threats to the profession and in markets could be understood. The salient features of this ideology have been an 'ignorant public', 'political strangleholds' and conspiracies based upon 'etatism', and the imperative need to maintain the independence of the legal profession. It is clear that what the independence of the legal profession entails for the Council is the maintenance of the market of the Law Society. It is certainly true that the politics of the Law Society have been symptomatic of a striving towards the sort of picture depicted by

Rueschemeyer (1973) in his account of the bargain theory of professions.

One fundamental question for anyone interested in the nature and function of ideology is 'At whom are the ideologies aimed?' It would be wrong to draw from the foregoing the conclusion that the rhetoric of professionalism was purely a vehicle for the furtherance of the economic interests of the profession or the bureaucratic interests of its governing body. More plausible is the explanation that the importance of the rhetoric, with all its notions of threats to freedom, vulgar ignorance, the independence of the profession and the rule of law, lies more in the direction of maintaining self-image than in the legitimation of the profession to the public. This is not to deny that the ideas have existed primarily as defences of solicitors' markets and Law Society autonomy from interference by the state or outsiders. None the less, these ideals have a profound cultural significance for many members of the profession, who see themselves, as the Council has encouraged them to see themselves, as members of an imperilled fraternal elite whose ideals are in danger from state interference actuated by malice and ignorance.

While the ideology of the profession should not be treated as the vacuous outpourings of the cynically self-interested, the contradictions between altruism and self-interest remain. For the Council these are quite easily resolved through the idea that the profession requires a sound economic base from which to practise altruism. That is to say that solicitors, by virtue of their calling, are entitled to high status and rewards. If, as Johnson (1972) says, the essence of the idea of a profession is that it is a means of controlling an occupation, then, as the argument of this paper suggests, one of the prime concerns of the sociologist of law should be to examine the ways in which control may be effected or attempted by the controllers, and the goals which the controllers are striving to obtain.

NOTES

1 Presidential address to the National Conference of the Law Society, Brighton 1961, 'Law Society's Gazette', vol. 58, p. 420.
2 Letters to the 'Gazette', 1960, 'Law Society's Gazette', vol. 57, pp. 40 and 280-1.
3 Letter to the 'Gazette', 1964, 'Law Society's Gazette', vol. 61, p. 421.
4 Editorial 1967, 'Law Society's Gazette', vol. 64, p. 145.
5 Editorial 1968, 'Law Society's Gazette', vol. 65, p. 145.
6 Statement by the Council of the Law Society 1968, 'Law Society's Gazette', vol. 65, pp. 242-4.
7 The future of the profession, by the Special Subcommittee of the Young Members, 1968, 'Law Society's Gazette', vol. 65, pp. 96-7.
8 Report of Subcommittee of Young Members on the Future of the Profession, 1968, 'Law Society's Gazette', vol. 65, pp. 198-200.
9 See P. Knightley, Law on the streets, 'The Sunday Times', 4 April 1976.

10 Legal Aid Editorial, 1973, 'Law Society's Gazette', vol. 70, pp. 208-9.
11 Letters to the Editor, 1973, 'Law Society's Gazette', vol. 70, p. 2622.
12 Ibid.
13 Representation before Tribunals, 1974, 'Law Society's Gazette', vol. 71, p. 337.
14 'Report of the Law Society and Comments and Recommendations of the Lord Chancellor's Advisory Committee 1973-4' (24th Report), London, HMSO, p. 40.
15 Question to the President, 1976, 'Law Society's Gazette', vol. 73, p. 202.
16 Ibid.
17 The Hillingdon Affair, 1976, 'Law Society's Gazette', vol. 73, p. 393.

BIBLIOGRAPHY

ABEL-SMITH, B., ZANDER, M. and BROOKE, R. (1973), 'Legal Problems and the Citizen', London: Heinemann Educational Books.
AUERBACH, J.S. (1976), 'Unequal Justice: Lawyers and Social Change in Modern America', London: Oxford University Press.
ASHWORTH, W. (1969), Neighbourhood Law Firms, 'Law Society's Gazette', vol. 66, pp. 182-3.
BARR, D. (1976), To Hell with Lawyers, 'Law Society's Gazette', vol. 73, p. 234.
BENNION, F. (1971), The Plight of the Professions, 'Law Society's Gazette', vol. 68, pp. 87-91.
CHAVASSE, C.P.G. (1964), Diminishing Returns and Rising Overheads, 'Law Society's Gazette', vol. 61, p. 93.
HADFIELD, B. (1975), Two Models of the Legal Profession, 'Northern Ireland Legal Quarterly', vol. 26, pp. 94-105.
HAYNES, Sir G. (1973), Legal Aid, the Community and the Lawyers, 'Law Society's Gazette', vol. 70, pp. 2531-4.
HUNTLEY, K.O.G. (1967), The Future (address to the Holborn Law Society), 'Law Society's Gazette', vol. 64, pp. 715-7.
JOHNSON, T.J. (1972), 'Professions and Power', London: Macmillan.
KIRK, H. (1977), 'Portrait of a Profession', London: Oyez.
KNIGHTLEY, P. (1976), Law on the Streets, 'Sunday Times', 4 April 1976.
LEACH, P. (1974), What Has the Future of the Profession Committee achieved in 3 Years?, 'Law Society's Gazette', vol. 71, pp. 1126-7.
LEACH, P. (1975), Report of the Future of the Profession Committee on a National Legal Service, 'Law Society's Gazette', vol. 72, p. 1219.
LEACH, P. (1976), Prospects 1976 - Bleak - Changing - Interesting?, 'Law Society's Gazette', vol. 73, p. 26.
LUND, Sir T. (1964a), Public Relations and the Profession, 'Law Society's Gazette', vol. 61, pp. 463-8.
LUND, Sir T. (1964b), Public Relations and the Profession, 'Law Society's Gazette', vol. 61, p. 827.
MONOPOLIES AND MERGERS COMMISSION (1976), 'Report on the supply of services of Solicitors in England and Wales in relation to restrictions on advertising', London: HMSO.

MONTGOMERY-CAMPBELL, H. (1968), Training of Unadmitted Staff, 'Law Society's Gazette', vol. 65, pp. 242-4.
NAPLEY, D. (1973), Review of 'Legal Problems and the Citizen', 'Law Society's Gazette', vol. 70, p. 1798.
NAPLEY, D. (1976), Threats to Freedom, 'Law Society's Gazette', vol. 73, p. 395.
POLLOCK, S. (1973a), Review of the Annual Report of the Council on Tribunals 1971-2, 'Law Society's Gazette', vol. 70, p. 1250.
POLLOCK, S. (1973b), Legal Advice and Assistance - the New Real, 'Law Society's Gazette', vol. 70, pp. 1508-9.
PYNCHON, T. (1974), 'The Crying of Lot 49', Harmondsworth: Penguin.
ROBERTS, J.K.D. (1960), Letter from a Council Member, 'Law Society's Gazette', vol. 57, p. 433.
ROWE, H.E. (1960), Letter from a Council Member, 'Law Society's Gazette', vol. 57, p. 479.
RUESCHEMEYER, D. (1973), 'Lawyers and their Society: A Comparative Study of the Legal Profession in Germany and the United States', Cambridge, Mass.: Harvard University Press.
SARGENT, H.E. (1968), Inaugural Address of President of the Law Society, 'Law Society's Gazette', vol. 65, p. 654.
SINGLETON, E.H. (1975a), Whither the Profession, 'Law Society's Gazette', vol. 72, p. 181.
SINGLETON, E.H. (1975b), Help and Self-Help, 'Law Society's Gazette', vol. 72, p. 605.
ZANDER, M. (1976), 'Cases and Materials on the English Legal System', 2nd edn, London: Weidenfeld & Nicolson.

Chapter 2

MAINTAINING THE GOOD FACE OF JUSTICE: THE CASE OF PLEA-BARGAINING*

Colin May

INTRODUCTION

English criminal justice falls within the ambit of a state which claims liberal-democratic foundations. It is important, therefore, that English criminal justice is seen as holding a mandate from the community for the exercise of its considerable reservoir of powers. One essential feature of the claim to hold such a mandate is thought to be the image of criminal justice, which emphasizes the safeguards that the system itself grants individual members of the community against the potential coercive exercise of these powers. In the most general terms, this image is characterized by two features. First, the system is open to scrutiny, so that in any individual case the community can 'see justice being done'. Second, the system places the highest value on the fairness of its procedure so that it is better that 'nine guilty men go free than for one innocent man to be convicted'. (1) This image stands as the exemplar of a reciprocal relation between the criminal justice system and the community. In other words, this image acknowledges that the criminal justice system's accountability to the community involves the safeguarding of the community against the immoderate exercise of powers the community has vested in the police and the courts.

Any threat to this image is a serious matter as, potentially, it can damage the criminal justice system's claim to legitimacy. This paper concentrates on one major issue in English criminal justice, plea-bargaining. I will argue that plea-bargaining, and in particular the suggestion that it is a regular feature of Crown Court practice, poses just such a threat. Plea-bargaining challenges the favoured civil rights image of criminal justice as its occurrence implies that 'openness' and 'fairness' are not pre-eminent. (2) The challenge posed by plea-bargaining does not go unmet, and a section of the paper is devoted to how the legal authorities meet it and struggle to sustain 'fairness' as being the appropriate image of criminal justice. (3)

The study of criminal justice by social researchers has, for a considerable period, been dominated by the notion of a dichotomy between the 'theory' of criminal justice and its concrete 'practice'. (4) The emphasis has been on the 'practice' side of the dichotomy, in the way enforcing the law is carried out, for example, by policemen on the beat. (5) The suggestion in this paper is that to understand how criminal justice maintains its legitimacy, it is necessary to turn our attention to official accounts of justice which emphasize civil liberties. Just as violations of civil liberties may be functional in ensuring organizational goals, so the image of criminal justice as embodying civil liberties may be functional in sustaining the legitimacy of criminal justice. (6)

As a final point in introduction, we must raise the issue of what interests are served by the official ideology of criminal justice. The official ideology grants legitimacy in the first place to law as the guarantor of justice. The ideal of a fair trial is held to be a just conclusion to the investigation of a possible misdemeanour. If law itself was found to be corrupt in some way, then the assurance that it provides for fairness would be lost.

In a classic statement, Arnold (1962, p. 134) draws out a different implication of the official ideology of criminal justice:

> The notion that every man however lowly is entitled to a fair trial and an impartial hearing is regarded as the cornerstone of civilized government. Before this notion considerations of efficiency in the administration of law must give way. Even a criminal caught in the act is still entitled to present his defence to a tribunal which must be ignorant of the event. This ideal is as old as Western civilization, and its significance in our culture is tremendous.

The ideology, then, has a function for the state, as the state must be seen to maintain order by fair means. Also, as in official ideology of liberal democratic societies, the state and the law are held to be distinct; the individual, in theory, is shielded from injustice inflicted by the state as the state itself can be taken to law. As official ideology projects law as fair, it grants support to the liberal democratic state. So, the official ideology of criminal justice serves the state's interest in maintaining its legitimacy.

SPOILING THE IMAGE: PLEA-BARGAINING AND THE CROWN COURT

In terms of the image of criminal justice, the major institutions of law enforcement, the police, the Magistrates' Court and the Crown Court, are not of equal importance. An indication of this disparity is the way the legal authorities react differently to social research which criticizes the three institutions. The suggestion that the police exercise their discretion in an arbitrary, and often coercive, way on the streets and in police stations, is one that is frequently made. (7) Carlen (1976) argued strongly that the Magistrates' Courts offered, at best, only criminal safeguards to protect the defendant against the coercive potential within the institution. Notwithstanding its consciously less critical tone, her argument is supported by the work of Bottoms and McClean (1976). Yet, these studies of the police and of the Magistrates' Court, in spite of the criticism they level at these institutions for systematically failing to realize criminal justice which is fair and open, have not moved the legal authorities to any sustained defence.

The reaction of the legal authorities, or rather their lack of one, does imply an acknowledgment that either the police and the Magistrates' Court are unimportant in sustaining the liberal image of justice, or that it is too hard to link this image with these institutions. In the case of the police, it would seem to be particularly difficult for the legal authorities to present them as giving a high priority to civil liberties when the police themselves have sought to promote the view that civil liberties are an unnecessary obstacle in their work. The police campaign to remove the defendant's right of silence is only the latest battle in the war the police have been waging against civil liberties. (8) In the case of the Magistrates' Court, it may be that their character as institutions of mass justice serves to neutralize the possibility of any strong association with the image of criminal justice. The rapid turnover of cases and the fact that the Magistrates have little legal training could be seen as robbing the proceedings of this court of the dignity and deliberation consonant with the image of justice as fair. We are left with the Crown Court.

In contrast to the police and the Magistrates' Court, the Crown Court has been the subject of far less research which draws critical conclusions. This might itself be an indication of the legal authorities concern to sustain the standing of this institution in particular. The recent study by Baldwin and McConville (1977) does make the strong criticism that in the Crown Court plea-bargaining occurs extensively, and violates the standard of 'open' and 'fair' justice. This piece of research has been the target of a hostile reaction from legal authorities including an attempt to stop publication and, that having failed, an attack on the credibility of the authors' credentials as researchers. (9)

This differing reaction can only be understood in terms of the prime importance of the Crown Court. There are at least three reasons for this importance. First, because it deals with indictable offences, the possibility of 'rough justice' which may be regarded as tolerable in the Magistrates' Court is unacceptable in the higher court. This links to a second, more significant reason: the Crown Court, in offering the opportunity of a trial before judge and jury with full legal representation, is widely regarded as the symbol of an adversary procedure which puts 'fairness' and 'openness' into practice. Third, not only is the Crown Court meant to safeguard the individual from its own coercive potential, but it also has a role in rectifying any coercion experienced by the individual in the police station and in dealing with appeals against injustice made against the Magistrates' Court. Thus Seifman (1977, p. 552) has no qualms admitting that

> Plea bargaining in the 'bargaining' sense does exist, but at a much earlier stage than is currently supposed. Inducements at the arrest and charging stage are not uncommon and are one of the many weapons in the vast arsenal of police techniques of securing vital information ... [because] such imperfections are generally corrected with full legal representation before a judge and jury.

Any suggestion that Crown Court practices are less than 'fair' threatens not only to severely damage that institution's claim to legitimacy: because of its supervisory and symbolic roles, if Crown Court practices are said to exhibit failings, there are serious implications for the image of criminal justice as a whole.

Plea-bargaining refers to out-of-court discussion, usually between defendants and their barristers, which frequently result in the defendants pleading guilty in the belief that they will receive lighter sentences than would otherwise be imposed on them if they were found guilty after going to trial. This process often occurs at the last possible moment, with defendants changing their plea only when they are about to enter a courtroom, which has been prepared in the expectation that what is about to ensue is a full-scale trial. (10)

Plea-bargaining is only one of a number of out-of-court practices which can effect the outcome of a case in the Crown Court. (11) It is, however, the most important in terms of the image of the Crown Court, as any suggestion of a concession over sentence in return for a plea of guilty implicates the judge as party to the negotiations. Plea-bargaining soils the image of criminal justice because, as Seifman (1977, p. 552) says, it implies

> 'Innocent' defendants being coerced to plead guilty for the convenience of the judge and counsel. It pre-supposes 'behind the scenes' justice and bartering for sentences.

The impression that plea-bargaining produces is one much at variance with the official image of Crown Court proceedings: fairness is supplanted by coercion, and public scrutiny is negated by decision-making being moved 'behind closed doors'. The suggestion of judicial involvement violates the image of the judge as an impartial arbiter who applies a presumption of innocence, and gives 'behind-the-scenes' justice its coercive character.

A strong case can be made for the regular occurrence of plea-bargaining at Crown Court level. Plea-bargaining circumvents the trial through strong pressure being exerted on defendants to plead guilty. This is functional for the Court faced as it is with a heavy work load. But a high number of guilty pleas not only facilitates getting the work done, but also serves to legitimate the law enforcement process and particularly police decisions to arrest and to charge. A guilty plea also forecloses any discussion of improprieties that might have occurred prior to the court appearance.

The practice of plea-bargaining does not, of course, account for all guilty pleas. (12) But, given the utility of guilty pleas for the court, the practices of plea-bargaining will account for a significant proportion. In other words, plea-bargaining is not a matter of isolated cases but a set of practices which, though they do not have a highly organized character, can be regarded as a general phenomenon. (13)

Defendants are pressurized to submit to plea-bargaining as the result of two institutionalized features of the criminal justice system. The first is the private, unsupervised character of the police station and the activities within it, which makes it very hard for defendants to mount successful challenges to police evidence in court (Baldwin and McConville, 1977, p. 69):

> The importance of police verbals in this context is that their force is never spent until after sentence. If the defendant wishes to challenge a statement or verbal allegations in court, his barrister will often quickly make clear that this is impossible or, at least, that it is a course so fraught with danger that it must not be undertaken.

The second institutionalized feature is the 'sentencing discount'. It is judicial policy that defendants who plead guilty should be granted a reduction in the sentence they otherwise would have received if they had been convicted following a trial. The Court of Appeal has stated that this policy should be made known to defendants. (14) The official justification for this practice is that a plea of guilty amounts to a display of remorse and that this is deserving of recompense. This is not, however, the way the 'sentencing discount' is viewed by the defendants themselves. Research indicates that they perceive the promise of a reduction in sentence not as a reward earned through remorse, but as an incentive to induce them to plead guilty and forgo their option of going to trial. (15)

In addition to these two pressures, those barristers and judges who are members of the local Bar form a tight-knit network both professionally and socially. As Cain (1976, p. 241) puts it, 'The world of the successful barrister may be both closed and close.' This creates the potential for frequent and pervasive co-operation so that (Heberling, 1973, p. 440): 'the fraternal nature of the English Bar creates an atmosphere conducive to plea negotiations.'

Given this institutional background of the police, of the 'sentence discount' and of the organization of the Bar, it is not surprising that defendants often experience extreme pressure to plead guilty. Often this leads to their pleading guilty even though they believe in their own innocence. (16) In the face of the strong and varied institutional pressures which promote plea-bargaining, the rules laid down by the Court of Appeal in R. v. Turner (1970) to regulate private discussions between judge and counsel provide a very weak and ineffective safeguard for the defendant.

I have argued that the practice of plea-bargaining in the Crown Court is built on substantial institutional foundations. Its systematic occurrence implies that the idea that it is better for 'nine guilty men to go free than for one innocent man to be convicted' is no more than empty rhetoric. As such, plea-bargaining threatens the image that Crown Court practice gives priority to the principle of fairness, and so, potentially, weakens the criminal justice system's legitimacy.

MAINTAINING THE IMAGE OF JUSTICE

The previous section outlined how plea-bargaining can be seen to have damaging implications for the image of criminal justice. I now go on to examine how the Court of Appeal deals with Crown Court cases in which it is alleged that plea-bargaining took place. The way that the Court of Appeal treats such cases amounts to an attempt to nullify the threat that plea-bargaining poses to the image of criminal justice.

The Appeal Court, in attempting to maintain the image of criminal justice, would appear to be faced with a difficult task because there are a number of obstacles, both formal and informal, which have to be overcome before a case actually reaches a hearing. (17) As a result, the cases dealt with by the Appeal Court are ones in which plea-bargaining seems to be particularly blatant, as only the more extreme examples are likely to reach this stage. In addition, the Appeal Courts' task has not been made any easier by the widespread publicity of Baldwin and McConville's study. (18)

In the cases examined below, all of which came before the Appeal Court after the study's publication, the defendants evidently faced judges prepared to grant considerable sentencing concessions if they pleaded guilty. If the defendants resisted the offer, opted to fight and were then found guilty, they were apparently given a more severe sentence than they would otherwise have received. (19) Accounts presented in the Appeal Court of what occurred in the Crown Court tell a tale of judicial activity to encourage guilty pleas in direct contradiction of the favoured image of judicial impartiality.

As an example, we will take the case of R. v. Bird (1978, p. 237), in which the defendant was charged with stealing £200 from his employers: 'Before the trial commenced, the trial Judge invited counsel into his room and indicated that if B pleaded guilty he would probably go free, but should he be convicted by the jury he would probably be imprisoned.' This was not revealed to Bird, who continued to maintain his innocence. His case developed as follows:

> The trial started. Almost at the end of the prosecution's case the Judge again summoned counsel to his room. At that stage a deficiency of over £2,000 had been admitted by the Defence. The only issue for the jury was whether there had been dishonesty on the part of B or whether someone else had taken the money. The Judge again indicated that a plea, even at that stage, would result in a suspended sentence but that a conviction by the jury would result in immediate imprisonment.

When faced with this sort of account of Crown Court practice, how does the Appeal Court meet the threat these cases present to the idea that the priorities of criminal justice are the principles of fairness and of adversary procedure? The arguments used by the Appeal Court often exhibit a tortuous logic that in some cases is almost incomprehensible. But behind them, we see the Appeal Court engaged in a struggle which reveals the commitment to maintain that 'fairness' and 'justice' is the true face of justice.

The main theme that recurs is the Appeal Court's presentation of these cases as showing a lack of concern for 'fairness' and 'openness', which is exceptional. In R. v. Grice (1978, p. 171), for example, the Court said of the recorder who presided at the trial:

> He indicated that he would not pass an immediate custodial sentence if the appellant pleaded guilty, and that had the effect of, so we are told, making the appellant change his mind, having determined up to that point to plead not guilty. That was the clearest form of 'plea-bargaining' and the clearest example of the very thing that should not be done. In our view the occasions that the judge should discuss sentence with counsel are rare indeed and when there is such a discussion, the recorder or the judge, should take the utmost pains to comply with the directions in Turner. It is quite clear that in this case the learned recorder completely disregarded those directions.

The forthright manner in which the recorder is berated contrasts with the more circumspect evaluations the Court usually makes of the actions of recorders and trial judges. But what is characteristic of the Appeal Court's response to plea-bargaining is the way the case is 'explained' as departure from a set of procedural rules (R. v. Turner, 1970). The argument runs that, under English procedure, sentencing is entirely in the hands of the judge, so that if plea-bargaining is to occur the judge must be involved. Though the judge can hold discussions with the prosecution and defence both prior to and during a trial, the Turner rules lay down that such discussions should not touch on any possible reduction in sentence stemming from the defendant's pleading guilty, rather than being found guilty. There is a grey area which does allow for exceptions to this rule, but the high standard of professional practice insisted upon by the Bar is held to safeguard the defendant from any exploitation of this loophole. The combination of the procedural rules with the ethics of professional practice should leave no scope for plea-bargaining. Hence, any instance of plea-bargaining is explained away, by the Court, as atypical. Invariably, the occurrence is accounted for in terms of the failure of an individual judge to act in accord with the rules. This individualistic mode of explanation distances plea-bargaining from the normal operation of criminal justice and, thus, serves to characterize its occurrence as exceptional. For the Appeal Court it could hardly be otherwise, as 'Plea-bargaining has no place in English criminal law' (R. v. Atkinson, 1978, p. 463).

The Court's method of preserving the image of criminal justice through assigning failure to individuals and thus absolving the system may not, however, be wholly successful. The disadvantages of this argument, which the Appeal Court seems itself to recognize, is that it could lead to some judges being seen as having unscrupulous motives. Such an interpretation would further neither the good image of criminal justice nor the Appeal Court's account of the unlikelihood of plea-bargaining, which assumes high ethical standard in professional conduct. Of course, it may be suggested that any individual involved in a case of plea-bargaining is simply a 'bad apple' in an otherwise good barrel. (20) But the danger of this sort of reasoning is that, if used frequently, it undermines its own credibility. Hence the Appeal Court's apparent circumspection in evaluating the actions of judges who fail to follow rules and their care in suggesting the possibility that the actions of these individuals spring not from any Machiavellian intent but, on the contrary, from the best of motives. The Court of Appeal evidently does make a point of implying that, if individual judges fail, their failure is not necessarily because they are 'bad' men. Thus in R. v. Howell the court says: 'The trial judge may have meant well, but what he did could quite readily be interpreted as pressure to obtain a plea of guilty' (1978, p. 239); and in R. v. Ryan 'It was not a case where the deputy judge was putting on pressure. It was done with the best of motives' (1977, 'The Times', 13 December 1977).

These statements do not attempt to maintain the image of justice simply by offering reassurance as to the good character of judges. More importantly, they hint at the role of intentions, whether good or bad, and their relationship to the rules of criminal justice. In both the cases quoted above, the Court of Appeal treats the judge as having failed to follow the rules, and hints at the possibility that this is linked with bringing intentions, albeit good ones, into play. This link indicates that the idea behind rules is that they are a way of dealing with intentions and the problems of unfairness that intentions can cause: problems of bias and of arbitrariness. Judges who fail are those who give free rein to their intentions rather than letting themselves be governed by rules. The point of following rules is to control intentions to the extent that any question of intentions having an influence, for example, on how a judge does his work becomes irrelevant. The Appeal Court, in asserting the primacy of rules, is simultaneously denying that intentions have a place in criminal justice. This assertion is consistent with the Appeal Court's concern to present criminal justice as being 'fair', for a fair criminal justice system is conceived of as one in which there is the rule of law (i.e. rules) and not the rule of men (i.e. intentions).

The image of 'fair' practice and procedure is promoted by the court in the way they deal with cases by another method. In some of the cases the Appeal Court implies that the original result is correct; but, of course, a correct result arrived at unfairly is not to be equated with justice. Here the Appeal Court reasserts the favoured image by saying the ends cannot justify the means: 'When the court was left with the impression that there was no appearance of justice, it could not sustain the conviction however correct the rest of the details, of the trial had been' (R. v. Llewellyn, 'The Times', 3 March 1978); and again (R. v. Bird, 1978, p. 238):

> No one could have complained at the sentence in the absence of the prior procedure adopted by the judge. [But] the circumstances that had lead up to its passing were so irregular that it could not be supported. In order to preserve the good face of justice the court felt obliged to quosh the sentence.

The concern of the Court of Appeal is to see not only that justice is done, but also that it is seen to be done.

This concern is because of a preoccupation with the appearance of justice presented to the public (R. v. Atkinson, 1978, p. 462):

> In this sensitive area, the appearance of justice is part of the substance of justice and it will not do if a prisoner at the general public derive the impression that it is possible either openly or in a pre-trial review, as in this case, or by private discussions between convict and judge, to achieve a bargain with the court.

As the quote suggests, the appearance of justice is felt to be part of the substance of justice. Because the public sees little other than the presented image of justice, then the court itself will be judged by the impression it gives. In the case of R. v. Atkinson (1978) the Court of Appeal emphasizes that the impression given that a bargain may be made with the court, is a false one: 'Of course the trial judge was not striking a bargain with the defence.' The impression received from this appearance is, in this case, dismissed as misunderstanding. The implication is that the layman is one who is moved by the impression he is given, because he lacks any resources of his own to assess criminal justice. The legal professional understands the workings of law, whereas the layman does not have the experience and expertise of the lawyer. In this respect the relationship between the law and the public is unequal, as the legal professionals are held to have a wealth of resources in their knowledge of law and the public lacks these qualifications. The image of law may be seen as the public's one resource regarding law. Therefore, the presented image must be favourable to the courts' claim to exercise justice. Although in comparison to the courts' experience this kind of understanding is felt to be of little value, this is all the public has. Therefore what the court may dismiss as misunderstanding the layman may interpret as injustice.

Hence the Appeal Courts' concern that the layman be given the impression that contributes to sustaining the image of the Crown Court, and to maintaining the legitimacy of criminal justice.

CONCLUSION

The Court of Appeal is concerned with appearances and impressions. In cases where plea-bargaining is established the Appeal Court is often condemnatory, but its actions have as much concern with preserving the image of criminal justice as with countering possible injustice. This response to plea-bargaining does not affect the institutional features of the criminal justice system which are the root of plea-bargaining. There is, therefore, every reason to expect that plea-bargaining will continue to be a regular occurrence in the Crown Court, notwithstanding any declarations the Court of Appeal may make to the contrary. The Court of Appeal will continue to be confronted with cases of alleged plea-bargaining, and will struggle to nullify the recurring threat that plea-bargaining poses to the good face and to the legitimacy of criminal justice.

NOTES

* Geoff Mungham made helpful comments on an earlier draft of this paper.

1 This point has been made in more formal terms by the Court of Appeal: 'There is something more than convenience and expedition. Above all there is the proper administration and the criminal justice to be considered' (R. v. Coe, 1969).

2 For a discussion of the courts which use civil rights as the standard for assessing the quality of justice, see Cox (1975). Note, he sees plea-bargaining as evidence that the courts fall short of the standard (see pp. 212-18).

3 By legal authorities, I refer to the leaders of the profession and, in particular, to the Court of Criminal Appeal.

4 For a discussion of the different forms the dichotomy has taken and the way it has permeated research, see McBarnet (1978).

5 See Cain (1971).

6 In making this point, Blumberg (1967, p. 32) is exceptional among most recent social researchers into criminal justice.

7 For an overview of police discretion and its coercive potential see Box (1971, Chapter 6), and Rock (1973, Chapter 4).

8 The Association of Chief Police Officers stated that they 'will fight hard to have the silence of anyone arrested or being investigated for a crime made "cause of comment" at any subsequent

trial' ('Guardian', 15 August 1978). In evidence to the Royal Commission on Criminal Procedure, Sir David McNee, Metropolitan Police Commissioner, put forward the view that 'Society must recognize that utopian measures introduced to ensure excessive protection of the individual citizen also lessen the chances of criminals being caught and convicted, which increases the risk of further rises in crime' ('The Times', 3 August 1978). Not only are civil liberties 'excessive' and 'utopian', but McNee implies they are an indirect cause of 'rises in crime'.

9 One of the most interesting reactions was that of Sir David Napley, former president of the Law Society: commenting on the research report of Baldwin and McConville, he wrote, in a letter to 'The Times' (12 October 1977): 'It would be helpful to ascertain to what extent the present breakdown in law and order is attributable to the repeated denegration of lawyers and the legal system.' Though it is misleading, the research does not denegrate lawyers; the comment in linking criticism of the legal system with the 'breakdown of law and order' (Napley's terms) reminds us that an uncritical respect for legal ideology is often regarded as essential for the maintenance of public order. For the researchers' own account of the legal authorities' reaction see Baldwin and McConville (1978b).

10 See Baldwin and McConville (1977, p. xiii).

11 The other main practices are dropping the more serious charges on the indictment against the defendant, and the defendant being pressurized by his barrister to plead guilty without there being any suggestion of a plea bargain.

12 See Baldwin and McConville (1977, p. 28).

13 Ibid., p. 27.

14 See R. v. Cain (1976).

15 See Baldwin and McConville (1977, 1978a).

16 See Baldwin and McConville (1977, pp. 59-82).

17 The main formal obstacle in the filtering process that cases go through prior to reaching a hearing in the Appeal Court is the review conducted by the single judge. The main informal obstacle is that defendants often find it difficult to enlist the support of a barrister for their appeal. On the basis of informal conversations I have had with barristers, it seems that a significant factor is that appeal work is often regarded as inconvenient, especially if the barrister works on provincial circuit and is faced with having to travel to London for the appeal. For some illustrations of the difficulties facing appellants, see 'Justice' (1978, pp. 10-16).

18 The widespread attention included the printing of a large extract from the book in the 'Sunday Times' (18 September 1977), editorial comment in the 'Daily Telegraph' (27 September 1977) and 'The Times' (24 September 1977). The BBC radio programme, 'Checkpoint', also devoted one of its editions to plea-bargaining (22 September 1977).

19 In general, the difference was a custodial rather than a non-custodial sentence. See, for example, R. v. Bird (1978), discussed later in the text.

20 Seifman (1977, p. 552) is one commentator who employs the bad apple argument: 'It would be naive to assume that ethical mal-

practice does not exist. However, in England, it is the exception rather than the rule.'

BIBLIOGRAPHY

ARNOLD, T. (1962), 'The Symbols of Government', New York: Harbinger Books.
BALDWIN, A. and BOTTOMLEY, A.K. (eds) (1978), 'Criminal Justice: Selected Readings', London: Martin Robertson.
BALDWIN, A. and MCCONVILLE, M. (1977), 'Negotiated Justice', London: Martin Robertson.
BALDWIN, A. and MCCONVILLE, M. (1978a), The Influences of the Sentencing Discourse in Inducing Guilty Pleas, in Baldwin and Bottomley (eds) (1978), pp. 116-28.
BALDWIN, A. and MCCONVILLE, M. (1978b), Plea Bargaining: Legal Carve-Up and Legal Cover-Up, in 'British Journal of Law and Society', vol. 5, no. 2, p. 69.
BLUMBERG, A.S. (1967), 'Criminal Justice', Chicago: Quadrangle Books.
BOTTOMS, A.E. and MCCLEAN, J.O. (1976), 'Defendants in the Criminal Process', London: Routledge & Kegan Paul.
BOX, S. (1971), 'Deviance, Reality and Society', London: Holt, Rinehart & Winston.
CAIN, M. (1971), On the Beat, in S. Cohen (ed.), 'Images of Deviance', Harmondsworth: Penguin.
CAIN, M. (1976), Necessarily Out of Touch: Thoughts on the Social Organisation of the Bar, in P. Carlen (ed.), 'The Sociology of Law: Sociological Review Monograph 23', University of Keele.
CARLEN, P. (1976), 'Magistrates Justice', London: Martin Robertson.
COX, B. (1975), 'Civil Liberties in Britain', Harmondsworth: Penguin.
HEBERLING, J.L. (1973), Conviction without Trial, 'Anglo-American Law Review', vol. 2, pp. 428-72.
'Justice' (1978), '21st Annual Report', London: Invicta Press.
MCBARNETT, D. (1978), False Dichotomies in Criminal Justice Research, in Baldwin and Bottomley (eds) (1978), pp. 23-34.
R. v. Atkinson (1978), 2 'All E.R.', p. 460.
R. v. Bird (1978), 'Crim. L.R.', 237.
R. v. Coe (1969), 53 'Cr. App. R.', 57.
R. v. Cain (1976), 'Crim. L.R.', 464.
R. v. Grice (1978), 66 'Cr. App. R.', 167.
R. v. Howell (1978), 'Crim. L.R.', 239.
R. v. Llewellyn (1978), 'The Times', 3 March 1978.
R. v. Ryan (1978), 'Crim. L.R.', 306 and 'The Times', 13 December 1977.
R. v. Turner (1970), 54 'Cr. App. R.', 352.
ROCK, P. (1973), 'Deviant Behaviour', London: Hutchinson.
SEIFMAN, R.D. (1977), The Plea Bargaining Process: Trial by Error?, 'New Law Journal', vol. 127, pp. 551-3.

Chapter 3

DEFENCE AND MITIGATION IN THE JUVENILE COURT: THE ROLE OF THE SOLICITOR IN JUVENILE JUSTICE

Howard Williamson

INTRODUCTION

The role of the solicitor in juvenile court proceedings has, with few exceptions (e.g. Anderson, 1978), been neglected in both theoretical and empirical studies of juvenile justice, which is surprising in light of the increasing legal representation of young offenders in juvenile courts. There is of course a danger in attempting to generalize from the study of any one juvenile court for, as Anderson (1978) has noted, the solicitor's function and behaviour is very much dependent on the particular orientation of the particular juvenile court in which he works. In a court with a legalistic orientation (where stress is placed on the individual's culpability) the solicitor's skills are useful and appropriate to the court setting; in a court concerned with the child's needs, greater confusion surrounds the role of the solicitor, for criteria based on the assessment of personal and social factors are not relevant to the legal representative's normal field of professional competence. However, Anderson's typology of 'legalistic' and 'welfare' juvenile courts is somewhat misleading; the court I observed (1) could not be comfortably allotted to either category. Indeed, its orientation was very much dependent on the composition of the personnel on any particular day. Solicitors were adept at determining the specific orientation of the court on each occasion and tailoring their behaviour and arguments accordingly.

HISTORICAL CONSIDERATIONS

Historically, the solicitor in the juvenile court has been conspicuous only through his absence, perhaps because representing juveniles was hardly lucrative. Yet ever since the inception of Legal Aid, solicitors have been considerably slower to appear in the juvenile courts than in the adult criminal courts. The persisting absence of solicitors from the arena of juvenile representation may be attributed to the early conception of the juvenile court as primarily a welfare-oriented forum. The notion that the young offender should be 'helped' rather than 'punished', and the resultant emphasis on individualized justice, together with the wider 'framework of relevance' utilized in the juvenile court, has, historically, distinguished the organization of juvenile justice from that of adult criminal justice. As a result of such distinctions, the value of a solicitor in such a (theoretically) welfare-oriented court was perceived to be a limited one, since the juvenile court performed a predominantly social, rather than legal, function.

It has also been argued that, the more 'legality' and 'due processes' are emphasized in juvenile court proceedings, the more treatment opportunities may be lost. For when consideration of the child's welfare is upmost in the court's mind, it is not fair on the juvenile if procedural requirements or legal objections inhibit the imposition of the most 'appropriate' treatment.

Precisely because the juvenile court is still a criminal court (unlike the American juvenile court, which is a civil court), and so technically conforms to the rules of criminal procedure (Giles, 1967; Ford, 1975), there has never been undue concern for protecting the juvenile's legal rights; nor has the juvenile court often been charged with exercising 'rampant' discretion. Nevertheless, the value of providing legal representation for the juvenile defendant has been increasingly recognized. There does appear to be some consensus of opinion regarding the role of lawyers in the juvenile court: it is felt that they can effectively ensure that justice is done, or at least is seen to be done, and that they can see that the child's interests are efficiently represented (though one might question whether such efficiency is more beneficial to the court than to the child).

In many respects, the solicitor in the juvenile court today performs the same duties as his contemporary in the adult criminal court. In the case of 'not guilty' pleas he attempts to prove the innocence of his client. In cases of 'guilty' pleas, or where a finding of guilt has been made, he attempts to secure a 'favourable' outcome for his client. However, the solicitor performs an additional role in the juvenile court. By virtue of the 'treatment' philosophy of the juvenile court, he undertakes the role not only of the legal expert but also of the 'expert witness' (the social expert), adding his assessment of home background, parental concern, or signs of remorse on the part of the offender to more narrowly legal arguments. As most juvenile defendants do plead guilty, the solicitor's expertise in presenting social arguments (as pleas of mitigation) may often take precedence over his expertise in legal matters.

For solicitors, the specific characteristics of juvenile justice have two important implications. First, the growing acceptance of social and psychological theories of crime causation (particularly in relation to young offenders) and the consequential stress on the need to provide individualized treatment has given the solicitor in the juvenile court new bases for evidence on which to bargain in the interests of his client. Second, the juvenile court's seeming lack of concern with questions such as deterrence or retribution, and its concentration only on the rehabilitation of the juvenile offender, offers the solicitor greater opportunity for arguing in favour of a lenient disposition, if only he can demonstrate to the court that the cause of the juvenile's delinquent behaviour has now been removed. So the juvenile court solicitor potentially has a far greater range of mitigating arguments than his counterpart in the adult court. However, the value and success of mitigation in the juvenile court is limited, for the course of action taken most frequently is that recommended by the social worker or probation officer, not the solicitor. I will also argue that the key value of the solicitor in the juvenile court is to the court, rather than to the defendant: the presence of a defence solicitor facilitates the smooth running of court proceedings. An unrepresented defendant can often prove to be a 'spanner in the works' - interrupting at the wrong moment, wasting time (both deliberately and unintentionally), changing his plea, or because of ignorance (which is often construed as 'awkwardness') involving the court in a time-consuming debate as to whether a 'guilty' or a 'not guilty' plea should be entered. As Carlen points out, 'Solicitors can aid court administration by informally ... straightening out what, owing to either a defendant's lack of courtroom competence or his deliberate strategy, threatens to be a "messy case"' (1976, p. 47).

THE SOLICITOR IN THE JUVENILE COURT

Though representation of juvenile offenders is steadily increasing, not all defendants in the juvenile court are legally represented. In my own study, one-third of those appearing for criminal offences remained unrepresented even on the most critical occasions, namely when the plea was entered and when disposition was made. For those who do seek legal representation there is effectively a very limited choice. Tis is not to deny that a large number of solicitors spasmodically appear in the juvenile court, but, as one court usher observed,

> There are really only two solicitors who do much juvenile court work, and they're always down here. Another one used to be quite a regular, but now he's more often up the top [referring to the magistrates' courts]. You see a lot of different faces, but they're the main ones.

Indeed, these two solicitors readily acknowledge their de facto 'monopoly' of juvenile court work and explain it in terms of the following argument: that they work for large, well-known firms of solicitors; consequently they have been allowed to develop an expertise in juvenile court advocacy; and, given such expertise, they carry out all juvenile court work taken on by their firms; further, given 'networks' of juvenile criminals, and having represented one or two juveniles from such a 'network', their name is passed on when others in the 'network' get into trouble. Both factors lead to the establishment of good reputations ('because we are good juvenile court advocates') and a resultant demand for their services. This demand is fired both by the court, which demonstrates a concern that juveniles should be represented, and by parents, who, prior to a juvenile's court appearance of when 'something serious' (meaning a custodial sentence) appears to be imminent, adopt the conventional lay view that, if you are to appear in court, you need a solicitor. It is of interest that, between the first appearance and the appearance when the juvenile 'may get stuck down', parents often consider that having a solicitor is a 'waste of time'; the reasons for this view are rarely articulated, though one might speculate that working-class parents may feel that smartly dressed, smooth-talking solicitors waste not only their 'time' but also their money. However, while the solicitor may actually do very little for his client, nevertheless there remains substantial client demand for his services.

What, then, are the implications for the defendant and for the court, arising from the presence of the solicitor in the juvenile court? As regards the offender, Carlen (1976) has suggested that the defendant in criminal proceedings may be viewed as the 'dummy player'. Yet the 'treatment' philosophy, which theoretically underpins juvenile court proceedings and the consequential relaxation of formal rules of process (when such relaxation is perceived, by the magistrates, to be beneficial to the case), might suggest that the juvenile defendant is less a 'dummy player' than the defendant in the adult court. Unrepresented juveniles who do speak up at the 'wrong time' are occasionally given an immediate hearing by the magistrates and allowed to make their point; they are not always automatically ruled out of order, out of place, or out of time, as Carlen (1976, p. 82) argues is typical in the Magistrates' Courts. However, once a juvenile is represented, proceedings immediately become more formalized - the solicitor becomes the spokesman for the defendant, and the defendant does regress into a 'dummy' role. In one case, the police were relating the 'facts' of the case and included a report of the defendant's abusive language, to which the defendant started to object. But before he could say very much, the clerk of the court told him to sit down: 'you've got a solicitor to speak for you'. However, the solicitor did not take issue with the police version of the 'facts'. It is apparent that, in the event of conflict or disagreement between the juvenile defendant and his solicitor, it is the solicitor's, rather than the defendant's, word which is accepted by the court. The solicitor controls his client to the extent of refuting in open court statements made by his client. Such disagreement may partially damage the solicitor's reputation in the eyes of his client, but it does not threaten his credibility before the court. A threat to the solicitor's credibility before the court occurs primarily on these occasions when the solicitor undertakes representation of an 'awkward' client.

The 'awkward' client poses considerable problems for the juvenile court solicitor. An awkward client is one who looks cocksure, who fidgets in his seat, who chews gum in court, who appears to show no remorse for his behaviour, and so on. It is crucial for the solicitor to successfully manipulate such a client, to show the court that the defendant is genuinely sorry for his 'bad' behaviour - 'he just doesn't show it very well' - or that his lack of courtesy towards the Bench is a product of 'stage fright' rather than, for instance, some sort of recalcitrance which might lead the Bench to categorize the defendant as a 'no-hoper'. In other words, the solicitor attempts to use aspects of the 'awkwardness' of his client as a contribution towards his plea of mitigation. And one must accept that a lenient sentence which can be interpreted as the result of a successful plea of mitigation (whether it actually is or not is irrelevant) is, to the solicitor and usually to his clients, indicative of adept and profitable legal representation. However, the awkward client poses a considerable threat to the credibility of his solicitor before the court, and particularly before the Bench. 'He must have been mad to have taken that case on', 'that kid obviously doesn't give a damn what happens to him; why is he [the solicitor] trying to get him off', are typical reactions of other court personnel to cases where the solicitor is representing an individual perceived to be an awkward client. The only way in which the solicitor can regain his credibility is by incorporating the awkwardness of his client into his argument for the defence or into his plea of mitigation, thereby suggesting that the reasons for his client's awkward behaviour in court are (in part at least) the same reasons why his client's needs should be given careful consideration by the Bench and a more lenient disposition imposed. Unless this course of action is taken by the solicitor, he will lose face before the court. If he draws attention to the defendant's behaviour but does not attempt to use it as a mitigating factor, he is thought to be doing his client a blatant disservice, so why is he representing him? If he makes no mention of such behaviour, yet pursues his plea of mitigation, he is made to look stupid, for the courts see a solicitor asking for leniency and consideration for an apparently recalcitrant young offender. His only other choice is the one I have described. One example of this approach in dealing with an 'awkward' client will suffice. A boy of 12, with seventeen previous appearances before the court, spends the early part of his case staring out of the window, 'popping' his mouth, laughing and singing. This behaviour becomes increasingly worse while the magistrates are reading through his Social Inquiry Report, and just before the boy's solicitor is about to address the Bench the magistrates give the child a severe warning: 'Behave yourself. Stop making those noises and pay attention to [your solicitor]. He is doing his best for you.' With this background, the solicitor still attempts to make a case for a lenient disposition:

> What, then, is the appropriate action to take today? ... The school feels that he can make progress and be rehabilitated. The school is optimistic.... In my submission, it is still not appropriate to make a Care Order. I don't think the boy understands the severity of his behaviour. This is quite obvious by his demeanour in court: not paying attention, singing, looking out of the window....
>
> This shows how little he understands about the seriousness of his offences....

This was a desperate, and temporarily successful, effort to avoid a 'custodial' sentence being imposed upon his client. The solicitor implicitly denied that the defendant's awkward behaviour was the product of some fatalistic resignation to a 'severe' sentence or of any deliberate opposition to the court; he explicitly asserted that both the boy's criminal behaviour and his awkward behaviour in the court could be traced to the same roots So, although acknowledging the severity of the boy's offences, the solicitor points to the defendant's youthfulness; this young boy does not understand how serious his actions have been, hence his conduct in court. Any rationality behind a defendant's awkward behaviour in court is necessarily categorically denied by the solicitor.

These, then, are some of the implications for the defendant who is legally represented in the juvenile court; what are the implications for the court of the solicitor's participation in juvenile court proceedings? Just as the awkward client proves problematic to his solicitor, so does the unrepresented defendant general problems for the juvenile court. When the juvenile does not have a solicitor, the burden of dealing with the awkward defendant, or any defendant who does not 'know the ropes' or who chooses to obstruct the smooth running of the court, falls on other court personnel, in particular the clerk and, to a lesser extent, the magistrates. As a result, in any case which threatens to be a 'messy case', the court does its utmost to persuade the defendant or his parents to seek legal advice, especially in cases when there is uncertainty as to whether a guilty or a not guilty plea should be entered.

The presence of the solicitor in the juvenile court causes problems of administration and procedural dilemmas for other court personnel; and by the nature of the solicitor's relationship both with his client and with the court, he has little choice but to deal with such problems himself, if he is requested by the court to do so. The solicitor in the juvenile court is himself presented with a number of problems generated by the 'treatment' ethos which is so central to juvenile justice. Solicitors develop tactics to resolve such problems, as I will suggest below. However, a key problem for solicitors is located in the dependence by the juvenile court upon Social Inquiry Reports (SIRs).

SOLICITORS AND SOCIAL INQUIRY REPORTS

Social Inquiry Reports are written on the vast majority of those appearing before the juvenile court and are of crucial importance in relation to the final dispositional decision. As one magistrate in my survey observed, 'The Reports are central to our final decision. In almost all cases, we follow the recommendation of the Report.' This view was reiterated by magistrates on numerous occasions. In many reports, recommendations are on the 'lenient' side, if contrasted to a more tariff-based system of sentencing whereby the disposition reflects the severity of the offence. As a result, the solicitor frequently places the SIR recommendation at the centre of his address to the Bench. In this way, his role is merely to add weight to a suggestion which he considers to be in his client's interests. In these cases, the solicitor does no more than restate the more favourable aspects of the report (though he may contradict or question the validity of some minor adverse point) and conclude, 'I would therefore ask your worships to follow the recommendation made in the Social Inquiry Report.... I can assist your worships no further.' Such pleas of mitigation 'cribbed' from Social Inquiry Reports are a source of irritation for the social worker or probation officer who has prepared the report. Certainly the solicitor offers very little additional information or argument to the court in such instances.

However, in some cases the solicitor is instructed, or feels it necessary, to oppose SIR recommendations. This is usually when the report proposes a custodial sentence, or when it appears that a report and the accompanying recommendation are written for a number of different court appearances in anticipation of findings of guilt for a number of offences. In both these circumstances, opposition to the report is due to concern that the disposition imposed on the juvenile will be a punitive one. A third reason for opposition to report recommendations is when the recommendation is 'lenient in the absurd'. To ask the court to follow such a recommendation would make the solicitor look foolish before the court. The situation is highly problematic for the solicitor. In 'normal' cases, he is either following and accepting SIR recommendations or asking for a more lenient disposition. In these cases, he must demonstrate the absurdity of the report recommendation without implying that something far more severe is appropriate. Once again, the solicitor is treading the flimsy ground between his duty to his client and his credibility before the court.

TACTICS OF MITIGATION

Closely related to the role of solicitors in dealing with SIR recommendations is his role in mitigating for his client. The function of the defence solicitor in the juvenile court, as in any court, is to furnish the court with information which may establish the innocence of the defendant (in contested cases) and, when the defendant has pleaded guilty or been found guilty, to help the Bench in their dispositional decision. Naturally, the information offered by the defendant's representative is likely to be favourable to the defendant, the objective being to show the Bench that a lenient rather than a punitive sentence is more appropriate in the particular case.

The growing body of knowledge relating to the social and psychological aetiology of crime and delinquency and its acceptance in courts of law (indicated by the ever-increasing demand for social, psychiatric and medical reports) has furnished the lawyer with a wider range of potential mitigating arguments. This is especially applicable to juvenile justice. Yet the range of mitigating tactics remains surprisingly limited, though combinations of arguments give the impression of a wide variety of pleas of mitigation. One solicitor admitted that he preferred mutations of the same basic argument whenever possible, for it was an argument which appeared to 'get results' more often than it failed. There follows a catalogue of the juvenile court solicitor's 'choice' of tactics of mitigations, which are carefully combined for each case to produce an apparently 'individualized' plea. They are presented in an order of decreasing importance.

(i) 'Good home background'

There are numerous implications to this argument, the more important being that parental control is in general effective and sufficient, that the juvenile has 'prospects' if he is not scarred with a criminal label, and that he is unlikely to re-offend in the future: he has learned his lesson, and further punishment is simply unnecessary.

(ii) 'Bad company'

Unfortunately, the juvenile 'got in with a bad crowd', and was led along by other boys, some of whom had long histories of delinquent behaviour. However, he has now severed his relationship with such characters, and so will not be involved in such behaviour again. In these circumstances, a token penalty is in order.

(iii) 'Similarity of offences'

Though the juvenile is appearing before the court for a number of offences, these offences are all of the same nature, and all have the same roots (for instance, absconsion offences - offences which are 'necessary' if a boy is on the run). It must be made clear that the court is not dealing with a case of a hardened, adaptable criminal. Any disposition must involve the eradication of the cause; the offender will then no longer be a problem.

(iv) 'Adverse effect of dispositions'

This argument is utilized in cases where there is a strong likelihood of the offender receiving a custodial sentence. Though the Bench may be considering imposing a punitive disposition, and quite justifiably, given the nature of the offences involved, it is important that the magistrates should be aware of the following points. The solicitor then indulges in one of two key assertions. First, he may assert that the defendant has managed to secure a reasonably well-paid job (there is an implicit suggestion here that a stiff fine may be more effective and more appropriate); if he is sent away, he will lose that job. The job may be the biggest factor in keeping him out of trouble. Employment is not easy to find, especially in view of the prevailing economic climate, and if the boy comes out of custody and remains unemployed for any period of time, he may well slip back into his delinquent ways. By imposing a custodial sentence, the Bench may be ensuring that the juvenile will persist in his delinquent ways. Second, the solicitor may assert that the juvenile has been through the 'institutional mill'. He has just settled down, after years of uncertainty and instability, which themselves have contributed to his criminal behaviour. To send him away would merely re-awaken that insecurity and instability, just when he appears to be settling down for the first time in his life. The Bench may be doing society a disservice by imposing a custodial sentence on this particular individual.

(v) 'Cost of institutionalization'

This may be interpreted as an argument of desperation, when no other convincing mitigating factors are readily apparent. The solicitor's argument is short and to the point. He stresses the enormous costs of institutionalization, and acknowledges that the defendant has committed serious offences (for which the magistrates are quite naturally thinking of making a custodial disposition), but then suggests that it is about time the offender put something back into society, and that a custodial sentence will not enable him to do this.

(vi) 'Recognition of the severity of the offence, and remorse'

Whether he is sincere or merely bluffing, the solicitor maintains that the defendant came to court anticipating a custodial disposition, and contends that this is a clear indication that the defendant recognizes the seriousness of his behaviour. The juvenile is very sorry for what he has done, and is full of remorse and contrition. The court appearance has come as a shock to him. The solicitor stresses that he believes that this will be both the juvenile's first and last.

(vii) 'Turning point, critical stage in life'

This tactic is brought into play for older juvenile defendants for whom there is a distinct possibility of a custodial disposition. It emphasizes how recently the offender left school, the difficulty in obtaining employment ('though he has been trying extremely hard, he tells me that he has been to six different places this week ...'), the fact that the 'boy' is now possibly the highest potential wage-earner in his household. In all, it is a turning point for the boy, a transition into adulthood. A custodial sentence at this stage would have an extremely adverse effect on him at such an important time in his life.

(viii) 'Not the "normal" case of ...'

There are some forms of anti-social and illegal behaviour which, at times, elicit extreme reaction and condemnation from the media and other public spokesmen, and a concomitant demand for heavier penalties in order to 'stamp the problem out'. Recent examples might include 'mugging' or, in the context of my own work, football hooliganism and bus vandalism. During the course of these 'moral panics' the courts are likely to impose more severe penalties on those convicted.

Even the juvenile court, with its dominant emphasis on individualized justice and treatment, is not immune to this 'public' opinion, and responds by stressing to defendants that such behaviour will not be tolerated, and by making more severe dispositions for these offences. Deterrence objectives intrude on the reformation goals of juvenile court-sentencing policy. In such cases, the solicitor cannot make use of his usual repertoire of defence and mitigation arguments which have all been carefully constructed around a 'rehabilitation of the individual' model, for the dispositional decisions in these cases are not based on those criteria. What the solicitor must attempt to impress upon the court is that the juvenile's behaviour was, in this particular instance, not the 'normal', typical, case of hooliganism or vandalism 'with which the courts today are unfortunately only too familiar'. Indeed, the solicitor must make the court realize that, despite the public pressures for consistent, heavy penalties, this case - precisely because of its special circumstances - still warrants individualized consideration.

(ix) 'Full co-operation with the police'

One tactic which is increasingly used in juvenile court advocacy involves stressting that, despite the juvenile's criminal behaviour, he has still co-operated fully with the police, and the court should give him credit for this. The implicit suggestion is that, given a defendant's anti-social ways, one would expect him to be awkward and obstinate in the face of police investigation. That he is not must be to his advantage. The increasing centrality of this argument in pleas of mitigation can be explicated by the growing concern throughout the criminal justice system about the public's treatment of, and attitude towards, the police. The lack of respect for 'our law enforcement officers' is viewed in all the courts as a matter of intense concern. Consequently, co-operation with the police, previously taken for granted, now places the defendant in a favourable light, and as a result is now a positive and valuable component in a solicitor's catalogue of mitigating tactics.

(x) 'Victim of the system'

Once again, this approach is relevant only to those defendants who are likely to be sent to detention centre or to the Crown Court with a recommendation for Borstal training. In some respects, it is a pertinent argument. The solicitor blames the juvenile justice system itself for the continuing delinquency on the part of the defendant. The argument is exemplified in one specific case: 'This girl is the product of a court which could not effectively deal with her at an earlier age. She has a lack of respect for authority because of the way authority has dealt with her before....' Blame can no longer be attributed to the defendant himself, and if the court recognizes the truth in the solicitor's contention, it has little choice but to give the defendant 'one more chance'.

(xi) 'Amateur criminologist'

The majority of the arguments presented above touch on some form of social theory of crime causation. However, at times the solicitor espouses a cohesive and explicit theory as to why a certain course of action should not be followed, or why a certain disposition should be implemented:

> Personally I agree that the boy must be shown boundaries or he'll end up in court all the time.... The Probation Officer says that a Detention Centre Order is appropriate. This would cer-

tainly show him the boundaries ... or would it just add to his status within his delinquent peer group?

With the 'amateur criminologist' plea of mitigation a 'theory', whether it relates to the environment and delinquency or to the 'contaminating processes of penal establishments', forms the substance of that plea.

(xii) 'Public commentary'

Solicitors are reluctant explicitly to acknowledge the responsibility of certain offences, for this will jeopardize their chances of securing a relatively lenient disposition for their clients. However, there are times when they resign themselves to the inevitability of their client receiving a punitive sentence. When this is so, they offer what I have termed a 'public commentary': that juveniles who have committed these kinds of offences should be punished; that the juvenile himself realizes that the court has a duty to protect society, or that it has a duty to teach him a lesson. For 'regular' juvenile court solicitors, this is an expedient move. By propounding such beliefs when a punitive outcome to the case is anyway inevitable, they pave the way for putting forward the same views in future cases, but then contesting that a custodial sentence should be automatic: 'One couldn't really complain if your worships said "This city has had enough. We must teach them a lesson." But would it do any good? Juvenile courts are not there just to punish but to assist....'

In documenting this detailed catalogue of mitigating tactics, I have attempted to illustrate how certain very general pleas of mitigation may be astutely blended by solicitors to form what appears to be an individualized plea based on the specific circumstances of the individual defendant. Though the solicitor will incorporate some aspect of the real-life situation of the defendant, many mitigating arguments bear little resemblance to the offender's true circumstances and appear to be no more than a technical construction of points which the solicitor believes will be most effective before certain magistrates.

SOLICITORS AND MAGISTRATES

First, it is important to reinforce the idea that solicitors representing defendants in the juvenile court are continually trying to seek a balance between a powerful (and possibly successful) defence and mitigation, and losing credibility in front of the magistrates. This is well illustrated by a solicitor who, having made an address to the Bench opposing an application for a care order on a boy who had committed numerous and regular offences over the previous few months (and having successfully opposed a similar application some months before by arguing that the boy would not offend again), commented to some other members of the court personnel, 'I've a very nasty feeling that Mrs _____ [magistrate] has set on this case before when I've been there.... Oh dear....' In other words, he had suddenly realized that the chairman of the Bench would recognize the flimsy nature of his argument, because she had already sat at previous hearings involving the same boy (and the same arguments!).

But in general the relationship between the defence solicitors and the Bench may be described as one of 'polite disagreement'. Solicitors make it clear that they quite understand why the magistrates may be considering a particular disposition; however, by the very nature of their role within the court, they are obliged to oppose such a course of action: 'Your worships probably feel that Borstal is appropriate in this case. However, I cannot agree with such a recommendation. I must ask you: will yet another institution really be of any good....?'

As I have already argued, SIR recommendations are usually implemented by the Bench. Solicitors frequently have to oppose such recommendations. Consequently, their work is often a thankless task. But their 'failure' is rationalized by the fact that they were 'very close' to 'succeeding'. This rationalization is made possible because the dispositional decisions are made by at least two, and usually three, justices. Unanimity of opinion about what to do with a juvenile is, in the first place, unlikely in many cases. Additionally, it is quite feasible that one magistrate feels that the solicitor's argument and resultant proposals are realistic and valid ones; however, he or she stands down in the face of opposition from his or her colleagues on the Bench. This may or may not be so; it is not possible to comment on the group dynamics of magistrates' decision-making. But true or not, this is how solicitors argue when their pleas of mitigation have 'failed': 'What did you think of that then? A bit harsh, I think. Mrs ____ [magistrate] was all in favour of a deferred sentence. She was just unlucky to be sitting with Mr ____ [chairman of the bench].'

However, the likelihood of 'failure' is further reduced by a number of improvised strategies on the part of solicitors. Naturally, some magistrates are more receptive than others to the pleas made by solicitors; with other magistrates the solicitor's plea of mitigation may well fall on deaf ears, because their minds are already made up (because magistrates know best), or because they have more faith in the recommendation included in the SIR (because social workers know best). In a court where certain solicitors are 'regulars', they get to 'know' the magistrates well. I am not implying some form of conspiracy and collusion between the Bench and regular solicitors, but rather that magistrates who are receptive to defence and mitigation arguments are distinguished from those who are not. The latter are best avoided, and to accomplish this solicitors think up any possible reason to ensure that a case is adjourned, in the hope that next time the case may be heard before magistrates of the former type: 'It's very important to know your magistrates.... The number of times I've thought up a flimsy excuse for an adjournment purely because I didn't think that the particular magistrates that day would be any good for my client....'

Solicitors also 'manipulate' the Bench in another way. This arises when they are in conflict with another professional group in the court, usually the police. In the event of an apparent stalemate, the solicitor will appeal to the liberal, treatment-based ideology of many juvenile court magistrates. His strategy in this instance is to make it clear that what he wants for his client (and what, by implication, what the police object to) is perfectly in accordance with the philosophy of the juvenile court and the general attitudes of magistrates, so how can it be objectionable? One example was a case that was adjourned, the defendant was released on bail, with both reporting and curfew conditions. (2) His solicitor requested that the curfew be lifted while the boy went to scout camp. The police objected saying that the boy had committed offences and that a curfew was thought to be necessary, so the scout camp should 'go by the board'. No agreement could be reached until the solicitor appealed to the Bench: 'I object strongly to the attitude of the police. This is the boy's first offence.... Your worships are always trying to encourage extra-mural activity.... It seems wrong to stop a legitimate scout camp....' As soon as the Bench concurred with this appeal, the police lifted both the curfew and the reporting conditions altogether.

As may be seen from the above example, magistrates show considerable respect for the solicitor. He may 'lose' a substantial number of cases, but so long as he does not lose the credibility of the Bench the magistrates will help to maintain his credibility before the court, and before the defendant. Likewise, solicitors are aware of the importance of maintaining their own credibility before the Bench, to the point of retracting objections which do in fact have legal validity. In one case, the defendant was being cross-examined by the prosecuting solicitor who asked, 'You've been in trouble before?' The boy's solicitor objected to this question, and demanded a re-trial, claiming that by the very nature of the question it was obvious that the boy did have previous convictions. The magistrates countered this objection: 'Mr _____ [solicitor], this is a dreadful waste of time. How are we ever going to get through all the juveniles in this city if this is going to happen every time...?' After brief contemplation the defence solicitor accepted the point made by the Bench and agreed that the case could proceed.

Magistrates recognize the value of the solicitor to the juvenile court, and appear anxious to consolidate his function within the juvenile court setting. Thus the Bench will often precede its 'judgment' and dispositional decision by saying the defendant (and therefore to the whole court): 'Your solicitor has made an eloquent plea on your behalf, and made us give your case very, very careful consideration. However ....' Only then will the Bench implement the report recommendation. The 'polite disagreement' between solicitors and magistrates remains, but their mutual value is not forgotten.

CONCLUSIONS

If the juvenile court is practically, rather than just theoretically, concerned with providing help and treatment for the young offender, should not the offender take a far more active and positive part in the proceedings (by means of a statement perhaps, or in response to questioning from the Bench) than he does when represented by a solicitor? The solicitor in a more restricted role might still serve a useful function (regarding points of law and issues of procedure), but should he relegate the juvenile defendant to the role of a 'dummy player'?

Although I have suggested that theories supporting the 'external' causation of crime may provide the solicitor in the juvenile court with a wider range of potential mitigating arguments than his contemporary in the adult court, these theories might also contribute to the ultimate decrease and demise of solicitors in juvenile justice. By supporting social and psychological theories of crime causation, the lawyer is stating the case for the increasing relevance of specialists (for example, psychologists and social workers) in official procedures. If this process continues, the determination of any kind of 'leniency' will move to these 'expert witnesses' and will then be right outside the lawyer's control. The use of SIRs and the juvenile court's dependence on them for guiding dispositional decisions is indicative of this process.

Since a large proportion of juvenile court work involves dealing with perceived petty offences ('Mickey Mouse stuff'), a fact that is accepted and even a point of criticism by solicitors, why the need for legal representation? In juvenile court cases where there is a possibility of the offender receiving a custodial sentence, it is obligatory to offer the defendant the services of a solicitor. But in the adult courts, it is thought that legal representation is unnecessary for those defendants who have committed 'minor' offences. Indeed, this is reflected by the fact that those defendants who do choose to seek legal advice for summary offences are frequently ordered to pay legal aid costs in the event of a finding of guilt. Why should the juvenile court be any different? Unless there is great concern about the 'rampant discretionary power of the juvenile court' in England and Wales, and a consequential perceived need for a solicitor to protect the juvenile's legal rights (and the contradictions inherent in the solicitor's role in juvenile justice makes even their ability to do this questionable), it would appear that legal representation is hardly necessary in many juvenile court cases (although Lemert, 1976, contests this point), particularly when the recommendations made by SIRs are likely to be implemented and the course of action taken is likely to be 'lenient'. The solicitor's function in mitigating for his client in such cases is scarcely applicable and usually quite ineffective.

To conclude, it would seem that the key value of the solicitor in the juvenile court is to aid the smooth running and administration of the court by 'sorting out' the 'awkward' defendant, by providing a line of communication between accuser and accused unhindered by language problems (Fears, 1977) (that is, other than those problems between solicitor and client, which are not usually conveyed to the court), and by showing that not only is 'justice' done, but is seen to be done (by giving the defendant his own spokesman) - all in all, to ensure that the processing of juvenile offenders is as smooth and unproblematic as possible.

NOTES

1 This paper is based upon an eight-month observation of juvenile court proceedings in a large city. During this time I

monitored 350 cases (not all of which were legally represented). In addition to being allowed into the court to watch its deliberations, I also had the opportunity to talk to magistrates, magistrates' clerks, solicitors and police as well as the juveniles themselves.

2 This meant that he had to stay indoors between 7.00 p.m. and 8.00 a.m. and report to his local police station at 6.00 p.m. each day. The times may vary according to individual circumstances and the offences committed.

BIBLIOGRAPHY

ANDERSON, R. (1978), 'Representation in the Juvenile Court', Routledge & Kegan Paul, London.

CARLEN, P. (1976), 'Magistrates' Justice', Martin Robertson, London.

FEARS, D. (1977), Communication in English Juvenile Courts, 'Sociological Review', vol. 25, no. 1, pp. 131-45.

FORD, D. (1975), 'Children, Courts and Caring', Constable, London.

GILES, F. (1967), 'The Criminal Law', Penguin, Harmondsworth.

LEMERT, E. (1976), Choice and Change in Juvenile Justice, 'British Journal of Law and Society', vol. 3, no. 1, pp. 59-75.

Chapter 4

POLITICAL TRIALS IN CONTEMPORARY WALES: CASES, CAUSES AND METHODS

Zenon Bankowski and

Geoff Mungham

INTRODUCTION

It is a paradox that all trials, all law in process, are 'political'. Since all courts are agencies of government and judges and magistrates are part of the state apparatus, then all decisions in law can be considered political ones. At the same time there is a steadfast refusal by the state, in this country, to acknowledge the existence of political trials in the legal order. The traditional way of getting over this point and giving the term 'political trial' a specific meaning has been to see it as a prosecution launched with a political (in a narrow sense) purpose. In this paper we are not so much interested in this narrow definition; rather, we will study what happens when defendants take their politics into the courtroom.

This becomes important in times of crisis when, as we can sometimes see happening now, the law begins to deal with more contentious and political issues and different styles of political activity develop, especially confrontation politics and the like. These factors often mean that the confrontation spills over into the court and the trial becomes an important means of denying the authenticity or true nature of the defendant's activities. The court becomes a representation of that confrontation in stylised form; for it is the point where abstract ideology meets those caught in the meshes of the law. The lesson of the trial is the transmutation of political activity into legal processes. This is done not only by translating these activities into legal language but also, through this, by making the defendants symbolically act out their activities in a legal way in the trial. Solzhenitsyn, when talking of the Moscow trials in the 1930s, summed up well the point of them for the Soviet state (1974, p. 374):

> On the threshold of the classless society, we were at last capable of realizing the conflictless trial - a reflection of the absence of inner conflict in our social structure - in which not only the judge and the prosecutor but also the defence lawyers and the defendants themselves would strive consciously to achieve their common purpose.

Our suggestion is, though we impute no consciousness of purpose, that the trial in the United Kingdom can be viewed in a similar light - as showing British society in a consensual light. Viewed in this way, the trial becomes a modern morality play which ends in the triumph of abstract and universal justice.

In British trials, as opposed to the Moscow ones that Solzhenitsyn was referring to, the consensual nature of the world is shown in the appearance of conflict. The British trial takes the form of the adversary system, where two opposing sides battle it out over what is to be considered as the truth of the matter or who has the most coherent vision of reality. But though this is the case in form, there is great pressure to minimise and change this form. If the courts are viewed as bureaucratic institutions then we may begin to see how the proper performance of the adversary system can inconvenience the 'regulars' in the court (by whom we mean not the defendants but those who spend most of their working lives in the courtroom - police, court staff, judiciary and lawyers), by upsetting the smooth running of the courts, the disposal of cases and the relations of 'regulars' with each other. Studies of plea-bargaining and the like show this process quite clearly. (1) They also show how the court can function only if there are extra-legal arrangements to help this process along and, to some extent, settle the case 'reasonably' before the actual trial. The argument that what is at stake is not a contest but the disinterested pursuit of truth can be seen with concern over those modes of legal action (such as certain rules of evidence and procedure) which are regarded by some as hindering the ability of the court to arrive at that truth. The claim that the relaxation of these procedures inevitably leads to more state power is countered by saying that what is at stake is solely truth. And so the trial, far from being a contest, becomes something arranged beforehand with the defendant a bemused spectator on the outside.

Studies of the failure of the due performance of the adversary system apply mainly to the lower courts, but the style that results permeates the whole trial system. We are not concerned here with conscious collusion as such, or with the determining of actual results (though this also goes on); rather, we are concerned with the form that the adversary system thereby takes on. Here one can view the trial as Barthes sees a wrestling match (1973, p. 22):

> It is easy therefore to understand why out of five wrestling-matches, only about one is fair. One must realise, let it be repeated, that 'fairness' here is a role or a genre, as in the theatre; the rules do not all constitute a real constraint, they are the conventional appearance of fairness. So that in actual fact a fair fight is nothing but an exaggeratedly polite one: the contestants confront each other with zeal, not rage; they can remain in control of their passions, they do not punish their beaten opponent relentlessly, they stop fighting as soon as they are ordered to do so, and congratulate each other at the end of a particularly arduous episode, during which, however, they have not ceased to be fair. One must of course understand here that all these polite actions are brought to the notice of the public by the most conventional gesture of fairness: shaking hands, raising the arms, ostensibly avoiding a fruitless hold which would detract from the perfection of the contest.

The general context of the staging of the trial can be defined as a model comprising exclusively the following categories of active participant: the judge, and his auxiliary staff; the defendant(s); the public prosecutor(s); the defence lawyer(s); witnesses for the prosecution and defence; and the jury. And it also encompasses a further passive group, the spectators. By agreeing to accept the part already written for them in the 'drama', radical defendants, without a word being said, have submitted to the morality and procedures of the court. They take their place in a social world characterised by highly formal patterns of interaction between participants. It is accepted that the judge 'guides' the trial; it becomes taken for granted that a defence lawyer speaks on behalf of his client, who should not speak out for himself; it is thought 'proper' to ask only particular questions of witnesses: those put in a particular style and order. Witnesses, for their part, answer only those questions put to them by court officials and do not 'volunteer' information. This reflects an orderly consensual view of the world and shows the paradox in the traditional definition of the political trial (as that of a prosecution launched with a political purpose). For those who hold to this position the political trial becomes totally apolitical in that it reflects the traditional trial and consensus society.

It is into this situation that defendants who see themselves as political come. They take part in a fight in which the rules and meanings and the style of the fight have been 'fixed' beforehand. If they take part on these terms it means that the meanings of their acts have been transformed. They may win legal victories but these are only pyrrhic, since they have only the meaning the law cares to give them. Making the trial political, then, involves transforming the drama and making it give an entirely different message, by keeping the meaning of the activities as those the actors had for them before the trial. Thus what is important is the way that the trial is managed and its relation to outside activities of the defendants and not the actual charges.

We are here making a distinction between being tried for political acts and making the trial political; (2) our concern, in this paper, is not to look at the general considerations we have talked about so far but rather to examine in detail how some specific trial activities are made political. We attempt this in the context of different litigation tactics where the defence is part of a wider political struggle. This is no easy task for the radical defendant, for it involves a rejection of what Goldman calls the 'bourgeois distinction between either persuading the jury or making propaganda for the outside' (1944, p. iv). To be properly a trial it must actually take place in the trial forum and this, of course, makes for certain constraints. It involves, at the very least, some participation in the trial. Refusing to recognise the court would be difficult to categorise, in our sense, as a political trial, for two different things would be going on simultaneously. First, there would be a trial in the ordinary sense and second, there would be someone standing outside of it. Turning the trial into a surrealist farce would do the same sort of thing. Both these options have been taken by political defendants, as has the adopting of a purely legal defence. We are not however here concerned with prescribing what is to be done; rather, we describe what happens when defendants take their politics into the courtroom and try to overcome the 'bourgeois distinction'.

For radical defendants who have collective goals and ideals, presenting these in a legal forum which has the language of individual rights and duties is doubly difficult. In this respect it is often easier to do so in institutions which display what Tay and Kamenka have called the bureaucratic-administrative form of law, a point demonstrated in some of the Claimants' Union's cases before social security tribunals (Rose, 1973).

This shows another problem for the radical defendant, since it is not enough just to 'send up' the court. If the political message, the alternative reality, is to have any general impact, then links with a movement outside and publicity are crucial - otherwise defendants may satisfy their souls and little else. They must perform the difficult balancing feat of being both inside and outside the court at the same time. The best analogy for this is Brecht's notion of the materialist theatre. Bourgeois theatre, Brecht argues, takes for granted that a drama performance should directly reproduce the world. This finished 'real' object is then given directly to the consumers, the spectators, to accept uncritically - there being no possibility of seeing how things might be different. This prevents the audience from reflecting critically on both the mode of representation and the actions represented. Against this, for Brecht, the task of theatre is not to show this fixed reality but to show how characters and events are historically determined and produced and can still be changed. To do this needs a more open theatre, and one of the ways of achieving this is the 'alienation' effect where the actors in the play distance themselves from their roles and critically reflect on them.

We now turn to examine these problems in the context of political trials in Wales. This we do in the context of the Welsh language issue and Welsh nationalism, and how the British state attempted (and, indeed, is still attempting) to defuse them. The type of trial activity that we are interested in then has a significance far beyond the details of actual courtroom encounters. The specifics of these 'political' trials can be fully appreciated only when placed in the broader context of the current agitation for a new political settlement in Wales. The trials we discuss here represent only one point of conflict and confrontation between Welsh nationalist groups and the British state. As such these courtroom struggles have obvious, though complex, links with other, wider, political developments within Wales. Ultimately, the causes must be sought in what Nairn has called the emergence of 'the new national questions' in British politics. In discussing cases and methods, most of our work necessarily deals with the law-breaking and trial activities of the Welsh Language Society (WLS), the most conspicuous of the nationalist pressure groups. First, however, we deal with a trial held in 1936: one which was crucial, for, in many ways, the tactics of the accused came to serve as a model and inspiration for the WLS activists who came later.

CASES, CAUSES AND METHODS I: THE 'PENRHOS THREE'

In 1935 the British Air Ministry proposed to set up a bombing range in Lleyn, in the centre of what is often called the 'Welsh heartland', the core of Welsh-speaking Wales and an area of historic Welsh communities. Much of the opposition to the proposal was mobilised by the newly formed Welsh National Party (WNP) (3) and turned upon the argument that the development of the range would 'destroy the essential home of Welsh culture, idiom and literature ... [and] ... shatter the spiritual basis of the Welsh nation'. (4) Protests about the plan were widespread in Wales, but went ignored outside. In 1936, when the building had begun, three men set fire to the RAF aerodrome at Penrhos: Saunders Lewis (a lecturer in the University of Wales), D.J. Williams (a schoolteacher) and the Rev. Lewis Valentine (a non-conformist minister). Lewis was president of the WNP and the other two were noted party activists. After their sabotage, the three gave themselves up to the police; in statements they asked to be judged by a jury of their own countrymen and claimed that the 'moral law' guided and justified what they had done.

The three men were first tried at Caernarvon Assizes in 1936, in a trial which displayed many of the case characteristics and methods which came to typify the trials of WLS members in the 1960s and 1970s. Some of the defining qualities were well captured in Lewis's final address to the jury. (5) He began by protesting against the refusal to grant an 'all-Welsh' trial (cf. a request for the trial to be conducted entirely through the medium of Welsh). Speeches which had to be translated bit by bit from Welsh into English lost their force and direction; it gave the Welsh speaker what one observer was later to call a part in an 'abominable ... and inferior trial'. Because of these constraints, Lewis elected to speak only in English. His appeal was to the jury's 'moral sense'. He - like the others - admitted to a 'technical guilt', but (Jones and Thomas, 1973, p. 115)

> we hold the conviction that our action was in no wise criminal, that it was an act forced upon us, that it was done in obedience to our conscience and to the moral law, and that the responsibility for any loss due to our act is the responsibility of the English Government.

His attempt to invoke the idea of 'a universal moral law' and the 'essential rights of nations' was stubbornly resisted by the judge (Jones and Thomas, 1973, pp. 116-17):

> You are telling the jury - and I say this in your own interests - the reasons why you took the steps you did and burnt down the aerodrome; and I tell you that that is no excuse in law, and that the more you persist in telling the jury your ideas about Welsh nationalism and Welsh culture, the less excuse there is for having committed this act. So far your argument has been totally irrelevant to the charge.

In the struggle between the judge and Lewis, we see made plain the contest between those who wished to politicise the trial and those who sought to maintain its criminal character. The attempt to hold to a strict separation between the 'criminal' and the 'political' is, as we know, a predictable response of trial managers when confronted by assertive and politically conscious defendants. The particular style of Lewis's defence was said by some to have been 'revolutionary'; it was, argued Thomas (a writer with strong nationalist sympathies), a defence 'very much as Castro's was at Moncada' (Thomas, 1973, p. 56). In the event the jury to whom Lewis had made his sustained appeal failed to agree on a verdict and the trial was transferred to the Old Bailey. There the three spoke only in Welsh and Lewis (with the others) made clear his attitude from the outset: 'I do not intend to defend myself in this court, the authority of which I cannot recognise in the trial of this case, because it has been transferred from my own country' (Fishlock, 1972, p. 77).

This time the outcome was predictable. Each man got nine months in a trial which attracted little publicity and where it was impossible for the defendants to engage the sympathies of jurors (and spectators) as had been done in the first trial in Caernarvon. But, as Thomas and others have pointed out, while the verdict represented a tactical success for the British government, it 'turned out to be a great strategic mistake' (Fishlock, 1972, p. 56), the trial came to achieve an enormous symbolic importance in nationalist demonology; it came to be regarded as the first tremors of resistance and insurrection in Wales, the first bid to arouse what Lewis had called a 'psychologically subdued community', the Welsh. Here, specifically, the particular configuration of the trial of the 'Penrhos Three' re-emerged and was embellished in many of the trials of WLS activists after 1963.

CASES, CAUSES AND METHODS II: THE WELSH LANGUAGE SOCIETY IN COURT

The immediate origins of the WLS are traceable to Saunders Lewis's radio lecture in 1962, 'The Fate of the Language'. In his talk Lewis pointed to the decline of the Welsh language and foresaw its extinction unless efforts were made for its survival. Lewis argued:

> The Welsh language can be saved.... Let us ... make it impossible for the business of local and central government to continue without using Welsh.... It will be nothing less than a revolution to restore the Welsh language in Wales. Success is only possible through revolutionary methods.

The formation of the Society in 1962 by a group of students and teachers in and around the University of Wales was the first response to Lewis's programmatics, and was to become 'the major factor in the language struggle in Wales'. But this reaction was conditioned by something more than Lewis's rhetoric. Two factors were involved. The first was the failure of the WNP to make any real progress after 1945. According to Morgan (1963, p. 303), in thirty years (1926-56) the Party did not once come 'appreciably near' to winning a seat in Parliament. In 1959 the Party made its most ambitious attempt to do so, but twenty candidates attracted only 82,000 votes. Nor had the WNP been seen to have had any great success in lobbying for Welsh interests by constitutional means. (6) The failure of the 1955-9 campaign over the Tryweryn dam site was taken to be a good illustration of the progressive enfeeblement of the Party. The second factor lay in the appeal of Lewis's speech to those who believed that to save the language 'is the only political matter which it is worth a Welshman's while to trouble himself about today': (7) more important, even, than the pursuit of self-government. This point is crucial, for on it turns the tensions which have marked the relationship between the WLS and the WNP - and which in turn have had a bearing upon the character and intensity of the trial tactics and general strategy of the WLS and its membership.

Lewis's rage was against what cultural nationalists regarded as the 'infamous' s. 17 of the Act of Union 1536 with England, which provided for the exclusive use of English in all legal proceedings and by all public office holders. This deeply felt sense of cultural and political oppression has surfaced again and again in WLS campaigns and trials, and much of its activity has been justified by appeals to ancient grievances and wrongs. For Lewis and those, like the WLS, who took their cue from him, the meaning of the struggle for the language - the entire justification for the campaigns of civil disobedience and protest and the subsequent trials - was largely derived from this sense of historical neglect. There were no 'trivial issues' where the defence of the language was concerned, for its preservation was intimately bound up with a particular sense of 'community' and nationhood. For this reason the fight against s. 17 was not a matter of social or legal policy, but stood instead for the resurrection of history itself.

The first of several campaigns of civil disobedience centring on the language issue was launched in February 1963. According to Davies (1973, p. 251),

> It happened that certain members had asked for, and had been refused, Welsh summonses to a Cardiganshire court, but the matter goes deeper than that. The summons, the pre-emptory call to the citizen to answer for his misdeeds, symbolised perfectly the power of the State - and that power must, it was ... said, be exercised in English alone. Moreover, it provided a perfect opportunity for a symbolic act of law-breaking.

Several dozen WLS members stuck posters on government property and other public buildings. The police refused to be drawn, so 'a fair number of members eager to secure a summons, then blocked [road traffic] by sitting down on the road. There was some public hostility and violence, but no summonses' (Davies, 1973, p. 251).

Several points of interest mark this first, rather tentative, encounter, because they help serve as a kind of introduction to the attitudes adopted and postures struck in later and more substantial struggles, including the contest of the trials. Perhaps the first point to note is the low-key approach of the police; their unwillingness here, as elsewhere, to stage the drama sought by language activists. The second is the pursuit of law-breaking by WLS members for the purpose of orchestrating a courtroom procedure which they could present as a 'show trial' and use as a platform for propaganda; a political trial - in their terms - in which not merely an individual or even a group would be put on display, but an entire nation and its culture. Third is the tacit - and often more overt and explicit - support of some segments of the Welsh intelligentsia (their significance becomes clearer in the last section of this paper), especially Welsh-speaking teachers and ministers, but also including influential groups of state functionaries of different kinds. Fourth is the evident sympathy of some police and factions of the lower judiciary, in a predominantly Welsh-speaking area, with the aims and tactics of the WLS. In other words, the law was not able in 1963, or at any time since, to present itself as a monolith in the face of nationalist pressures. The local state, in many parts of Welsh-speaking Wales, was ready to listen, to ignore or do a trade in sympathy with WLS law-breakers. Fifth is the resentment of some sections of the public to the road-blocking, which Davies noted was in part an expression of the strong antagonisms the language issue stirred up, even among some Welsh-speakers. At base, we are talking here of the anxieties of the monoglot English and Welsh about their possible future in a fully bilingual and separate Welsh state. And finally - and by way of sharp contrast to these local fears - there is the responsiveness of the central state to the language issue and the apparent willingness of the British government to listen to the demands of the WLS and its supporters.

As proof of this last point a Government Committee (8) was set up in 1963, shortly after the first round of demonstrations, to clarify the legal status of Welsh and to consider changes. The Committee sat for two years, during which time the WLS suspended all campaigning. A general election was held (1964) in this interval, and again the WNP made no progress - a failure that seemed to confirm once again the futility of contesting elections. The Committee finally reported in October 1965; it endorsed the principle of 'equal validity' for the Welsh and English languages, and its recommendations on the use of Welsh in public life formed the basis of the Welsh Language Act 1967. The 1967 Act purported to repeal s. 17 of the Act of Union, and - where the courts were concerned - it gave 'any party, witness or other person' the right to speak Welsh in trial proceedings.

But the Report also became a launching pad for new WLS campaigns. In November 1965 post office buildings were occupied in various parts of Wales, as part of a demand for more official forms to be made bilingual. According to Davies, the leaders' expectations were vague, but included the assumption that there would be summonses, fines and even imprisonment - and by this route a chance to take the struggle into the law courts and against the law itself. In the event, however, the vision evaporated: 'the authorities failed to respond and the demonstrations came to an end'. The following year a campaign was started for road fund licence application forms to be made bilingual. On this occasion there was a reaction; the secretary of the WLS was jailed along with two other members, for driving untaxed motorcars. Incarceration, though brief (none got more than two months and this after persistently offending), was viewed as a valediction: 'These imprisonments, the first serious confrontations, were a turning point; at last the hidden oppression of the Welsh language had been made clear and explicit' (Davies, 1973, p. 255).

We suggested earlier that political trial activity in Wales required to be placed in the context of broader struggles for nationalist objectives, for a full appreciation of their development and significance. This point is partially confirmed by events in 1966, a general election year. The election was a triumph for the WNP; it won its first parliamentary seat and did well in several constituencies. The results seemed to indicate that the parliamentary road to self-determination was at last open. This deduction would appear to explain partly the diminution of WLS activities in the next three years. What may also help account for the subsidence was the interest in watching the progress of the 1967 Act. Thus the re-emergence of active campaigning on a large scale in 1969 is thought to be largely attributable to the realisation that the 1967 Act did not make the principle of equal validity effective as of right. As Butt-Phillips put it, 'Much still depended on the willingness and liberalism of individual government ministers and local authorities in following up the Welsh Language Act' (1975, p. 233).

The WLS decided to call attention to the situation by starting a campaign for bilingual road signs in 1969. Before the end of 1969, eighteen members of the WLS had been arrested and fined. One such trial involved the then chairman of the WLS, Dafydd Iwan, yet another student of the University of Wales, and - more significant - a well-known Welsh pop singer. Iwan refused to plead, refused to recognise the court, and chose only to make a final defence speech, in the course of which he said (quoted in Davies, 1973, p. 59):

> You accuse me of inciting my fellow members to act; but I am afraid that I do not deserve that praise ... like me ... they have been moved by the crisis of their nation and language ... incited and terrified by the possibility of the death of that nation and language.

Similar litigation tactics and political defences were favoured in many other trials of the time. There was a confused and divided response among the Welsh to the campaign; the WNP blamed their poor showing in the local elections of 1969 on 'language militants'. Yet it was clear that the WLS could count upon sponsors and sympathisers influential in Welsh cultural life. In one instance the Archbishop of Wales publicly declared: 'it would be a pity if unreasonable and stupid official attitudes to reasonable demands should seem to encourage the violence we all deplore' (quoted in Butt-Phillips, 1975, p. 234).

What is of interest here is not simply the manifestations of that kind of moral crusading opinion that would regularly invoke itself in support of the WLS, but also the fear - expressed at other times too - that a refusal to condone or 'understand' such acts of law-breaking might have the effect of driving a segment of Welsh youth to political extremism. The spectre of Northern Ireland was summoned up; from this perspective, any refusal to consider the weight of Lewis's 'moral law' might propel some Welshmen into desperate sectarian violence.

At the end of 1969 the WLS decided to suspend the road signs campaign for one year to allow, it was said, local authorities to reconsider requests for a fully bilingual policy. But it is much more probable that suspension had a connection with the Society's new campaign against the investiture of the Prince of Wales at Caernarvon Castle in the summer of 1969. The attacks on the ceremony increased interest (outside Wales, in particular) in the WLS. Their criticism, which mobilised a wider strain of middle-class radicalism in Wales, drew upon the support of those members of the Welsh intelligentsia who were, in Butt-Phillips's terms, 'alienated from the norms of Anglo-Saxon culture [being] anti-establishment, anti-cosmopolitan ... and anti-monarchist' (1975, p. 234). A similar point was made by Thomas, who argued that the campaigns of 1969, together with the trial activity they generated, meant the steady 'radicalisation' of older members of the Welsh-speaking community, as the non-constitutional and extra-legal opposition of the WLS seemed to be the only vehicle prepared to agitate seriously for the cultural nationalist interest. While there is some evidence to support this thesis, there was more convincing evidence still of the polarising effects of the 1969 struggles, even within the Welsh heartland. In the 1970 general election the WNP lost its only seat and blamed defeat on the 'extremism' of the WLS. There was also renewed hostility between sections of the public and WLS activists, leading to sporadic outbreaks of violence.

Thomas's belief about a process of 'radicalisation' probably drew its inspirations from a quite separate civil disobedience campaign in 1969, dreamed up by the Welsh literary magazine, 'Barn'. The editor launched a crusade for a bilingual road fund licence disc by urging people to sign a pledge not to display a disc unless these were printed bilingually. In all, 642 took the 'Barn' pledge; but it was not the numbers that were important, but the social connections and credentials of those who signed: 40 per cent were schoolteachers, 14 per cent university lecturers, 14 per cent ministers of religion, and several were senior staff members of the BBC in Wales. Within eight weeks the government gave way; this example illustrated yet again the readiness - and the practical effectiveness - of one stratum of the Welsh intelligentsia to defect on the language issue and to set up, albeit in a small way, in opposition to prevailing state policies.

In the period 1969-71, the WLS was constantly in the news, in a cycle of court cases, imprisonments, demonstrations and occupations of courts and BBC buildings. In January 1970 Iwan was again arrested and jailed for refusing to pay fines on a 1969 road sign charge. Twenty-one magistrates contributed to a fund to pay the fine and secure his release. The originator of this move was a former national librarian of Wales, who wrote a letter to forty lay justices arguing it was necessary to begin to heal the growing chasm between the older and younger generation of Welsh-speakers. One magistrate, in sending money to the fund, wrote: 'I feel there is a difference between a criminal act and an act of conscience.' (9) It was a sentiment taken up and repeated in many other similar cases. The significance of this development lay not in any general 'politicisation' of the community elders in some more radical direction, but in the fracturing of the law enforcement machinery of the state. It is no exaggeration to say that by this time the loyalty of those who manned the lower courts in the Welsh heartland to 'English law' was increasingly problematical.

The road signs campaign was not exhausted by Iwan's trial. In 1971 there was staged the biggest and most politically charged of all such cases in Wales, and again Iwan was involved. This trial and the setting up by the Secretary of State for Wales of a committee to investigate the question of bilingual road signs, were widely regarded in Wales as peaks in the language campaign.

The trial involved eight members of the WLS, arraigned on conspiracy charges. At the first hearing at Aberystwyth Magistrates' Court, the defnedants asked that the Bench recommend they be committed for trial at Carmarthen Assizes, claiming that it was important that the trial be heard by a Welsh-speaking judge and jury, in a Welsh-speaking area. The Bench agreed. Even during this stage of preliminary hearings, there were accusations that the trial was 'political'; over sixty WLS members who staged a sitdown in the court were ejected. As this happened, another twenty-five demonstrators outside dumped a mass of English road signs on the steps of the court building. As the hearing started there were impromptu speeches and singing from the public gallery.

From Aberystwyth the case moved to Carmarthen, where the application for proceeding with conspiracy charges against the eight was considered. All eight refused to plead or recognise the court. Before the hearing there were protests outside the building; inside, fifty WLS members who sang and shouted from the well of the court were all imprisoned for a weekend for what the judge called 'the greatest contempt of court' he had ever seen. After listening to the defendants' statements the judge ruled:

> Although in the main they were political speeches I appreciate the strength of their feelings. But this court has nothing to do with politics. It is only interested in administering justice. The same applied to the assize court at Swansea. This case will be transferred to Swansea where justice will be done.

Swansea is an anglicised area of South Wales. At the Swansea Assizes the eight defendants demanded an all-Welsh trial, with an all-Welsh-speaking jury, basing their appeal on the provisions in the Welsh Language Act 1967. The judge refused their request on the grounds it would amount to a 'secret trial', and translations were ordered instead. This decision by the judge had two ramifications. To begin with, the defendants refused to plead or to recognise the court, or to respect any of the usual courtroom conventions basic to the criminal trial. Two of the accused said they wanted nothing further to do with the trial and asked to be locked in their cells and for the case to be heard in their absence. Second, the use of translations made the presentation of any sustained or effective oratory or argument impossible. In the words of one observer of the trial, 'beautiful spasms of Welsh were followed by the interpreter's precise, though sometimes stumbling, English'. The business of translating caused great confusion at certain points; for instance when a policeman quoted in English a statement made originally in Welsh, which had then to be translated back into Welsh for the accused, who gave an answer in Welsh, which then had to be turned into English. (10)

Throughout the trial, as part of its background, there were protests and demonstrations outside the court. Inside the court those defendants who chose to contest the trial tried to fight in on their own terms. Iwan called his father, a minister, to testify at one point; the result gives some flavour of the trial proceedings. His father refused to take the oath, endorsed his son's actions and urged the jury to do the right thing 'before this little country follows the bloody path followed by other countries oppressed by the English'. On the last day of the trial, all eight made long and emotional speeches, during which women in the public gallery wept. They quoted extensively from Welsh poetry, philosophy and hymns. From one defendant,

> We are not criminals secretly conspiring, but workmen rolling up our sleeves in the winter to cut a furrow towards the spring. If you call us Welsh extremists the name is a tribute. New states all over the world are full of people who were called extremists by the English.

All eight were found guilty, after the judge had warned the jury not to capitulate to 'emotional blackmail' or any other kind of 'outside pressure'. The defendants were given suspended sentences of three to twelve months; it was a verdict which reflected the judge's idea of clemency. In his words, 'I have come to the conclusion that a happy ending to this case would be to wipe the slate clean, to give just one more chance for reason to prevail.'

But according to nationalists, the judge was moved by considerations not of mercy, but of fear; a fear, that is, generated by what was thought to be an upsurge of support among 'good respectable Welshmen' for the accused at Swansea. 'Had the sentences ... been actual rather than suspended,' argued Davies, 'the impact would surely have been tremendous.' Such an outcome appeared highly unlikely (later trials, involving larger numbers and severer sentences, provoked no reaction at all, outside of the 'heartland' areas), but it served the purpose of persuading one segment of nationalist opinion that, even in its moments of apparent beneficence, the British state was still, at heart, a craven creature.

By 1971 the characteristics of this sort of trial were becoming clear. Their internal characteristics comprised attempts by defendants to deny the legitimacy of the courts and the law, to run a political defence, to appeal to 'a world that we have lost', to draw in local eminences as witnesses (thereby trying to dignify and add authority to their claims), to refuse to respect or partake of courtroom ritual and convention, to exploit the problems of translation to the full (by delaying proceedings), to encourage spectator participation (as a means of pressurising jurors, by heightening the emotional atmosphere of the courtroom) and to draw - consciously or unconsciously - upon the tactics and rhetoric of the 'Penrhos Three', with the emphasis on the ideas of 'over-riding moral imperatives', 'technical guilt' and 'moral right'.

The response of the judiciary seemed by now equally well set. There was the insistence that the trials were 'criminal' and not 'political' ones; there was the declaration that defendants' beliefs were irrelevant to the charges, and a markedly high threshold of tolerance for the behaviour of defendants and their supporters. This willingness almost to parley with language activists was probably best expressed in the relatively light sentences put forward, even when treating with persistent and unrepentant lawbreakers like Iwan and Ffrancis(see below). The talk of 'showing mercy' itself seemed to concede something of the defendants' arguments - that here, indeed, were people who were different and special; people against which the usual canons of judgment in criminal cases did not apply, even if it was necessary to insist on a criminal trial for them.

The external characteristics of this trial activity type were just as clearly discernible. For the defendants there was the strong movement support, the readiness of a segment of the Welsh intelligentsia to testify as witnesses and to petition more generally on behalf of defendants, and the varying degrees of sympathy among sections of the police and the lower judiciary. Taken together, these reflected a broad base of support for the WLS in 'Welsh Wales'. It was a support strong enough to persuade the prosecution and the higher court judiciary that it would be difficult to run a successful criminal trial involving WLS members in much of the Welsh heartland. A recognition of this factor helps explain why many cases which had their roots in those areas where the WLS was strongest were transferred elsewhere for trial.

Although the Swansea trial was the most celebrated of all road sign cases, there were further, more intermittent, courtroom encounters around this issue. For example, there were trials at Swansea at the end of 1971 and at Carmarthen in 1972 involving twenty-five WLS members. The Carmarthen case was of particular interest. There the three defendants were 'kidnapped' to prevent their appearance at the assizes. Twenty-eight people claimed responsibility, including university lecturers and professors, BBC broadcasting staff and solicitors. It was done, they said, to draw attention to the 'neglected' rights of Welsh-speaking defendants in courts. On this occasion, as on others, the authorities when faced with a more generalised civil resistance elected to do nothing. When the defendants eventually got to court they were conditionally discharged, though all had previous convictions for kindred offences. The judge made it clear that it was a case which could have been dealt with in a lower court, but had had to be transferred to a higher one. The reasons for the move were twofold: the prevalence of this type of crime in the area, and the known sympathies of many local lay justices for those accused of 'language-related' offences.

In the autumn of 1967 the WLS had announced the beginning of a campaign for an 'adequate' Welsh broadcasting service. This objective was, at first, largely subordinate to the Society's activities on other fronts: post offices, official forms, road signs and the investiture. But after 1970 a serious effort began against television transmitters and studies, organised around the demand for a Welsh-only channel. We can usefully pick up the chronology of the ensuing trials in February 1971, when four WLS members were accused of maliciously damaging a window at the Palace of Westminster. The trial followed a by now familiar pattern. The defendants began by refusing to plead, answer questions or recognise the court; there was the common backcloth of vociferous spectator support. According to one of the defendants, Ffred Ffrancis, in his speech to the Bench at Lambeth Magistrates' Court, 'Our purpose was publicity. We did not break into the House of Commons for personal gain. We did not go through the window in a spirit of vandalism. This was a responsible act.' All four were conditionally discharged; but their actions, in effect, initiated a campaign of protest, disruption and sabotage against television installations which still continues today. Perhaps the most spectacular of the 'political trials' which arose from this issue came in 1971, when seventeen members of the WLS were charged with conspiring to interfere with television and radio transmissions.

The preliminary hearing was held at Mold Magistrates' Court, Flintshire. The session ended in uproar after a request to have the case heard in Welsh was refused. Four translators were called instead, but all declined to serve, 'as a matter of principle and conscience'. As a result, the morning session ground to a halt. As the officials left, defendants and spectators rose and sang the anthem. Interpreters were found for the afternoon, but when being sworn in defendants protested saying they would not accept translations. As the oaths were administered defendants stood with their backs to the Bench and began singing Welsh hymns. The public gallery had to be cleared after disturbances. At this point the prosecutor applied to the High Court for leave to prefer a private Bill of Indictment; 'That course becomes necessary by reason of the conduct to which the court has been subjected by defendants.'

In October 1971 the defendants came before the Flintshire Assizes, in a case that was to be the focus of endless demonstrations and controversy over the use of Welsh in the courts. The seventeen accused asked repeatedly and always unsuccessfully for the trial to be conducted in Welsh. One defendant refused to recognise the court 'because it debased the Welsh language', and was placed in the cells at his own request. Thirteen were allowed to leave on bail, for separate trial. The remaining three included Ffrancis, who shouted out as the charges were being read: 'I am not prepared to take any part in this political trial and I speak for the other two defendants when I say I am not prepared to let the trial go on.' The three began singing, accompanied by the public gallery. The gallery was cleared and the defendants carried to their cells. But the dispute over the legal status of Welsh was carried a good way beyond the court precincts. The day the trial started, fourteen men prominent in Welsh public life wrote to 'The Times' pointing to the moral weight of the defendants' argument on the use of Welsh in trial proceedings. The remainder of the trial was a mosaic of refusals, protests and interruption. The three were found guilty (of occupying and damaging a television studio), at which point Ffrancis demanded to make a statement. This was refused on the grounds that he would have an opportunity later. Ffrancis retorted, 'These political shows are getting much like pantomimes.' As the judge began his summing up, Ffrancis's girlfriend (the daughter of Gwynfor Evans, the first WNP candidate to be elected to Parliament) tried to throw herself twenty feet into the well of the court from the public gallery. Before being sentenced (Ffrancis got two years, his co-conspirators one year each), Ffrancis was given, and took, the opportunity to address the court:

> The destruction of property may be essential to prevent violence to people, and it is a positive duty to anyone who feels any responsibility to his fellow man to be ready to take this course of action.... In Wales, broadcasting equipment is being used as a means of oppression against the language and personality of the Welsh people.

The judge countered, predictably, by stressing the distinction between the criminal and the political trial:

> I want it understood ... that every court is loath to sentence to prison men who in their belief commit offences. I have to sentence you for the offences concerning the destruction of valuable property.

Similar sentences and trial patterns were voiced and enacted elsewhere, inside and outside of Wales. Some examples give a sense of the scale and nature of the activity. In trials in 1971 there were demands for all-Welsh hearings, protests at the use and quality of translations, refusals to plead, recognise the court or engage in any aspect of conventional courtroom behaviour. Through all this, defendants were encouraged and sustained by an articulate and uncompromising spectator and movement support.

These trials brought more sharply into focus the ability of the WLS to involve members of the intelligentsia and to capture the tacit and, on occasions, the active support of members of the lower judiciary. The former were everywhere active in the wings during the process of the trials, prompting, organising, testifying and lobbying. The involvement of the latter came to a head in 1972-3. In June 1972 an Aberystwyth magistrate resigned after being criticised by the Lord Chancellor for publicly disagreeing with a decision of other lay justices to imprison a student over the non-payment of a fine (arising from a road signs case). One year later, nine WLS members were given a conditional discharge on charges of burglary and causing damage at a television transmitter. After the verdict, the defendants - protesting that the trial was 'political' - sang the anthem in court and were joined in this by the five lay justices who had tried the case, the police and court solicitors. The Lord Chancellor asked for an official explanation: there had been at least six previous incidents where the actions, comments and decisions of lay magistrates adjudicating in the 'Welsh areas' had been investigated. Most of these inquiries had come after pressure from Labour MPs complaining of the 'political bias' of some Benches - an event which hinted at the wider political tensions in Wales, as the ruling Labour Party has tried to ignore, subordinate or accommodate the various manifestations of new nationalist sentiment.

The trials again revealed the continuing willingness of judges and the police to strike a bargain rather than a punitive posture in relation to WLS offenders. While at pains to deny the political claims of defendants, many judges went some way, by implication, towards acknowledging the unique properties of this type of law-breaking and trial activity. Thus:

> As you can see we have been unusually tolerant in allowing you to use this court as a platform for your views. We respect your views but we are custodians of the law and we are quite clear about our duties.
>
> I love the language as much as you do ... but we must keep within the bounds of the law.... This is not a political court or a political platform, but a court of law.

These extracts suggest the extent to which the judiciary were prepared to sanction departures from the usual procedures of a criminal trial while, paradoxically, striving to deny the style of political defence put forward by the majority of defendants.

The generally low-key reaction to language-related offences by the judiciary was matched by the reluctance of the police to launch any systematic policy of arrest or detention of known law-breakers. The emphasis, instead, on selective and partial (and probably partisan) law enforcement was strikingly borne out in the police reaction to a major act of sabotage, causing £25,000 damage, at a television transmitter in North Wales early in 1977. All thirty-one members of the Senate (the collective leadership) of the WLS signed a statement admitting responsibility. The police ignored this. In their subsequent house raids they were concerned only with finding the equipment used in the action, deliberately looking past papers, maps and photographs.

The aim of the Senate was a 'show trial', a big conspiracy case aimed at drawing in the entire leadership of the WLS. The police preference for working in this way made it difficult for the WLS to force and exploit confrontations with the authorities. More recent examples of their failure came in 1977, and were serious enough to provoke a section of the WLS leadership into questioning the tactics of the search for 'confrontation'. In 1977 warrants were issued for the arrest of eight WLS members on the non-payment of fines. The WLS was hoping for a collective arrest, jailing and eventual release, for the likely publicity value. They achieved none of this. Instead, the eight were processed individually and prison authorities learnt to forestall 'welcome outs' by releasing WLS members early. The developments of these and other 'refinements' in law enforcement meant that having members in prison was of much less value to the WLS than before, since it generated little media coverage. The chairman of the WLS complained of 'collusion' between the authorities in planning a strategy of defusion. But a more plausible explanation should be sought in the slackening interest in the WLS after the general election successes of the WNP in 1974, together with the growing commitment of central government to the idea of some measure of 'devolution' for Wales (we return to this point at the end of the paper).

A further aspect of the 'television-related' trials - though of course it was a feature of other trials as well - was the dispute over the use of translators. There were various attempts at compromise, but the fundamental position of the language activists was clear enough:

> Translators are abominable. The right to translation is to my mind the right to have an inferior trial.... You know you will never sway a jury by cold argument alone: all this would be spoilt by the intervention of a translator.

Or, more pointedly,

> Many people will say fair play to the authorities - they have given you a Welsh judge and Welsh translating equipment. But it reminds us of our position and the position of the Welsh language.

The reluctance of judges to give a generous interpretation of the provisions of the Welsh Language Act 1967 has been guided largely by the judge's declaration in the 1971 Swansea conspiracy trial that to grant an 'all-Welsh' trial would be, in effect, to sanction a 'secret trial'. The retort to this is the claim by the WLS that if this is so then the trials of all those Welsh people who have felt more at ease in Welsh, but who have been denied an all-Welsh trial, have just as emphatically been 'secret trials' - the more so in those cases where the defendants have refused to recognise the legitimacy of the law, its agents and its procedures.

SUMMARY AND CONCLUSION

We have only been able to set down the sketchiest account of the range and number of trial activities involving members of the WLS in the period 1963-77. The Society started with a founding membership of 12 in 1962, and has probably never had more than 300 active members at any one time, though the formal membership list now numbers about 1,300. Their success as a pressure group, pushing their own kind of 'expressive politics' has been impressive. So, too, has been their ability to rework conventional definitions of the 'political' and to force a collapse (to the satisfaction of themselves and their supporters, at least) of cherished orthodoxies concerning the distinction between the idea of the 'criminal' and the 'political' in much of their trial activity. Yet despite all this, the forces which carried the WLS along have never been exclusively self-generating; and just as the victories of the Society were inextricably linked to wider political currents in Wales, so too is the decline in the Society's campaigns and successes after 1974. Consequently, if we are properly to complete our study of the causes of political trial activity in contemporary Wales, we need to look some way beyond the WLS bloodstream, to a broader refusal and resistance - principally the reluctance of an increasing number of Welsh people to accept traditional political arrangements, institutions and choices.

NOTES

1 See Bankowski and Mungham (1976, Chapter 4).
2 Bankowski and Mungham (1976, pp. 123-30).
3 For good accounts of the genesis and career of the WNP see Morgan (1963) and Butt-Phillips (1975).
4 Lewis, in Jones and Thomas (1973, p. 115).
5 The full text of his address is printed in Jones and Thomas (1973, pp. 115-26).
6 The significance of this struggle (over the British government's drowning of Welsh villages in order to construct reservoirs for use mainly by English cities) is discussed in Butt-Phillips (1975).
7 Emyrs ap Iwan, quoted in Jones and Thomas (1973, p. 54).
8 For details of the Committee and its recommendations, see Davies (1973) and Lewis (1969).
9 For a fuller discussion of this particular agitation, see Fishlock (1972, p. 90).
10 Reported in Fishlock (1972, p. 100).

BIBLIOGRAPHY

BANKOWSKI, Z. and MUNGHAM, G. (1976), 'Images of Law', Routledge & Kegan Paul, London.
BARTHES, R. (1973), 'Mythologies', Paladin, London.
BUTT-PHILLIPS, A. (1975), 'The Welsh Question: Nationalism in Welsh Politics 1945-70', University of Wales Press, Cardiff.

DAVIES, C. (1973), Cymdeithas yr laith Gymraeg, in Stephens (1973, pp. 248-63).
FISHLOCK, T. (1972), 'Wales and the Welsh', Cassell, London.
GOLDMAN, A. (1944), 'In Defence of Socialism', Pioneer Publications, New York.
IWAN, D. (1972), Cymdeithas yr laith, the Courts and the Police, 'Planet', no. 12, pp. 14-16.
JONES, A.R. and THOMAS, G. (eds) (1973), 'Presenting Saunders Lewis', University of Wales Press, Cardiff.
KAMENKA, E. and TAY, A. (1975), Beyond Bourgeois Individualism; the Contemporary Crisis in Law and Legal Ideology, in Kamenka, E. and Neale, R. (eds) (1975), 'Feudalism, Capitalism and Beyond', Edward Arnold, London.
LEWIS, R. (1969), 'Second-Class Citizen', Gwasg Gomer, Llandysul.
MORGAN, K.O. (1963), 'Wales in British Politics, 1868-1922', University of Wales Press, Cardiff.
NAIRN, T. (1977), 'The Break-Up of Britain', New Left Books, London.
ROSE, H. (1973), Who can De-label the Client?, 'Social Work Today', vol. 14, no. 13, pp. 409-13.
SOLZHENITSYN, A. (1974), 'The Gulag Archipelago', Fontana, London.
STEPHENS, M. (ed.) (1973), 'The Welsh Language Today', Gomer Press, Llandysul.
THOMAS, N. (1973), 'The Welsh Extremist', Y. Lolfa, Talybont.

Part II

SOCIAL ORDER AND THE LAW

Chapter 5

POPULAR JUSTICE AND THE LAY MAGISTRACY: THE TWO FACES OF LAY PARTICIPATION

Rose Pearson

> I think that one of the best methods of radicalising an individual today is to have him spend a day in court witnessing the way we are unceasingly railroaded into the jails and prisons. Now even the facade of democracy is beginning to fall. [Davis, 1971, p. 185]

> Alternative universes co-exist. Probabilities clash and possibilities wink out for ever. [Piercy, 1976, p. 177]

INTRODUCTION

I preface my remarks with quotations from the writings of two radical American women, which may strike many people as somewhat inappropriate for the examination of an institution such as the lay bench, which summons images of all that is traditional, slow-moving and above all stable in British society - an embodiment, perhaps, of our obstinate resistance to social change. But it is both possible and plausible to regard the historical period we are now entering as one that will be in many ways extraordinary, characterised by social dislocation and disruption of a kind not seen in this country since the violent upheavals of industrialisation. This is not to assert that history is about to repeat itself, but rather to point to a more general parallel between the early nineteenth and late twentieth centuries, as it becomes clear that the economic crisis of capitalism is to be marked by massive technological innovation which will, like the industrial revolution before it, create radical social upheaval. According to the recent Clayton Report (1978), and to those various private agencies which 'forecast' economic trends, something between three and seven million jobs will be lost in manufacturing industries and offices during the next two decades. Indeed, without the development of a mini-computer industry Britain will become uncompetitive in world markets, so the necessity of change, and the consequent inevitability of unemployment, is curiously recognised yet not recognised by government. Politicians speak in a latter-day 'white heat of technology' vein of a future free from oppressive drudgery, yet fail to expose the obvious fact that an economy geared to the maximisation of profit cannot engage in such a beneficial utilisation of that technology. However, two assumptions can be reasonably made concerning the immediate future: first, that the reserve army of labour will be transformed into an enormous, permanent and, in productive terms, totally superfluous population, and second, following from this, that we can expect a correspondingly large increase in crime and disorder, matched by intensified levels of state repression. Clearly, any sociological analysis of legal institutions in contemporary Britain must locate the latter within the concrete conditions of a society in crisis.

There are two senses in which mass unemployment of the kind I am referring to will create novel situations for the legal system. On the one hand, political confrontation, when it steps outside the parliamentary arena and becomes a demonstration or a riot, is redefined as a problem of civil order, though it is widely recognised for what it is - political repression. But I am here interested in the rise that can be anticipated in the 'ordinary' crime rate, for the crisis that produces political protest will also produce an enormous criminal sub-culture, in the sense that economic collapse creates for millions of individuals the problem of how to exist, and many eventually and consistently choose crime, both petty and organised, as one possible means of survival. I am interested, then, in how the growing problem of 'non-political' crime (which is of course political, in the sense that it is caused by, and is a response to, economic inequality) will be handled by the state, and in what possible defensive responsive against the courts could be devised.

Magistrates' courts, in England and Wales, handle over 90 per cent of all those brought to trial, and as the institutions responsible for the ordinary, routine operation of law and order, their immediate future is of obvious importance. The questions I want to raise are concerned with how these courts are currently staffed, but they are also intended to identify dilemmas and to point towards possible strategies for change. I place the discussion within a wider perspective of what a socialist legal system might look like, and what the relationship between the capitalist courts and such a system is likely to be, and argue that the process identified long ago whereby key members of the working class are co-opted and incorporated into the system will continue to act as a source of stability for the state unless greater working-class involvement, rather than less, is demanded. The crucial issues concerning the particular area of the magistracy are, namely, the problem of democratising the composition of the lay bench, and that of defining present and possible future government policies towards the bench in the period of the 'exceptional state'. Before examining these issues in detail, however, we can usefully point to some alternative conceptions of justice, and counterpose the practice of lay justice in contemporary Britain to systems of popular justice in socialist societies, indicating something of the range of possible systems for the everyday law-keeping in complex industrial societies.

WHAT IS POPULAR JUSTICE?

The distinguishing features of popular justice systems are easily discernible when we compare the variety of judicial systems produced by different societies. There are several ways of classifying the types of law found in differing social formations, but without becoming engaged in a detailed study, four major types can be abstracted. First, there are the law-keeping mechanisms of hunter-gatherers; second, there are those of stratified agrarian societies, referred to, using Tonniës's term, as the Gemeinschaft type of social regulation. These two types have often been incorrectly collapsed into one by some commentators, as a general mode of social control which predates industrial societies (Kamenka and Tay, 1971, 1975). The third major type is legal justice, or law as it is recognised in our society; finally, there is the law of post-capitalist societies, referred to here as 'revolutionary justice', or 'popular justice'.

It is always rash to make over-arching generalisations about hunter-gatherer societies because these have for the greater part of human history been the predominant form of social organisation, with the result that the variety of institutions to be found even within the limits of our knowledge of such societies is enormous. Weber (1948), in his categorisation of major forms of law, makes the distinction between systems of formal and of substantive justice. Formal justice is characterised by strict rules of procedure and could involve, for instance, magic, reference to an oracular source of judgment, or trial by ordeal. Substantive justice occurs when justice is dispensed not according to rules, but according to the particular circumstances of the case, as in so-called 'kadi' justice. Weber is, of course, talking here of ideal types, and the systems he describes are abstract models which do not, in reality, occur exactly as described so that real judicial systems contain mixtures of different elements, although there is an overall predominance of one kind. Thus Matza (1974), in pointing to the similarities between contemporary American juvenile justice and other substantive justice systems, uses, illustratively, the term 'kadi justice'.

To return to the question of law-keeping among hunter-gatherers: the most notable feature of such systems is that matters of justice occur not as sequences of events isolated from other aspects of life, but as part of the corporate life of the community; for, as Tonniës demonstrated, pre-capitalist forms of social organisation are marked by a lack of separation between the 'public' and the 'private'. Turnbull, speaking of traditional African law, stresses the way in which it flows from face-to-face contact in a society where people 'could be truly social' because they 'had time to socialise and were expected to do so'. His description of African systems is also a defence (Turnbull, 1976, p. 107):

> Each action has to be assessed in context, and the co-operation of all those concerned is demanded. The focus is on justice rather than law, and this demands the co-operation of society as a whole. It is not relegated to a few specialists and a jury of twelve, who are not in any way personally concerned.

When elements of seemingly incomprehensible ritual do occur, they are usually present for a functional purpose. Thus, when among the Papuans is found the 'shouting reproaches and the dancing of the mad dance in front of the squatting defendant' (Poposil, 1958), or among the forest peoples of Africa the plaintiff is judged according to the standard of his or her singing (Turnbull, 1976), the rationale is similar: to persuade the person on trial to adjust his or her behaviour without having to take the somewhat drastic step of stigmatising a member of society as a guilty one, or criminal. The motivation is always to integrate the individual back into society, rather than to deter or punish.

The Gemeinschaft form of social control, to be found in feudal-type societies, is superficially similar to that of small-scale societies, but surface likeness masks a fundamentally different set of motivations; in addition to being the product of a closely knit, rurally based face-to-face society, this form of social control is one operated by the land-owning minority in highly repressive and rigidly stratified societies.

Elements of magic, religion, taboo and blood-ritual shift from functioning as mechanisms of social integration to become utilised by landowners and their propagandists (the priests) as weapons of domination and terror in the struggle to reinforce and justify the subordination of the majority of men (peasants) and all women. The point is more than merely academic; arguments which reject the existence of a specifically post-capitalist form of justice are developed from a typification of forms of social control as those of only the Gemeinschaft and Gesellschaft (market capitalism), to which a non-historically specific category, known as bureaucratic-administrative law, has been added (Kamenka and Tay, 1971). All law systems are viewed as a reformulation of these three basic types, which may occur in different combinations; but may never be superseded. For example, contemporary Chinese justice is seen not as a new, popular form, but as resulting from the blend of Gemeinschaft and bureaucratic-administrative systems. In fact, as I have tried to show, the repertoire of modes of justice and social order is wider, historically, than this. The 'three types' model is a clear illustration of the sociologically useful device of creating typologies, becoming, in its turn, an intellectual straightjacket, inhibiting the consideration of further categories which do not fit the scheme. In this instance, the possibility of truly democratic justice becomes precluded, providing an excellent example of what Marcuse (1964) refers to as one-dimensional, non-critical thought.

Legal justice is the justice of capitalist society. It is characterised by the existence of a separate legal sphere, in its turn marked by what Weber (1948) called the rationalising and accounting tendency within modern societies. There are institutionalised courts and trained, paid personnel to run them. The system is formal, the law is written down, and rules are followed in detail. The professed aim is absolute objectivity, that one person should be treated exactly like another. Such law guarantees certain basic rights to the individual. It was developed in the struggle against royalist autocracy and so offers, theoretically at least, protection from arbitrary totalitarianism which substantive justice, being irregular and discretionary, could not be relied upon to furnish. However, legal justice, although promising equality of treatment

\Quote

within the courts, also promises the retention of inequality outside, where the anarchy of the private market ensures an unequal distribution of wealth. The law protects private property rights as a basic form of social organisation, while retaining the rhetoric of equality and fairness for dealings within the courts, so that the notion of justice becomes a contradiction in terms. The concept of justice as we recognise it is, Quinney explains, 'an accumulation of ideas that have formed in the course of the development of capitalism' (1977, p. 2), while Miller argues that 'rather than justice being egalitarian, equality in the strong sense constitutes one way of interpreting justice' (1976, p. 21). This notion of social justice speaks not of equality, but of reasonable or tolerable treatment; and it, too, is embedded within market relations, with the result that ideas such as a minimum wage, or fair rent and security of tenure, never seriously challenge the concept of ownership embodied in legal justice (Miller, 1976, Parts 1 and 3).

Popular justice is the justice of a socialist society, and it exists today only in embryonic form. Its seeds are present in advanced capitalist societies in so far as the notion of social justice shades over into the idea of distribution according to need; and it has been actualised in the course of all major revolutions since the 1640s in the form of revolutionary tribunals and courts. Well documented are the Anarcho-Syndicalist tribunals of revolutionary Spain (Bollerton, 1961); while perhaps the most recent examples were the shanty-town committees set up in urban areas during the Allende regime in Chile. These bodies merge the functions of social order and the re-distribution of wealth, so spanning the conceptual gap between capitalist notions of justice and egalitarianism, and superseding the law-and-order functions of the courts. (Though even in revolutionary periods the formal court system continues to function as long as it is permitted, and can easily remain intact to re-emerge at a later date, as was the case in Spain during the period 1936-8.) The emergent socialist society of a post-revolutionary era may institutionalise these bodies, but in all known examples of permanent popular courts, as opposed to those of the revolutionary instant, powers and scope are limited - sometimes severely so.

Popular justice is a collective enterprise which exhibits many features of pre-capitalist systems, in that justice is substantive and based on face-to-face knowledge of the individual; it is also public and non-formal. The popular tribunals of Cuba deal with all low-level crime. They are chaired by a lay person with minimal training. Anyone may take part in the proceedings, and the one criterion used in judgment is that of 'anti-social behaviour' (Berman, 1969). To take one example of their functioning, they have been able to deal with the growing consciousness of exploitation of women by enabling the previously assumed 'private question' of whether men will do housework to become a question of public concern. Similarly, the street-level committees of China have evolved as organs for dealing with all aspects of community life, including the control of crime, the running of nurseries, launderies and garment-mending shops, the discussion of marital disputes and, lately, programmes of birth control. The latter two concerns will strike most Westerners as extreme intrusion into individual privacy, particularly when they hear of groups of women in a locality deciding among themselves who shall have a child; such subjects do not seem appropriate for public discussion. But what is occurring is the practice of collective problem-solving of an open and participatory kind. In the instance just cited, the alternatives are either laissez-faire or a resort to force of the type used in India by the Ghandi government, involving the compulsory sterilisation of peasants (which was in the long run not only coercive but also ineffective).

The Chinese concept of law flows from early Marx, and was developed by Mao Tse Tung in his revision of Marxist theory which saw the peasantry as a revolutionary force and stressed the importance of collective human consciousness in the construction of socialism (Pepinsky, 1973). Written law is deliberately minimal in China, in order that a sense of social responsibility, rather than the enforced following of rules, may develop. Discussion and persuasion feature more prominently than punishment and, consequently, control becomes the business of every member of society (Lubman, 1967). The Cuban and Chinese systems have, then, certain truly 'popular' elements, in that mass participation is genuine and continuous; people learn and become more involved. In contrast, it should be noted, the so-called peoples' courts of Eastern Europe and the USSR are in fact closely controlled by party personnel and show notably low levels of public interest and involvement (Podgorecki, 1962; Hammer, 1963). None the less, the Cuban and Chinese popular courts have limited scope and function alongside more formal legal systems which deal with important matters of security and the state. This may be an unavoidable arrangement, but from our point of view it demonstrates the tentative and transitional character of those popular justice systems.

The particular law-and-order crisis of contemporary capitalism poses the question of popular justice in a rather different form. The extraordinary policing methods in the process of evolution arises in a society where social control is maintained - to use Althusser's (1971) terminology - by both repressive and ideological domination. It is therefore the case that even those institutions comprising what I (following Althusser) call the repressive state apparatus - that is the army, police and judicial system - are also ideological state apparati; that is, they function and presentthem themselves to the public in such a way as to justify their own existence and the existence of the capitalism they uphold (Althusser, 1971). The new measures adopted at this stage have to look as though they arise from public demand and anxiety, although the mechanisms for consulting this putative public and gauging the real climate and range of opinion are, of course, barely existent. This dilemma is expressed by Hall et al. thus (1978, p. 220):

> The capitalist state cannot remain securely founded on the legitimacy of popular representation and take severe and unusual measures to contain a threat to its foundation which the vast majority of the population does not believe exists. It must therefore continually shape and structure that 'consent' to whic which, in turn, it refers itself.

Public participation in the fight against crime can fulfil two functions: one of legitimising novel measures of control, the other

- and this against a background of permanent fiscal crisis is essential - of filling gaps in public policing. In this way 'citizens' are encouraged to join the fight against crime, but only in a limited capacity which procludes taking serious initiatives. However, there is here, as Quinney states (1977, p. 13),

> built into the state efforts at citizen participation ... a dialectic that supports autonomous community action removed from state control. Developing alongside the criminal justice system is a grass-roots approach that is beyond the design of the state. The dialectic undoubtedly will advance in coming years.

To return to the lay magistracy of England and Wales: as an institution which, like Parliament, has its roots in the pre-capitalist era, it has undergone changes which enable it to function within the orbit of formal legal justice, while retaining certain elements which are typical of the former system: namely that its staff are untrained in legal matters, and are unpaid; that magistrates have, within a limited scope, the ability to exercise wider discretion than judges in higher courts; and that there is a small democratic element in their selection. I want now to examine the relationship of the lay magistracy to the state, looking at those areas which appear to be particularly problematic in its present functioning. The material I draw upon was gathered during research over the last two years into the operation of one lay magistrates' bench, and is based on interviews with magistrates, investigation of methods of selection, and examination of the social composition of this particular bench.

SOCIAL CLASS COMPOSITION OF THE LAY MAGISTRACY

First, a caveat about the use of the term 'class' in this context. On one level, the concentration on the occupational class of magistrates to be found in the existing research is misleading, because the class character of the magistracy as a body has to be determined on the basis of its function within the capitalist legal system, which in turn must be regarded as part of a system of both repressive and ideological domination. The magistracy, then, derives its class character not from the sum of positions in the occupational hierarchy held by individuals who compose local benches, but from the functions within the legal system those individuals perform. Magistrates clearly perform functions of surveillance and control. They are agents not only of repressive domination, in so far as they pass sentence and inflict punishment, but also of ideological domination, in so far as magistrates' courts operate in an authoritarian manner invoking, to use Carlen's (1976) terms, remedial routines against those individuals who challenge the structure by attempting to enlarge the area of discussion. The two examples that follow are illustrations of instances where a defendant tries to introduce information which she considers to have a direct bearing on the case, but which the magistrate refuses to accept for consideration. The accused here are women drawn from a study of female defendants in magistrates' courts (Pearson, 1976):

Example 1: 'I was drunk, but I wasn't disorderly.'

'But the police came.'

'The police are always picking on me, wherever I go in this town.'

'We're not here to discuss your view of the police. One day's detention.'

Example 2: 'I can't afford that fine. I've got children to feed and the rent to pay out of what I get off the Social Security.'

'You should have thought of that before. If you don't pay, you'll have to go to prison.'

Although defendants of the second type are unlikely to end up in prison, the message is clear; there is no element of substantive justice, except on the magistrate's initiative. The defendant may ask questions, but cannot bring forward broader considerations he or she considers pertinent to the case.

However, the question of the occupational structure of those who constitute magistrates' benches is relevant in a different sense, if we see it as part of the increasing legitimation crisis of modern democracies. In the 1930s, for instance, the overwhelmingly middle-class composition of lay benches was the subject of considerable comment in the press, yet, interestingly enough, central government has since 1948 continually pressed for what the Lord Chancellor's Office refers to as 'a wider social spread' on local benches - a call often only reluctantly taken up by local advisory committees. Attempts to achieve greater working-class representation on lay benches have repeatedly failed. Research by Hood (1962, 1972), and by Baldwin (1976) show that members of the Registrar General's classes I and II - professional and managerial - consistently dominate lay benches, while semi- and unskilled workers seldom appear. Furthermore, their work suggests there has been only a slight change since 1945. My own research confirms their findings; my evidence shows not more than 10 unskilled or semi-skilled workers out of a total 140 magistrates. A comparison of the occupational distribution of a group of new JPs appointed in 1977 with a group appointed in 1957 shows that no significant differences have emerged over the twenty-year period.

But the explanation is not to be found in a lack of effort on behalf of those responsible for selection, though there is a great deal of complacency which leads some prominent locals engaged in selection to insist that there is, today, a 'wider social spread', a claim which they justify with reference to twenty or so trades union officials (Registrar General's social class II), a number of appointees - mainly from the Labour Party - who have working-class backgrounds, plus three oft-cited manual workers who are claimed to be 'typical of the new type'. The group of Labour Party magistrates mentioned above provide an interesting study in themselves, for it appears that appointment to the bench coincided with a process of upward social mobility made possible by political involvement. This is not to suggest any sinister motives of using political parties for self-advancement on the part of this group, for while this may have occurred in a number of cases, many of them are undoubtedly sincere and altruistic in their political commitment. Rather, it is the case that contacts made through the Labour Party lead inevitably to a widening of contacts and horizons so that the individual may, for example, consider retraining to become, perhaps, a teacher or youth worker, after which it becomes quite natural to move house and develop new friendships. Appointment to the bench may be part of this process, or it may mark its completion, in cases where appointments are awarded for political services. Labour members of the local advisory committee are particularly anxious to widen the social basis of the bench - so much so that they will, on occasion, use their power to create JPs who are not politically sympathetic but have what are seen to be the right social qualifications. Why, then, do efforts to increase the number of working-class magistrates meet with such a lack of success? Obviously on a practical level, manual workers do not have the time to devote to being a magistrate, and the by now often desperate attempt to find some who do repeatedly fails. More significant is the closed nature of selection, described below.

Is working-class participation on lay benches a matter of importance, and can it be said to constitute any extension of the popular element within the lay magistracy? The dilemma is a genuine one for a handful of left-Labour magistrates in my study who feel dubious about their own involvement; while on the other hand the situation is a source of indignation to those groups who, like the local trades council, are consistently unsuccessful in pressing for their nominees to be appointed. There is no consensus within working-class organisations on attitudes towards the lay bench, but a full discussion of the question needs to include something of the experience of those members of the working class who do participate, as a contribution towards an analysis.

My research suggests that working-class magistrates do, in fact, have certain attitudes which mark them off from the majority of justices, though these are not to be found in the areas where criminologists have traditionally looked, that is in sentencing policies (Hood, 1962, 1972). 'Soft' magistrates, that is those with a social work orientation who oppose harsh penalties, are invariably middle-class professionals in the 'helping' professions, though it is by no means true that the majority of those with professional occupations support such an approach. Managers, businessmen and trades unionists seldom advocate a 'soft' approach, but magistrates who see themselves as working-class are no less (but no more) authoritarian or 'hard' in their attitudes than others. Not only can we reject explanations based on assumptions of working-class authoritarianism, we can also find different reasons for what may appear to be similar approaches. A number of justices from working-class backgrounds feel some degree of personal identification with juvenile offenders and recall their own childhoods, yet feel that stiff first sentences may prevent a boy from embarking on a criminal career, which they know from experience can easily occur. Their belief in deterrence is, then, more caring in its orientation than that of a middle-class justice, who may have little direct knowledge of working-class life, but who clings to an abstract belief in clamping down on trouble-makers for the good of society. A more significant difference is to be found in the attitudes of the two groups towards the police. Male working-class magistrates in my survey all showed considerable scepticism towards police behaviour and of the evidence they gave in court, and this view was held among them irrespective of political affiliation; indeed, a prominent member of the local Conservative Party said of the police, 'Well, they tell lies, don't they?... They tell lies. Among middle-class magistrates attitudes range from unconditional support of the police, in that they would always grant them credibility, to a policy of warily scrutinising their evidence on some occasions. But belief in endemic police dishonesty is rare, and where it does exist is usually seen as a reflection of a total breakdown of standards throughout society. I highlight attitudes towards the police not in order to assess which group is right or wrong, but to illustrate differences in attitude which are related to social class.

The question of the significance of the participation of manual workers, however, should be approached not with reference to what they do or do not do as magistrates, but rather in the light of their legitimating function for the legal system, and of the implications of this participation for working-class consciousness. On the question of legitimating functions, a negative approach would cite the fact that this type of participation provides only an illusion of democracy and consensus and serves to incorporate and defuse potential critics, since those involved are usually exceptional individuals who are publicly active, confident and verbose. But since the policy of the inclusion of a handful of workers is unlikely to be reversed, the question becomes one of challenging the token nature of such representation. To take an analogy, most feminists would hardly oppose women who enter male-dominated professions on the ground that they are token women; rather, they would press for measures against discrimination and for equal job opportunities. The issue of the relationship between working-class consciousness and participation in lay bodies is a more complex one. We have to consider here both the subjective aspects of social class, and the perception of law-and-order that the working-class currently adheres to. In one sense, the mere participation by members of non-dominant groups may erode prevalent deferential attitudes, for if they exercise power no better than those groups who traditionally command authority, they are unlikely to do any worse. (Or so the history of social-democratic governments suggests.) More important is the question of experience in holding positions of authority, of running and controlling all aspects of life. Some workers have argued against the Bullock Report's (1977) recommendation that there should be worker-directors, on the grounds that capitalism is a system which oppresses workers, and they should not co-operate in managing it. The same could obviously be said of the lay magistracy, and, incidentally, of community councils, regional hospital boards, boards of school governors, and a plethora of other organisations established by the authorities to manage state enterprises at a local level. But an alternative view is that, since capitalist hegemony depends upon ideological domination, worker participation can lead to de-mystification; or, to put it another way, the more the workers understand and contribute to the running of capitalism, the more capable they become of taking power and establishing an alternative system - socialism. In the case of magistrates, it would be erroneous to believe that those who are non-middle-class necessarily like what they see when they join the bench; on the contrary, they are, in the main, highly critical of the practice of lay justice. The local bench has been described by some of its working-class members as 'more of a closed shop than anything I've got here' (full-time union official), 'self-selecting clique', and 'a bunch who don't know the first thing about how people live'. Numerous examples of class bias in sentencing are noticed, and the closed nature of selection is frequently mentioned. It can only be assumed that more magistrates of this type would mean more criticism.

Furthermore, working-class magistrates feel there is a job to do which has to be done (but not necessarily by solicitor or judges), and we can fairly suppose that the majority of the working class are in broad agreement. Theoretically formulated, this can be understood in terms of Gouldner's (1976) distinction between 'paradigms' and 'ideologies'. Gouldner makes use of Gramsci's term 'hegemonic class' to describe the novel nature of the capitalist class, which, unlike all previous ruling classes, is unable personally to enforce its own domination and so becomes exceptionally dependent upon ideologies which convince the population that its rule is legitimate and upon mechanisms through which the diverse social strate of society become integrated. Gouldner sees this process as one which occurs when a number of differing images of what comparatively small numbers of people want (which Gouldner calls 'paradigms', not to be confused with the wider use of the term 'paradigm' by Kuhn (1962), who uses it in connection with scientific revolutions) become merged into a more general programme - an ideology. A paradigm is a limited case of an ideology; it is concrete and specific, whereas ideologies are abstract and general. So the paradigm 'work for yourself' becomes, in ideological terms, a belief in hard work, while a belief that 'a woman's place is in the home' may be happily accommodated in the ideology 'all men are equal'. A paradigm is merely a particular case of an ideology, but by becoming subsumed into an ideology it is united with other paradigms as part of a broad generalisation. In this way the private views of the individual can find public expression as part of a package of ideas that lay claim to speaking in the public interest. But the point about such ideologies is that, although they produce an apparent facade of unity to achieve specific ends, the lines down which an ideology may split can always be seen if we look at the paradigms which compose it. When we apply this model to the ideology of law, we can view it as the product of a tenuous unity between bourgeois conceptions of law on the one hand - that is, a belief in equality before the law and the retention of private property relations - and the working-class desire to be protected from disorder on the other.
Young (1975, p. 79) has pointed out how

> The working class does have a real stake in genuine social order ... it is a simple fact that the majority of working-class crime is intra and not inter working-class in its choice of target, area of activity and distribution. Working-class people suffer from crime, confront daily the experience of material deprivation, undergo daily the ravages of disorganisation and competitive individualism. The ideology that this play on - bourgeois ideology - contains an element of truth, and touches on the genuine interest of the class, albeit in a distorted fashion.

Similarly, a small piece of research recently carried out among slum dwellers argued that their attitudes towards the police were favourable; and though attitudes towards courts were less enthusiastic, this was because the courts were held to give insufficient support to the police (Davies, 1978). To suggest that the working-class supports the police and courts because of its false consciousness is too crude an assertion, because it fails to understand what is behind such support, and in what manner the consciousness is limited. The existence of law is a social necessity in contemporary society, but what can be usefully questioned are the terms on which law is created and sustained, and what can be suggested are possible changes to bring it closer to the working-class paradigm. If Gouldner's model of ideologies is valid, it would suggest that the ideology of law is at its most vulnerable where the content of law, and the social composition of the judiciary are concerned.

THE SELECTION OF MAGISTRATES

This is a sensitive area as far as government is concerned, and 'great debates' are not invited. Three sets of problems lend themselves to analysis; first what are the considerations guiding the selectors? Second, why does working-class representation always remain at a token level in spite of attempts to extend it? And finally, what are the possible implications of schemes for changing the system that are suggested periodically, particularly the suggestion that magistrates should be elected?

The repressive nature of the magistracy means that its personnel must, from the state's point of view, be entirely reliable, yet from an ideological viewpoint must be seen to be fairly selected. The process of selection does not, however, stand up to close scrutiny. There are scandals - one piece of research found the bench in Rochdale to be a virtual extension of the town's rotary club, and questions were asked in the House as a result (Bartlett and Walker, 1975). But the normal situation I shall describe, one where there appears to be no obvious bias, is neither democratic nor open. Selection is shrouded in secrecy - indeed, it even appears to be a mystery to some of those who have sat on the local advisory committee which chooses magistrates. The composition of this committee is a secret; the magistrates who sit on it are allowed to tell no one, and do not themselves always know why they are chosen for what is usually a six-year term. Two-thirds of the appointments are made through political parties and one-third are 'non-political' (referred to as a 'balanced composition'). The same proportions are represented on the advisory committee. Each member of that committee is virtually assured of getting at least one personal nominee on to the bench each time a new group of magistrates is selected. Apart from these, appointments are made either politically or on the basis of 'contributions made to the community'. The political nominees fall into several groups. There are the active party workers - a place on the bench may be offered as a reward for running an election campaign or for sheer longevity in political life. Hence at any point in time there will be upwards of a dozen councillors sitting on the bench. There are a number of councillors' and ex-councillors' wives - a useful device, no doubt, compensating these women for the long hours spent alone at home while their husbands spent evenings at political meetings (Hart, 1976, discusses the kinds of strains such an appointment may alleviate). Among Labour nominees there are several trades union officials; there are also six Liberals. Other magistrates come in via certain well-trodden paths. Certain organisations, including the Fabian Society and the local Jewish community, regularly put forward names, some of whom are regularly selected. There is a strong contingent of men connected with sport, including officials of local sports organisations and some who have broadcast and written on sporting matters and, partially overlapping with this group, a number from the city's major gentlemen's clubs. Individuals who have done voluntary work for such organisations as the Red Cross, WVS, Townswomen's Guild or Girl Guides are likely to be considered. Youth workers, of whom there are only four at present, are a group spoken of favourably and may well represent the emergence of a more welfare-oriented class of magistrate. But over and above these groups are a considerable number of magistrates who appear to have no particular qualifications or special knowledge; usually they know someone who is a JP, either through bodies such as churches or clubs, or professionally. The vast mass of the bench is composed of professional men or their wives, or of businessmen. Particularly prominent are medics and quasi-medics, and prominent among wives are those of doctors or solicitors. Wives of local power figures also appear on the bench.

How does this brief profile square with the rationale presented to justify methods of selection? The fit is certainly not a good one. The so-called political balance is in fact a self-perpetuating Conservative majority, mainly because, although the 'non-politicals' may not be active in political life, many say they are Conservative voters, and nearly all express Conservative attitudes. I have yet to meet in my research a non-political appointee who admits to Labour sympathies. No conspiratorial thesis is needed to explain this state of affairs; it arises naturally from those attributes which are deemed to constitute 'suitability' for service as a magistrate. There is a certain amount of ambiguity expressed here, for while on the one hand some selectors defend the selection of individuals with no specific qualifications as an integral part of the lay element, in practice such individuals are usually expected to wield a certain amount of authority and are selected only if they appear to be likely to be able to do so with ease. In our society those who are accustomed to the exercise of authority are usually middle class. Left-wing members of the middle class who would consider taking on this office are likely to be already actively engaged in politics, while the personal nature of recommendation itself virtually ensures that magistrates reproduce their own kind. Yet selection methods are defended on the grounds that they ensure the elevation of the right kinds of people: those variously defined as 'having a wide experience of life', 'proven contribution to the community' or possession of particular special knowledge related to the community. A profile of the origins and careers of magistrates shows that well over half have done, or achieved, nothing more than successfully hold down a middle-class job or look after a growing family - solid achievements, certainly, but not ones exclusive to this group. Furthermore, many of the women who are housewives appear to have remarkably less experience of 'life' than one might desire of a magistrate, and their limited world view finds frequent expression in anachronistic sentiments about working mothers and delinquency causation (after all, over half the mothers in Britain work, but over half the children are not delinquent), bigoted attitudes towards immigrant families, and unrealistic expectations of men who lose money for time taken off from work; for example:

> You can always tell the type a man is by whether he turns up in his working clothes or takes the trouble to change into something tidy. It shows proper respect - a respectful attitude.

Middle-class prejudice may equally be directed towards fellow magistrates: 'one needs to speak correctly, you know, good Queen's English, to be a JP'; or 'some of the new ones we are getting now, they just haven't got the education - I mean they don't understand what's going on'; and, more extreme still, 'some of these trades union people just haven't got it up there'. However, if the weakest link in the magisterial system is selection, then the question of secrecy is the major point of friction and grievance. Secrecy is frequently attacked; in the area referred to here there have been twenty-six references to the question of the selection of magistrates since the war, and in six cases articles are headlined with reference to the secrecy surrounding selection. Yet there has been no co-ordinated drive among individual objectors, who have mainly been union officials. Part of the trouble is that the Labour Party itself uses the same explanations to justify its own practices of secrecy as those presently responsible for lay justice. When proposals are rejected without reason either by Transport House (in the case of, say, Labour parliamentary candidates selected by constituency parties but struck off the 'A' list) or by the Lord Chancellor's Office (in its vetting of those proposed by local advisory committees), the reason given for secrecy is often identical. The person concerned, so the argument runs, may have done something extremely reprehensible which the selecting body has come to know of but does not feel free to divulge, in fairness to the rejected individual. This possibility is used to justify secrecy in all cases and can, incidentally, be quite damaging in its implications for the person turned down. Actual reasons given to me for the rejection of particular people included a man having been married twice ('the Lord Chancellor doesn't condone wife-swapping to that extent'), another having been known to have smoked marijuana (though not convicted), and a third being known as 'generally dishonest'.

The argument for secrecy outlined above can easily be countered by the suggestion that any individual could be warned that his or her background would be investigated before agreeing to be considered for the office, and would be free to decide not to stand. However, we are dealing here not with rational argument, but with a device commonly used by those with organisational power to maintain control, which has its parallel in the keeping of secret files and the computer storage of information about private citizens, which are themselves features of our evolving criminal justice system. A second reason given for secrecy is that it prevents canvassing and bribery, which again is an argument used to defend co-option rather than election of lay personnel on to public bodies. The end served is that of retaining the oligarchical power of political parties, and once more the assumptions are suspect. Why should those who have power be any less prone to corruption or errors of judgment than anyone else? The recent history of local government corruption suggests that, the more opportunity for patronage exists, the greater the potential for malpractice becomes, and it is among those who have held power longest that corrupt practices seem most likely to emerge.

The direct election of magistrates is often suggested; a Bill put forward in 1977 aimed to hand over power to select the lay bench to local councils, about which 'The Times' (1977) was moved to comment 'this bill is unlikely to become law'. In fact, the selection of magistrates would, if these measures were adopted, remain substantially the same, that is selection through political parties. But the interesting question raised here is not so much that of making the lay bench into a popularly based institution when bourgeois democracy is itself not 'popular'; rather, it is the articulation between open discussion of institutions, grass-roots community organisation, and the development of genuine working-class forms of social control. It is perfectly possible to envisage schemes which would be more democratic; justice in the lower courts could become more localised and magistrates be elected for a small geographical area; or they could be chosen on the same basis as jurors from the electoral roll. But the lay bench is a very clear case of the intention to delegate limited and carefully managed power to groups of people considered 'responsible', and who are in the main already accustomed, through their class and occupational position, to the assumption that they have the right to control others.

Magistrates are carefully socialised, in so far as their general world outlook is channelled, in training, into the performance of specific tasks in an institutionalised manner. Before the introduction of compulsory training in 1966 all training was informal, taking place on a model somewhat akin to the apprenticeship system; but the large numbers of new magistrates recruited to the bench in the 1960s and early 1970s necessitated the rationalisation of this process. The content of training is strictly delineated - it contains no criminology or opportunity to discuss the aetiology of crime, but is confined to talks about procedure and to sentencing exercises. Further informal socialisation occurs when the magistrate comes to sit on the bench, particularly for those who, like housewives, may have little direct knowledge of the control of adults. It is here that magisterial attitudes are inculcated by the more experienced members of the bench, and they prove highly influential because they fill a partial vacuum, since no consistent philosophy is developed during training. There is a contrast here with a profession such as school-teaching, where radical notions may be developed during training, but prove inadequate for the probationer faced with a situation where control is a problem and ideal modes of teaching are inoperable. In the case of the teacher, the collapse of a system of beliefs may frequently lead to the replacement of that system by staff-room philosophy, or it may give rise to a genuine re-working of ideas to meet the new situation. Magistrates seldom have any advance conception of what the job entails, and the unquestioning nature of their training does not encourage such intellectualism, even where some measure of disillusionment is experienced. The problem becomes, then, one of knowing what to do, with only a superficial justification as to why it is being done proving necessary. It is in this light, rather than in terms of a theory of pure conspiracy, that the exclusion of members of the political left from lay benches can be understood, while those in unskilled and semi-skilled occupations who have not been previously inducted into roles of authority by political parties, unions or other organisations are equally unlikely to prove amenable to this implicit method of socialisation. To put it another way, training relates to technical matters only, assuming that the magistrate will happily adopt the control functions demanded of him or her in a relatively unquestioning manner. Those who cannot be relied upon to do this are not considered 'suitable'.

CENTRALISATION AND THE MAGISTRACY

The main body of sociological research into the lay magistracy has concentrated on sentencing discrepancies, notably Hood's studies (1962, 1972) of sentencing in magistrates' courts and the sentencing of motoring offenders. These studies clearly show the relationship between the social class of magistrates, the populations of the areas they sit in and the types of offence. All this is of some interest, yet in some respects the research becomes part of a process rather than an attempt to explain it. The underlying value expressed is that uniformity of sentencing is a desirable end in itself, whereas it is better understood as part of a drive towards centralisation, of which the eradication of regional discrepancies is one component.

In the case of the lay magistracy, the conflict between localism and centralisation dates from the industrial revolution, when the squirearchy in charge of law and order in the provinces proved inadequate to meet the new problems of urban and rural disorder manifested in Luddism and the risings of the post-Napoleonic War period. These troubles were met by the creation of a regular police force to take over the peace-keeping role formerly exercised by magistrates and the yeomanry. Throughout the last century, governmental bodies set up by the newly strong capitalist state constantly usurped magisterial functions. The Poor Law Commission is a case in point. It deprived magistrates of control over outdoor relief, and with it the right to fix minimum wages. The support of unmarried mothers where the task of justices had been to designate paternity and responsibility for maintenance passed to the harsh and rigorous Poor Law Commissioners who, as part of a drive to impose middle-class norms of sexual morality on working-class women, had such mothers taken into the workhouse where their infants remained as paupers (Finer, 1974). The emergence of central government control of welfare and health robbed magistrates of many other powers, the latest in this long line being, of course, the 1969 Children and Young Persons' Act. This is usually, and in some senses quite validly, discussed in terms of which group - magistrates or social workers - is better equipped to decide the fate of juvenile offenders. The Act is quite correctly seen as representing a shift in modes of social control, but it is more than this. Following Weber's central tenet that it is a characteristic of advanced industrial societies to rationalise and render accountable all aspects of social life, it can be seen that the 1969 Act enables a far more complete recording of all cases and a far more thorough documentation of details concerning offenders and their families. A further radical rightist critique develops from this analysis which argues for the protection of the rights of juveniles against such intrusion by strengthening the courts and introducing more lawyers into the juvenile system; but the argument becomes trapped in a closed circle where the merits of different professional groups are weighed and balanced, whereas in fact all modes of social control in contemporary society are class-based, and as such can be said to constitute an attack on the rights of working-class individuals.

Within the tendency to centralisation there is still a role for the lay bench, but it is one which involves sharing power with other agencies, coupled with tighter control over sentencing policy. Lower courts staffed by legally trained professionals would be ideal from the state's point of view, but the cost would be enormous. The compromise effected is that a few stipendiary magistrates deal with sensitive areas such as crimes involving individuals of high social status, or football hooliganism, and when this is not possible magistrates are instructed as to how to proceed. Thus when the winter of 1976 saw a large number of the latter cases, magistrates in my area were gathered together and briefed by the chief clerk to the courts that the policy was to be one of stiff 'deterrent' sentences.

An interesting instance of the limitations placed upon magisterial power is to be found in a series of cases in 1972 involving the Welsh language, which showed clearly how little autonomy lay justices have in practice. In January of that year ten Welsh language protesters who refused to buy television licences were tried in cases conducted in Welsh, and were given absolute discharges. The Attorney-General immediately issued a strong warning: the Lord Chancellor, he said, may have no alternative but to ask these magistrates to resign. Subject to a maximum penalty fixed by Parliament, magistrates' courts and all other courts had unfettered discretion, and 'it would be contrary to constitutional practice to seek to interfere with this discretion by executive enquiry into the sentencing practices of particular courts or with relation to certain classes or cases of defendants' ('South Wales Echo', 28 May 1972), but where magistrates had shown bias or contempt for law in their decisions the Lord Chancellor would have no alternative but to ask them to resign, or, in default, to remove their names from the Commission. Lip-service paid to 'constitutional practice' was, in effect, to be no barrier to strong action, and magistrates were left in no doubt as to the likely consequences if they refused to convict those who broke the law. But the matter did not end here; feelings were roused in the Welsh-speaking community, and later in the year magistrates in West Wales gave five more absolute discharges in similar cases, while those members of the Welsh Language Society who disrupted the auctions in Caernarvonshire of country cottages (an emotive issue at the time, since many were being sold as second homes to English buyers who were diluting the Welsh-speaking character of the villages they moved into) were also dealt with leniently. The outcry that followed was initiated by Welsh MPs, both Labour and Tory. One raised the question in strong terms with the Attorney-General in the House; another demanded the immediate resignation of the magistrates concerned; a third warned of the dangers of bringing politics into the law; while a fourth said of the auction affair that the time had come to show greater strength in punishing these law-breakers, 'otherwise Wales is going to be at the mercy of a gang of hooligans' ('South Wales Echo', 8 July 1972). The affair ended with the resignation of one JP and strong warnings by the Lord Chancellor to the rest ('Western Mail', 31 July 1972; 'South Wales Echo', 29 July 1972). The independence of magistrates has seldom, during recent years, been put to the test, but this series of incidents demonstrates that the discretion magistrates can in theory exercise is, in practice, now very limited.

THE WORK-WORLD OF THE MAGISTRATE

Frequently dubbed 'the great unpaid', this body of people most certainly work, albeit in a supervisory capacity. My comments here will be brief, but there are a number of strains to which magistrates are subject today, and further pressures could potentially endanger the whole operation of lay justice.

The frustrations experienced by declining sections of the middle class are experienced by JPs, namely loss of status, devaluing of privileges and increasing work-load and routinisation, all of which emanate from the centralising tendencies outlined above. In the immediate postwar period there were two sittings a week which seldom lasted until lunchtime, in an area where there are now six magistrates' courts in sessions daily, plus separate matrimonial and motoring courts. The juvenile court sittings come on top of this, though they are of course optional, but it is usually expected of the third of the bench who are women that they will sit 'in juvenile' after their first year to make up the obligatory one man-one woman quotient. A further compulsory training course has to be undertaken for juvenile court work. The system is largely kept going by the availability of non-employed women, who do a disproportionate amount of work; but for all, the obligation to sit once a fortnight, compulsory since 1948, can be burdonsome. Sitting in the motoring courts is most tedious work frequently described as 'rubber-stamping' - sixty or eighty cases, pleaded in absentia, may be dealt with in one morning - so it is hardly surprising that the Magistrates' Association recommends the introduction of fixed penalties for common non-criminal motoring offences. Such work is often undertaken by the most busy magistrates, because it is done in half-day sessions. There are a number of other keenly felt minor grievances, including inadequate parking facilities, the petrol costs incurred by travel to widely dispersed courts, and having to share the male lavatories with defendants in the juvenile court. More acutely resented are delays caused by inefficient organisation, of which there are many; defendants, solicitors or social enquiry reports may fail to appear in the right place at the right time.

The uncertainties created by status incongruence are manifold. To begin with, magistrates display a range of attitudes towards the power they wield, or feel they should be able to exercise. On the one hand, some are reluctant to fulfil a leadership role, and may, for example, refuse to take the chair, or permit an experienced clerk to control the court and conduct the questioning of defendants. The rapid expansion in the size of the bench leads many to describe themselves as 'new boys', although they may in fact be comparatively experienced. Yet the belief that 'we can't do anything now' is so widely held an attitude that it virtually constitutes a magisterial article of belief; an attitude held particularly in relation to juvenile court work, but which pervades feelings about the task in general. There are other professional groups appearing more often in court - more solicitors, since the introduction of the Duty Solicitor Scheme, and more social workers, as well as probation officers. Magistrates may or may not welcome this change of affairs. Many do, to the extent that even relationships with social workers, still regarded as incompetent idealists by some, have improved over the last four or so years; but the presence of professionals with a defined area of expertise in court can serve to diminish or perhaps dilute the importance of the magistrate. The response of some magistrates is a defensiveness which indicates unease with the role; very few have independently developed ideas concerning their actual or ideal function in this altered situation, and fewer still are prepared seriously to consider radical alterations in the system of lay justice. Yet there are a number who can be said to be more creative and flexible in outlook, although they constitute a small minority. Among most, there is a tendency merely to blame change and the times for their perceived lack of power.

There are, of course, still very real advantages which accrue from sitting on the bench: the title itself carries weight; friendships are formed by some; and the first experience of sitting on the bench may be intimidating but is undoubtedly an interesting one. But it is doubtful if the system can sustain further onslaught without serious repercussions; indeed, it was only through the persuasive skills of the chief clerk to the courts that mass defections from the juvenile bench were prevented in 1969-70 when power over the disposition of juveniles was handed over to social workers. A number did resign, and the majority are still not reconciled to the changes embodied in the Children and Young Persons' Act. It may become increasingly difficult to find men and women who are willing, or indeed able, to devote the necessary time and effort for a sufficient number of years to justify the expense of training and weekend courses.

POPULAR JUSTICE AND THE LAY MAGISTRACY

The magistracy and popular justice are fundamentally differing systems, for the former is class-based in functions and composition, and its decisions are strictly circumscribed to prevent it from acting in what the state designates as the political arena. Magistrates' powers may continue to diminish, but it is difficult to imagine that the lay bench could be abolished entirely in the foreseeable future, if only because its legitimation functions are necessary to the state in a time of anticipated rising social conflict. This is precisely why the key problems of selection and composition are ripe for concerted public challenge.

Attempts to reform the lay bench are seen by many people as irrelevant to the major conflicts raised by the crisis of capitalism, but such an approach ignores the mechanics of the development of radicalising tendencies. It is certainly true that changes in the lay bench would not change the capitalist legal structure or methods of domination. Were the bench to be reformed, (i) there would be little difference in its functioning, though, as I have argued, there may be some; (ii) in all probability its powers would be further curtailed. We would see doubts raised about lay justice, in just the same way as Robert Mark and others have begun to question the jury idea since the franchise was extended to all those eligible to vote (Bankowski and Mungham, 1976). The jury is historically a grass-roots institution, while the bench has always been an instrument of control, so an analogy between the two must be used warily; however, it is clear from the earlier account of the Welsh language question that when magistrates have some sympathy with those they are trying the system does not necessarily operate smoothly.

The changes people demand do not arise from nowhere, nor do they arise, as is sometimes suggested, from some mystical quality within the working class which leads to the setting up of the right kind of system at some particular revolutionary point in time. Popular changes, I would argue, are defined with reference to what already exists, and if those changes are achieved but fail to provide the desired ends, then the nature of existing power structures becomes clearer, and new proposals can be refined. The lay bench is unlikely to become 'popular', but starting from the assumption that popular justice develops as an extension of ideas of social justice, and recognising that social change is a many-sided process, in which attempts to reform existing institutions and the development of novel forms interweave, we can see that in this area the inconsistency between the theory and practice of bourgeois democracy is both obvious and crucial. The lay bench is a point at which different modes of domination meet; the abstract power of the law endorses, increasingly, the decisions of social workers or probation officers and can be seen in a less formal setting than in that of the higher courts. The magistracy constitutes a vital link in this chain of domination - powerful and visible, yet vulnerable in its own bourgeois-democratic terms; remote, yet the product of tangible local power systems. The state's defence is to deflect any discussion of the lay bench, from which we can surmise that the most appropriate strategy for those who would democratise justice is to demand that the question of its nature be publicly exposed.

BIBLIOGRAPHY

ALTHUSSER, L. (1971), 'Lenin and Philosophy and Other Essays', London: New Left Books.
BALDIWN, J. (1976), The Social Composition of the Magistracy, 'British Journal of Sociology', vol. 16, no. 2, April, pp. 171-4.
BANKOWSKI, Z. and MUNGHAM, G. (1976), The Jury as Process, in 'Sociology of Law', Sociological Review Monograph No. 23.
BARTLETT, D. and WALKER, J. (1975), Wheel of Influence, 'New Society', 25 December, pp. 694-5.
BERMAN, J. (1969), The Cuban 'Popular Tribunals', 'Columbia New Review', December.
BOLLERTON, B. (1961), 'The Grand Camouflage', New York: Hollis and Carter.
BULLOCK, Lord A. (1977), 'Report of the Committee of Inquiry on Industrial Democracy', Cmnd 6706, London: HMSO.
CARLEN, P. (1976), 'Magistrate's Justice', London: Martin Robertson.
CLAYTON REPORT (1978), 'The Application of Semi-Conductor Technology', London: HMSO.
DAVIES, C. (1978), Crime and the Police Courts, 'New Society', 23 February, pp. 424-5.
DAVIS, A. (1971), 'If They Come In the Morning', London: Orbach & Chambers.
DOUGLAS, J. (1967), 'The Social Meanings of Suicide', Princeton: University Press.
FINER, M. (1974), 'Report of the Committee on One-Parent Families', London: HMSO.
GOULDNER, A. (1976), 'The Dialectic of Ideology and Technology', London: Macmillan, Chapter 10, pp. 210-28.
HALL, S. et al. (1978), 'Policing the Crisis: Mugging, the State and Law and Order', London: Macmillan.
HAMMER, D.P. (1963), Law Enforcement, Social Control and the Withering Away of the State. Recent Soviet Experience, 'Soviet Studies', vol. 14, pp. 379-97.
HART, N. (1976), 'When Marriage Fails: A Study in Status Passage', London: Tavistock.
HOOD, R.G. (1962), 'Sentencing in Magistrates' Courts', London: Stevens.
HOOD, R.G. (1972), 'Sentencing the Motoring Offender', London: Heinemann.
KAMENKA, E. and TAY, A.E.S. (1971), Beyond the French Revolution: Communist Socialism and the Concept of Law, 'University of Toronto Law Journal', vol. 21, pp. 109-40.
KAMENKA, E. and TAY, A.E.S. (1975), Beyond Bourgeois Individualism: the Contemporary Crisis in Law and Legal Ideology, in Kamenka, E. and Neale, R.S. (eds), 'Feudalism, Capitalism and Beyond', London: Edward Arnold, pp. 126-44.
KING, M. (1958), Mad Dances and Magistrates, 'New Society', 14 September, pp. 564-6; quotation from Poposil, L. (1958), 'Kapauku Papuans and Their Law', New Haven, Conn.: Yale University Press.
KUHN, T.S. (1962), 'The Structure of Scientific Revolutions', Chicago: University Press.
LUBMAN, S. (1967), Mao and Mediation: Politics and Dispute Resolu-

tion in Communist China, 'California Law Review', vol. 55, pp. 1284-359.
MARCUSE, H. (1964), 'One Dimensional Man', London: Routledge & Kegan Paul.
MATZA, D. (1964), 'Delinquency and Drift', New York: John Wiley.
MILLER, D. (1976), 'Social Justice', London: Oxford University press.
PEARSON, R. (1976), Women Defendants in Magistrates' Courts, 'British Journal of Law and Society', vol. 3, no. 2, pp. 265-73.
PEPINSKY, H. (1973), The People v. the Principle of Legality in the Peoples' Republic of China, 'Journal of Criminal Justice', March.
PEPINSKY, H. (1975), Reliance on Formal Written Law, Freedom and Social Control in the United States and China, 'British Journal of Sociology', vol. 26, p. 330.
PIERCY, M. (1976), 'Woman on the Edge of Time', Connecticut: Fawcett Crest Books.
PODGORECKI, A. (1962), Attitudes to the Workers' Courts, in Aubert, V. (ed.) (1969), 'Sociology of Law', Harmondsworth: Penguin, pp. 142-50.
POPOSIL, L. (1971), 'Anthropology of Law', New York: Harper & Row.
QUINNEY, R. (1977), 'Class, State and Crime: On the Theory and Practice of Criminal Justice', New York: Longman.
'South Wales Echo' (see 'Western Mail' and 'South Wales Echo').
SZASZ, T. (1963), 'Law, Liberty and Psychiatry: an Inquiry into the Social Uses of Mental Health Practices', New York: Macmillan.
TURNBULL, C. (1976), 'Man in Africa', Harmondsworth: Pelican.
'The Times', 30 June 1977.
WEBER, M. (1948), in Gerth, H.H. and Mills, C.W. (eds), 'From Max Weber: Essays in Sociology', London: Routledge & Kegan Paul, pp. 6-221.
'Western Mail' and 'South Wales Echo': 16-19 March 1964; 25 and 29 July 1972; 7, 8, 10, 14 and 27 September 1972.
YOUNG, J. (1975), Working-Class Criminology, in Taylor, I., Walton, P. and Young, J. (eds), 'Critical Criminology', London: Routledge & Kegan Paul, pp. 63-94.

Chapter 6

POLICING THE COMMUNITY

Howard Williamson

INTRODUCTION

This paper examines the organisation of police work in a working-class area (which I shall call Milltown) on the edge of a large city. The paper is drawn from a wider study I have been making into attitudes in Milltown towards law and order and the courts' approaches to dealing with those who infringe the criminal law; to establish the reasons why there is support for law enforcement in an area of pervasive criminality; and to unravel the value-system of this particular neighbourhood in order to explain how certain attitudes and assumptions relating to law enforcement and law enforcers (in this instance, the police) are developed and sustained.

POLICE ORGANISATION IN MILLTOWN

The force normally consists of one superintendent, a chief inspector, five inspectors, ten sergeants and approximately eighty constables. Each day is divided into four shifts, which leaves a 'floating' allocation of men up to the rank of inspector. However, the numbers actually available are reduced as a result of training courses, illness and leave. This effectively means that there are few, if any, 'floating' men available: each shift usually comprises an inspector, two sergeants and about fourteen constables.

As far as policing practice is concerned, there has been a radical change in methods in Milltown. Panda car patrolling (considered to provide greater efficiency, control and mobility) has been reduced and an attempt made to return to foot patrol ('unit beat') policing, which theoretically places greater emphasis on the 'peace-keeping' rather than the 'law-enforcement' role of the police (Banton, 1964; Hall, 1975). Police in Milltown justify this change in operational tactics in these terms:

> 'The only time people would see a copper was when someone was being arrested; now you actually see a policeman laughing with people.' [uniformed constable]

Further policing on foot is an (economic) expedient, just as panda car patrolling was an (administrative) expedient when it was introduced. Moreover, the strains on manpower often dictate the use of panda cars in order that the available men have greater mobility; when this is necessary, beat patrolling is neglected. The attitudes of Milltown residents towards the police which are discussed below are based on police operation which is almost exclusively dependent on panda car patrolling.

POLICE ACTIVITY IN MILLTOWN

Just as the overall allocation of manpower and resources is a matter for discretion, so it is a matter for police discretion as to what priority should be given to different forms of criminal and other forms of behaviour which the police are expected to regulate. It is quite misleading to believe that the police are merely a proactive organisation (Skolnick, 1966); quite clearly, external pressures on the police (for example, 'client' or 'victim', or wider and more general pressures from the 'public' - the media, politicians, 'experts' - to deal with certain forms of behaviour) also make them a reactive organisation. However, as Cain (1973) has asserted, in the absence of these guidelines as to what police priorities should be the police may develop their own set of priorities in their 'fight against crime'.

It becomes apparent that a compromise view is appropriate when examining the types of behaviour with which the police have most contact in Milltown. Top of the list come domestic disputes and road accidents, closely followed by burglary, vandalism and rowdyism. The first two categories indicate essentially reactive involvement on the part of the police, whereas the latter two - although they too may be reactive - provide an illustration of the kinds of police priorities in an area characterised by a large number of burglaries and a high degree of vandalism (though it does not necessarily follow that the most frequently committed offences are accorded the highest priority by the police). It is interesting that, because of both limited manpower and more important priorities - such as offences involving violence - burglaries are diminishing in importance as far as the police are concerned. A few years ago there would be a detailed investigation and a personal follow-up; today, burglaries are often just 'logged' and the police do no more than wait for an admission or the chance discovery of property stolen.

POLICE ATTITUDES TOWARDS MILLTOWN AND ITS INHABITANTS

The central problem in attempting to document the attitude of 'the police' towards the area in which they work is precisely that the police hold no corporate view. Many writers justify presenting a corporate image of the police by arguing that structural and occupational constraints provide the conditions for the development of a common perception of their function as policemen and conformity within a police 'culture' (Westley, 1970). But this argument appears dubious in the context of Milltown. It is true that certain corporate views are held (perhaps the most pervasive is the policeman's belief that all those who appear in court are effectively already guilty, and not-guilty decisions may be blamed on legal technicalities, or the wizardry of lawyers), but different policemen view the area in different ways, and this affects their own behaviour towards those who live there. These differences may be explained in terms of variables such as the individual policeman's training, any knowledge he may have had of the area before he came to work in Milltown (external commentaries on neighbourhood life are usually negative), and his roots (was he born in the district, or did he grow up in it, or is he a complete outsider?)

Certainly, most policemen have adopted the 'community typification' (Cicourel, 1968) of the district as a 'delinquency area', though most officers feel that such a typification requires some qualification:

> 'When I said that I was going to be transferred to Milltown, I was told it would be like going to the Falls Road. It's true it's bad, but it's not as bad as that.' [sergeant]

But the majority of policemen working in Milltown conceive of it as a 'bad area' in terms of the degree of criminal activity, and these notions of a 'bad area' are closely linked to both potential 'solutions' to the high crime rate and to the apportioning of blame to certain groups who are thought to contribute to the perpetuation of this 'bad' situation.

Local police attitudes towards the neighbourhood may be broadly divided into two main categories - those who view the area as essentially all-delinquent: 'crime is their way of life; you'll never get rid of it'; and the feeling that most locals are 'OK', but there are a handful of persistent offenders who corrupt the rest. (1)

Most policemen who fall into the former and dominant category suggest that parents must be blamed for the continuing criminal and delinquent behaviour in the neighbourhood. They believe in a 'cycle of delinquency', by which parents inculcate delinquent values in their children from an early age so that children never come to learn the difference between 'right' (within the law) and 'wrong' (against the law).

This view of the neighbourhood as delinquency-producing through the mechanism of the socialising of children in delinquent values has some academic support (Herbert, 1977; Trasler, 1972), and important implications for police behaviour towards juveniles. As a result of this 'theory of a delinquent area', the prevailing view among policemen is that potential juvenile offenders must be caught early, for once they pass the age of twelve or thirteen they are 'beyond redemption'. However, the police are inhibited through legislation and through the actions of other levels of the criminal justice system from achieving their objectives. As one uniformed constable said,

> 'A clip round the ear'ole is sometimes the best answer; it makes them give us some respect. But you can't do anything these days, and these kids know that; even eleven- and twelve-year-olds today are quite capable of filling in a Police Complaints Form.'

So the attachment of blame to the 'system' is also closely linked to the 'pervasive criminality in the neighbourhood' perspective.

The police argue that crime is 'seen to pay'; frequent benefits are seen to accrue to the individual in contrast to the occasional penalty, and such penalties are usually 'soft' sentences imposed by the courts. The police claim their hands are tied: they can 'catch' people, but what happens to them after that? To the police, the whole weight of professional work (social workers, probation officers, solicitors) appear to side with the criminal. These people do their utmost to 'get their clients off', and generally they are successful, particularly with juveniles, because the courts (and especially the juvenile court) seem ill-prepared to consider the protection of the public, or the punishment of the criminal, but all too willing to make judgments solely in the interests of the offender. The consequences of these measures is that criminal behaviour comes to be regarded as profitable; the numerous 'last chances' given by the courts merely serve to undermine respect for the police in particular and for the criminal justice system in general. It is of interest that this police view is very much in accordance with the juveniles' own assessment of his criminal behaviour. What is crucial is that, at the very stage in the juvenile offender's life when the police sincerely believe that 'something can be done' (the 10 to 14 years age group), the unintended consequences of the actions of other parts of the 'system' (notably social workers and the courts) is to contribute to the persistence of the very (delinquent) behaviour which they are attempting to control and discourage.

But blame is not just attributed to other groups such as parents or 'namby-pamby' social workers. Interestingly, the police are not reluctant to elucidate their own contribution to continuing delinquency in the neighbourhood. Such police 'contributions' to crime have frequently been suggested in analyses of police-criminal and police-community interaction (Lambert, 1970; Young, 1971; Gill, 1977), but only by 'outsiders' (academics or the press); rarely has it been asserted that the police themselves are sometimes willing to acknowledge the contribution they may make to sustaining criminal activity. Milltown policemen argue that circumstances make them unwilling actors in this 'contribution' to criminal behaviour. One factor concerns the manpower problems faced the police force in general, and more crucially how this militates against the individual policeman's ability to develop a specific knowledge about the area. Police self-criticism is focused on this critical issue, though the root of the problem lies in undermining the high turnover of police personnel in Milltown, and the place of residence of Milltown policemen.

HIGH TURNOVER OF PERSONNEL

High rates of turnover within the police force in general and at Milltown Police Station in particular are closely linked to the problem of undermanning for two reasons. First, an officer is more likely to be transferred at short notice from one station to another which has an even more acute shortage of men. Second, vacancies will appear more often, which means that there will be more choice and scope for the ambitious policeman who is therefore likely to move on more quickly than in times when the force is at full strength. It is apparent that the high turnover of policemen at all levels (e.g., between 1974 and 1978 Milltown Police Station has had no less than five different superintendents) in the police hierarchy hampers police-community understanding in that, neither will the majority of policemen in their area of work have any detailed knowledge of that area, nor will the neighbourhood in question be able to develop its knowledge of individual officers.

High turnover not only undermines the policeman's ability to build up a comprehensive awareness of 'his' district, but it also militates against his desire to do so. He comes to believe there is little value in making any such effort, reasoning that he will probably be moving on to another base within a couple of years. This argument also applies to the public relations function of the police, which Milltown police state is their main concern today. The success of such public relations work is likely to be limited as a result of both undermanning and high turnover. Effective public relations work may be impaired by the shortage of staff, even though it is nominally a police work priority. Law enforcement styles still take precedence over other aspects of police work, and if there is strain on manpower resources, those resources which remain will be directed to the primary task of enforcing the law. Public relations activities (such as visitng schools and talking to pupils about the nature of police work and the role of the policeman) are shelved in the interests of more crucial police priorities. Despite the police assumption that a few hand-picked public relations police officers can improve the overall image of the police, local people in Milltown do not accept that policemen are essentially 'good' or 'bad', but develop their own ratings of individual police officers: 'Bert ______ is a big man, but he's fair, I'll give him that; he never oversteps the mark.' Thus attempts to present the police as a whole in a favourable light are not likely to succeed precisely because local residents are not prepared to accept such generalisations. Individual police officers who spend long enough in Milltown also come to realise that local residents do distinguish between them as individuals:

> 'I was getting known round here, and seemed to be getting on with people - you know, dropping into youth clubs, getting offered a cup of tea now and then. Then they started treating me more coldly, and one man told me that it was because of another copper who had been pushing a few people around. I went down the station and told him to stay off my beat because he was upsetting the residents ... and he was making life harder for me. [uniformed constable]

The problem is that most policemen do not feel that they have such a stake in the neighbourhood. They believe (usually correctly) that they will probably be moving on in a few years and that their location in the district is just a 'temporary' one, just one of many similar areas which he will pass through during his career in the force. Though most officers do recognise the potential adverse consequences of not attempting to get to know the place, they still do not do so because of the time and effort required to 'get involved'.

RESIDENCE

Only four of the policemen who work in Milltown actually live there, and only one was born in the district. This fact is important for understanding police attitudes towards the neighbourhood. First, many 'outsider' policemen dislike the area because of the problems it poses for the police, though some enjoy working in a place like Milltown because it is the type of area where there is 'plenty of action'. But it is a dislike of Milltown which helps enfeeble police-community relations. Second, some policemen almost resent the attention given to juvenile offenders by professional agencies:

> 'I live in _____. My kids go to a youth club once a week. The rest of the week there's nothing for them to do. If they lived round here, they'd always have something to do. They'd probably be taken on holiday for nothing in the summer.' [inspector]

This is an implicit reference to the fact that some Milltown children who have been identified by the social welfare agencies as in special need of 'care' are taken on free summer holidays. It is also an attack on the fact that 'decent' law-abiding children tend to be forgotten (precisely because they are so 'good'), while those identified as 'delinquent' or 'potential delinquent' are doted upon in terms of the kinds of services which are provided for them (though in fact there is a dearth of leisure provision for youth in Milltown). This point was made more explicit by another officer who had served in the district for some years:

> 'There's far too much concern about "problem" kids, I think. What about the good kids? What does anybody do for them? You know a few years ago, the station used to lay on a trip for Milltown kids down to _____ [seaside] and it was all paid for out of the Police Fund. Only kids who hadn't been in any trouble in the previous year could go. There used to be fantastic queues of kids wanting to go. It was a sort of incentive to stay out of trouble.
>
> What do they do today? They ignore the good kids and concentrate on these so-called problem kids. They take them on holidays and trips and then if they stay out of trouble, they think the holiday's reformed them and so they forget about them. The next year the only kids who go are the ones who've carried on getting into trouble.
>
> So you see it's the opposite of before. The only way some of these kids can guarantee themselves a holiday is to carry on being a problem.'

To return to the theme of policemen's residence, the main problem is again the ability to develop a stake in, and knowledge of, the district. This is where the 'local bobby' is accepted by policemen to have distinct advantages over the 'outsider'. One officer outlined the prevailing attitude of many of his colleagues towards 'indigenous' policemen:

> 'Coppers born round here are likely to be better than the others on two counts. First and obviously, they probably know the place inside out. Secondly, they usually have some pride in the area: they want the area cleaned up, but not just by getting a lot of arrests, but also by establishing a greater pride in the community so people can be bothered to look after it.'

Only occasionally was the converse argued: that the locally born and bred policeman might adopt more punitive attitudes towards offenders in Milltown based on the premise that, if he had managed to stay out of trouble, so could they. There was a general belief that the 'indigenous' policeman would be a better policeman, but most also agreed that the policeman, born and bred and working his entire career in the same neighbourhood, is a creature of the past: 'if you want to get on in this job, you've got to be prepared to move about, and go where they tell you to go' (constable).

In sum, then there is considerable diversity in the attitudes of Milltown policemen towards the area in which they work. However, certain dominant views may be summarised as follows:

(i) The area is thought to be a 'delinquent neighbourhood'.

(ii) Blame must be attributed to parents for inculcating delinquent values into their children.

(iii) The only solution is to 'get the kids while they're young', while they are 'redeemable'; but this is made virtually impossible by the actions and philosophies of the social welfare agencies and the courts (namely the juvenile court).

(iv) The police do not absolve themselves completely from blame for the persistence of delinquent behaviour in the neighbourhood - shortage of manpower, high turnover, and a non-indigenous police force leads to little incentive and even less opportunity to develop a detailed knowledge of the district, and the result is often indiscriminate police action which is likely to generate neighbourhood resentment.

COMMUNITY ATTITUDES TOWARDS THE POLICE

In some respects, the police view of Milltown as a delinquency-producing environment is a correct one, though there are other variables apart from parental influences and encouragement. Milltown is an area of low-income, low-status population which almost exclusively inhabits council housing built in the 1920s. The poor environment (concomitant with high unemployment rates) is likely to furnish favourable conditions in which a market for stolen goods can flourish, and indeed this is the case. 'Knock-off' (stolen cigarettes, lighters, radios, cassette recorders, jewellery, and so on) is a central feature of neighbourhood life. It is not considered criminal to be trading in goods which others have stolen; it is just a way of making 'a bit of cash on the side'. But though they do not consider trading in stolen goods to be criminal (in the daily context of their life-style), they are fully aware that such behaviour is against the law, and therefore illegal. This does not mean that all residents are involved in deviant action (the majority are probably not), but most will implicitly condone the circulation of 'knock-off' provided that it is beneficial to themselves and if any potential adverse consequences can be avoided.

Thus one might assume that there is a general distrust and suspicion of the police. On superficial examination, this assumption would appear to be correct. School 'essays' rarely refer to 'police' or 'cops'; instead, the most common descriptive term is 'pigs'. Children of 8 or 9 played a warped version of 'cops and robbers' where the 'cops' appear to play the role of 'baddies' - indiscriminately picking on anyone (the 'robber'?), beating him up and pushing him around. Presumably the game has been adjusted to comply with perceptions of the police which predominate within the local culture.

The local population is aware of the police assessment of the neighbourhood as 'criminal': this is reflected in the contemporary joke that 'if you live round here and "go quietly", the coppers usually add another charge: failure to resist arrest'!

Parents may privately condemn their chidlren's deviant behaviour, but they are more than likely to shield them in the face of police investigation, and even condone their behaviour in the event of police 'interference'. This of course gives the impression to the police that the area is a delinquency-condoning one, and forms the basis of the belief among policemen that parents often encourage, either implicitly (through an absence of sanctions) or overtly, delinquent behaviour by their children. However, it is by no means a universal attribute of the local population that they categorically condemn and resent police behaviour. In reality there is intense and considerable ambivalence to the point when the police may actually be called in to deal even with family disputes (hence the large number of domestic disputes in which the police become involved).

Residents are quick to categorise policemen into 'good' and 'bad' cops; those who fall into the former category are respected (though they may still be disliked); those who are assigned to the latter group are resented. This resentment of certain police officers frequently becomes generalised to all policemen in group conversations, and especially in discussions with other 'outsider' professionals. It is only among small groups of local people that the 'individualisation' of police officers takes place. The pervasive resentment of the police (the product not only of the behaviour of certain officers but also of the ease with which this group may be contrasted with 'good' policemen) is essentially because they are perceived as inconsistent, erratic and unpredictable.

DISCRIMINATING BETWEEN DIFFERENT POLICEMEN

There is a popular assumption that regular law-breakers have a necessary and intense dislike, even hatred, for the police. I have already suggested why this may be so, and there are further reasons for an indiscriminate hatred of policemen. For instance, one individual (aged 17) commented: 'I hate all coppers because they got me for something I never did'; while another (aged 16) complained: 'It's wrong that one of you gets let off, when they do all the others, I hates the law for that'. These observations hint that police inconsistency may be central to the generation of dislike of all policemen, but most young delinquents, reflecting the attitudes of both the criminal and law-abiding adult population of Milltown, do distinguish between individual policemen. (It is ironical that, while the recipients of the criminal justice system strongly resent others individualising them, they are quick to individualise those who deal with them.)

The following comments about the police illustrate the ways in which policemen are assigned to two broad categories:

> 'Most cops are only doing a tough job. Mind you, some are bastards, like those who try to pin offences on you which you didn't do. But it's important to see the difference between individuals. Most cops are only doing their job.' [boy, 17]
>
> 'Some coppers are helpful and fair. You know _____ [constable], he did his best for me.' [boy, 16]

The 'good' policeman in these terms is the one who 'plays the game', who 'treats you like a human being' (boy, 19). Moreover, when such a policeman makes mistakes, he is willing to acknowledge them:

> 'This copper picked me up yesterday about some job. He took me down the station and then found out it wasn't me. So he said he'd made a mistake and gave me a lift home. He was alright.' [boy, 17]

The interesting point is that the 'good' cop is usually also construed as the 'soft' cop, yet local residents realise that by sticking to the rules, he is unlikely to get very far in terms of being a successful policeman - one who arrests a lot of people. Many local people accept that the policeman has to break the rules to catch lawbreakers:

> 'They took me down the law shop and asked me who I was with. I was being all cheeky with them when one hit me in the face. The bastard was saying, "Now, let's have their names, or you'll get more of that.' So I told them, I didn't like them hitting me, but you know, if they'd said, "Come on John, be a good lad and tell us who you was with", they'd have got fuck all out of me.' [boy, 16]

But though efficient police work is equated with transgressing the rules governing police behaviour, even transgressions are rule-bound: for Milltown residents, rule-breaking is considered to be necessary only when it involves the use of physical violence in order to extract information or to instil fear or respect. Yet it is precisely this kind of behaviour on the part of the police which characterises the 'bad' cop. In Milltown, the necessity of the police breaking their own rules to carry out their duties effectively is perceived as quite natural to those who break the law:

> 'If I was a copper I'd do the same as them. I wouldn't take any cheek from kids like me.' [boy, 17]

In fact, most juveniles agree with the police that a 'clip around the ear'ole' would be more preferable to the institution of formal legal proceedings; it is when this is in addition to (rather than instead of) the formal process, and does not have any apparent purpose (such as securing information), that resentment and injustice is experienced.

The irony of the situation is that, while many residents do distinguish between 'good' and 'bad' police officers, the 'good' policemen - though in some ways they may be accorded respect - are considered to be a 'soft touch' in that they are relatively ineffective policemen. In direct contrast, while being labelled 'bad' police officers, the rule-breaking, often inconsistent and sometimes physical behaviour on the part of these policemen is acknowledged as the only way of doing their job speedily and efficiently, to the point where local people state that they themselves would behave in the same way if they were in the same situation. Yet ironically this is exactly the behaviour which creates the pervasive resentment of police activity. The police find themselves caught between the community they police, a community which recognises the need for the police to indulge in extra-legal actions and yet also condemns them for it, and also caught between the requirement to 'catch criminals' (which can only be done effectively illegally) and the court, which though indirectly imposing this requirement also continues to stress the need for legitimate 'due process'.

The resentment generated by these factors is exacerbated by an almost fatalistic feeling of helplessness and powerlessness in the face of what appears to be the overwhelming power of the police, both at an individual level and at the level of police organisation.

PERVASIVE RESENTMENT AND PASSIVE ACCEPTANCE OF THE OVERWHELMING POWER OF THE POLICE

While there is considerable verbal bravado in talk about the police among people who live in Milltown ('I'm going to get that copper, not with fists, but with bottles, knives and guns' (youth, 19)), face-to-face encounters are usually met with immediate subservience to the police, and at most facetious backchat:

Police: 'We're taking you in for being drunk and disorderly.'
Boy, 17: 'Don't I get a breathalyser?'
Police: 'That's only for people in cars.'
Boy, 17: 'Well let me go for a couple of minutes and I'll come back with a car - I promise.'

But even this kind of backchat is uncommon. When policemen are encountered, the norm is to do anything to 'get off', without (if possible) losing too much face. The adverse consequences of 'cheeking' policemen are part of local folklore:

'I was coming back from town with Slammer. I was having a piss in this doorway when I felt a hand on my shoulder. I thought it was Slammer so I said "Fuck off you raving poof". Then I turns round and there's the copper. He says "I'm having you for indecent exposure...." I think I only got done because of what I said to him.' [boy, 17]

Being picked up for such 'petty' offences forms the foundation for the growth of resentment of police behaviour and the general feeling that policemen who concern themselves with these kinds of incidents 'must be after promotion'. But resentment arises not just from personal, isolated experiences, but also from local general beliefs about the police, which may of course be developed from the cumulative experience of specific incidents at different stages of the police investigative process. I am concerned with both the general and the particular factors which create resentment of a police force, which is seen as holding a degree of absolute power and answerable to no one.

Neighbourhood sentiments concerning police behaviour are not usually confined to any direct specific experience (though this may reinforce attitudes), but rather are the product of the accumulation of 'knowledge' about police - community encounters over many years.

Subjective assessments of the way in which the police 'work' is often passed down through families, to the point where young children have already incorporated stereotypical attitudes towards the police prior to having any direct confrontations with them. The fact that many of Milltown's residents, especially juveniles, believe that the police can 'get away with anything' contributes to their fatalistic attitude and sense of resignation to a potentially unjust outcome. One individual, discussing the legality of fingerprinting juveniles, made the point that 'they're supposed to get permission but there's no point in objecting because they'll do it anyway'. Though the police may say that fingerprints are solely for the investigation of certain offences and if the individual is found to be uninvolved the prints will be destroyed, but who can guarantee that they actually are destroyed? The alleged unaccountability of the police and the perceived wall which protects policemen from criticism is a source of extreme resentment. Even if the police insult and provoke you, you cannot risk answering back for whatever the police may do there is no recourse to complaints (or so many think) and even if there is, who will believe your word against that of the police?

The picking on kids 'for something to do' is also strongly resented:

> 'I hate all the police because they're always picking on me for things I didn't do - you come to expect it, but it's wrong when you haven't been out screwing or anything like that, isn't it?' [boy, 16]

This raises the issue of the 'labelling' of offenders (see below); it also illustrates the hazy divide between general and specific resentment of police behaviour. Specific resentment of the police in Milltown is focused on a number of distinct but interlocking levels of police activity: stopping, searching and questioning; arresting, taking into custody, plea-bargaining and charging. In addition, there is the issue of 'verballing' when the police lie or distort the 'truth' during court cases.

Local residents are keen to recount occasions when policemen have 'just barged' into a home without a warrant. At least, they are thought not to have a warrant; even if they have, it would be asserted that the police rarely show it. Consider the following account:

> 'There was a knock on the door the other morning. I only had my nightie on and I was sleeping on the settee, so I went upstairs to get my dressing gown. Then I went to the door. It was ____ [policeman]. He was looking for Andy [relative]. He said he supposed I'd been upstairs to tell Andy to get out the back window. So he just pushed past me and charged round the house in all the rooms. I couldn't do nothing. I know he can't do that, but then what can I do about it?' [woman, 26]

It is the rough knowledge of what constitutes legitimate police behaviour ('I know he can't do that') which exacerbates feelings of antipathy and powerlessness in the face of what is regarded as illegitimate action by the police. The police are seen to be able to get away with anything - after all, 'what can I do about it?' Yet again it is crucial to reiterate that local people also accept that immediate action by the police - without the delays inherent in going through the procedures of applying for a warrant - is the only basis for effective police work in the area. What they do resent is the fact that (as they see it) they will 'get nowhere' if they attempt to make complaints about this illegal activity. Indeed, the only visible outcome of making complaints is perceived to be the greater likelihood of 'getting done', and being a continual focus of police attention. Police power and influence is seen as a stronghold which can never be breached.

The policeman has extensive discretionary powers concerning whom to question (or search), when to do this, and where to do it. The criterion of having to have 'reasonable suspicion' offers the individual policeman broad scope for deciding on 'who', 'when' and 'where'. For example, questioning might take place informally immediately the suspect and the policeman have a chance encounter, or (regarding juveniles) it may be arranged to take place in the parental home, or it may occur (immediately or later) at the police station. The final choice will often depend on the policeman's subjective reading of the situation. But the policeman does not just read the situation in a vacuum - his past experience with particular 'types' and his knowledge of certain individuals or areas will also affect his final judgment. It is these decisions which are problematic and to which many of Milltown's residents, and juveniles in particular, respond with subdued indignation. Two examples will suffice. One is the situation when a group of youths is confronted by the police. The group is suspected of having taken part in the commission of an offence (and in fact all the group had been involved). Despite this, the police only question two or three individuals and tell the rest to 'clear off'. There may be numerous (quite rational) explanations for such discrimination (perhaps witnesses have described only the ones who were detained by the police), but the reaction is one of perplexity: 'sometimes they [the police] nick all of you; today why are they picking on some of us and letting the others off?' Of course, the others may be interviewed or arrested at a later date, but the immediate perception of this police behaviour is one of unfair discrimination.

The second example concerns the unpredictable reactions of the police to denials by juveniles of involvement in criminal activities. On most occasions denials are 'accepted', in that the police 'withdraw' to assess any possible relevant incriminating evidence. But occasionally the police (anticipating admissions of guilt) become exasperated by denials which they 'know' to be untrue, but are unable to prove it:

> 'We took this car and we'd only just dumped it when the law drove up. One of them said to me, you've just got out of a stolen car. I said No, we'd been walking around. I went on saying No and I could see him getting really mad. And he suddenly gripped me and said "OK, but we'll make sure we get you for everything we can next time."' [boy, 17]

Of course there may well be a rationale for such police aggression: 'cheeky' replies from a suspect which are thought to undermine police authority; a 'certainty' about the suspect's guilt; an assumption that the suspect is likely to be guilty considering the length and nature of his criminal record. But central to the growth of resentment of the police in Milltown is local dislike of individualisation - both within the community itself, and in the context of police work, whether in effect it means 'favouritism' or 'victimisation'. The reasons for the development of local resentment of illegal police behaviour and the concomitant fatalistic acceptance of the power held by the police, which is perceived to militate against the likely success of instituting complaints against the police) have, I hope, been clearly explained. I turn now to other levels of police-community encounters, particularly those of arrest, custody, and charge.

The indignation felt when the police arrest on the vague charge of loitering with intent (and being a suspected person) has also been documented by Gill (1977) and discussed in a recent inquiry by the Runneymeade Trust (Demuth, 1978) following protests that the very haziness of charges under the 1824 Vagrancy Acts acts as an incentive for rampant discretion by the police and is therefore positively harmful to police-public relations (and specifically police-coloured youth relations). In a similar way Cohen (1973, p. 93) has pointed to the way the police utilise a 'situational logic' in order to control groups perceived to be a threat.

Being arrested and kept in police custody ('down the cells') is clearly linked to being charged with an offence or offences. But the nature of the charge or charges presents problems for the police who, being overworked and undermanned, look for the kind of charge which will be 'administratively efficient'. This is one which is likely to be 'acceptable' to the arrested person, and one therefore to which he will plead guilty, thus saving the need (for the police) to spend time collating evidence, interviewing witnesses, processing fingerprints, etc., which would be necessary in the event of a 'not guilty' plea. (2) The power of the police to 'negotiate' the charges with the accused is a considerable one on which they can impose many conditions. The purpose of such negotiations is not only to secure the administratively efficient statement of guilt, but also to ensure the good behaviour of the suspect, or to 'persuade' the accused person to 'grass' on other people and other offences, or to 'ask' for a number of other offences to be 'taken into consideration'. This last factor enables the police to improve their clear-up rate with little additional effort.

It is not the actual 'negotiation' which is the point of criticism - this can of course be beneficial not only to the police but to the accused as well. What is at issue is, first, the relationship between the police and the accused, one characterised by an imbalance of power which undermines the potential 'fairness' of any 'bargains' struck; and, second, the accused person's knowledge of the law. These two factors may often be interrelated. The power relationship and the detailed individual's ignorance of the law allows the police both to indulge in unlawful 'persuasion' and to renege on their side of the bargain. In both cases, the denial by the police that they violated the Judges' Rules, or that they made any 'bargain' with the accused, is likely to be accepted by a court, for the courts rarely find fault with the police unless there is strong evidence of police 'malpractice' from independent witnesses. Usually there is not. The word of the defendant carries little weight. The suspect's ignorance of the law means that the police may suggest that certain actions on their part are 'privileges' or 'favours' when in fact they are the suspect's legal rights. But once interpreted to the accused as a favour, the police stress his obligation to return the favour. If the suspect does not, then what else can he expect but a highly punitive disposition from the court; for the police will do him no (real) favours in court (such as not opposing bail, 'playing down' his criminal record) because he did not keep his side of the 'bargain'.

However, the police tend to underestimate both the suspect's knowledge of the law and his perceptions of police power. A sense of injustice and resentment is generated precisely because the offender has a 'vague idea' about the scope of the legitimate powers of the police, such as forcible arrest and forcible detention. Indignation arises because not only do the police have legitimate powers to 'dominate' the offender, but they also resort to the use of illegitimate measures to subdue and intimidate accused persons.

The outcome of these measures in the eyes of the accused individual is that he perceives an unfair pressure being applied by the police to secure compliance with their wishes, when he already feels that 'they've got all the proper power they need anyway'. And when an unintended consequence of this pressure is sometimes 'getting done for things I didn't do', the sense of injustice and resentment of police power is profound.

'LABELLING'

The term 'labelling' as I use it does not refer to the idea of 'labelling' as conceptualised in modern deviancy theory, though there are similarities, particularly when social control as operated by the police does lead to a 'negative self-image' (Erikson, 1962) or to a 'symbolic reorganisation of self' (Lemert, 1951, 1967). Parker has provided an alternative perspective to that of 'labelling' (in the context of juvenile delinquency) when he argues (1974, p. 194):

> Social control impinges on the Boys' circuit of social space, it partly defines territory for them.... The Boys are the losers, but they only lose battles, not the war; they refuse to be objectified and labelled as 'not good'....
>
> Isolated and with little power The Boys may be, but objects, accepting definitions stamped on them, they are not.

But neither perspective is universally applicable in Milltown. Parker's study was based on what was, in many respects, a delinquency-condoning community, one in which delinquent behaviour was acceptable so long as it did not affect local territory. Attitudes towards delinquency are by no means as clear-cut in Milltown. As I suggested earlier, there is frequent vacillation between overt and at least covert condonation and outright condemnation. A deviant label may therefore sometimes be assumed by delinquents in the area, though at no time is there felt to be a compulsion to indulge in criminal behaviour. Rather, it is accepted that a delinquent 'label' is not easy to throw off, and is likely to mean more 'trouble' from the police, even if the identified delinquent does make an effort to stay 'straight'. 'Going straight' becomes harder, and police surveillance and questioning comes to be interpreted as 'victimisation'. Such victimisation is almost stoically accepted. Further, 'labelling' and its consequences are closely related to the observations made above in relation to the resentment but resignation over the power of the police. The police are perceived to have the power to attach and enrich the criminal or delinquent label; they are also the only ones who have the power to remove it.

Both parents and other professional workers (e.g. social workers; probation officers) recognise this power of the police to 'impose' a delinquent label on individuals. While parents use this as an excuse ('The police are always picking on my boy, no wonder he's in trouble a lot'), social workers suggest how the labelling can be avoided, or, once the label is there, how a juvenile may reduce the chances of the label being reinforced.

Many young offenders are aware that they are the focal point of considerable police activity, yet rarely do they object to their delinquent labels. In fact, the only time when the delinquent label is vehemently denounced is by juveniles who have never been in trouble:

> 'I don't like being called a juvenile delinquent. I've never been in trouble, never, at least not with the police.' [boy, 15]

What remains problematic is why certain individuals come to be labelled by the police as 'vandals', 'delinquents' and 'troublemakers'. The concept of 'community typifications' (Cicourel, 1968), which are developed by the police and which affect police decisions concerning the allocation of manpower and other resources, lead not only to areas being classified as 'good', 'bad' or 'rough': on closer scrutiny it appears that even more specific categorisation occurs whereby the police identify 'respectable', 'rough' and 'tough' streets, families and individuals. The labelling of 'good' and 'bad' streets, for example, is recognised and adopted by local residents, but used in a different way:

> 'It's not surprising that he's always up in court, he comes from _____ Road.'

It is impossible to establish whether local people mean that the road somehow creates its own problems (for example, by newcomers being 'contaminated' by other deviant households) or whether they are making a succinct attack on local methods of policing whereby certain streets are more frequently under observation than others.

Police 'labelling' of certain young offenders does not reflect any kind of 'conspiracy theory'. What it does reflect is the need of the police to allocate resources somewhere, and the impact of hearsay and historical 'fact' whereby policemen new to the area are told to watch out for certain individuals, or to keep a special eye open in certain parts of the neighbourhood or in certain streets, or even on certain houses. The historical 'fact' is generated by this self-fulfilling prophecy: those people and places which are under the most surveillance are likely to provide the largest proportion of arrests and so the cycle continues, and they come to be observed yet more closely. The labelled deviant in many ways accepts his 'fate', for he expects the police to be watching him. When they are not, he anticipates their presence in a light-hearted way. However, while he accepts his 'label', he also feels victimised, for he knows that others just like himself are rarely 'picked on'. Resentment is experienced not because he has been 'labelled', but because others in a similar position have not. Of course, the demands on police resources effectively mean that some 'selection' must take place. Some juveniles must be 'picked on' and therefore differentially 'labelled', but such logical distinctions are lost on the young offender. For him, his mates are left alone while he is 'picked on', and that is blatantly unjust. The delinquent label in itself is a fact of life, and so no problem - he rarely resents his delinquent label, for quite clearly that is what he is. What he does resent, and resent intensely, should be reiterated: the abuse of power by the police; the apparent policy of 'random selection' by the police; and the juvenile's inability to do anything about it. The delinquent label in itself is acknowledged but not resented.

CONCLUSIONS

The relationship between the police and the community is one of intense ambivalence. Local people in Milltown accept that behaviour of dubious legality by the police is necessary for police work to be at all successful. But they also know that such behaviour is not procedurally correct, and their experience of police activities indicates that the use of illegitimate measures is subject to the same discretionary decisions which apply to legitimate modes of action. The police - when acting legitimately - are seen to have immense power and to be accountable only to themselves. So even when complaints against the police are thought to be justified, they are not made because there is a pervasive feeling of resignation that 'who will believe your word against that of the police?' Thus there appears to be a basis for suggesting that the resentment generated by this feeling of helplessness and powerlessness is likely to be exacerbated by the procedurally illegitimate methods which are often utilised by the police to facilitate obtaining admissions of involvement in criminal offences or to jump the gap between either theoretical and empirical guilt, or sometimes even between innocence and guilt. But in fact this supposition is not valid. A substantial number of Milltown residents do appreciate the problems faced by the police and state that they themselves would behave in exactly the same way if they were policemen working in Milltown. Even juvenile offenders adopt this attitude: 'if I was a copper I'd do the same, I wouldn't take any cheek from kids like me'.

Resentment of the police is therefore intensified not so much as a result of the unlawful behaviour of the police in itself, but rather as a result of the way in which it is applied. Inconsistency on the part of the police becomes injustice and victimisation in the eyes of the local inhabitants and when certain individuals appear to receive more than their 'fair share' of police 'abuse', neighbourhood resentment of police methods and of the police in general becomes pervasive and acute.

NOTES

1 This view may, of course, be expedient for any policeman working in a high crime area, for he can then dedicate himself to seeking out this 'hard core' of delinquent/criminals. This gives meaning to his work, for he can convince himself that such a group exists, and if it is detected, then a large amount of the crime problem will be solved. In contrast, acceptance of continuing widespread criminal activity suggests that any real effort by the police is likely to be futile.

2 Such a 'not guilty' plea may be both the formal plea of not guilty taken in court, in which case the police may accept the plea and the case is dismissed; or it may apply out-of-court - in this case the police station. In this context I use the term 'not guilty' 'plea' to mean either a persistent denial of involvement in the offence for which he has been taken into custody, or an indication that a not guilty plea will be entered on the suspect appearing in court.

BIBLIOGRAPHY

BANTON, M. (1964), 'The Policeman in the Community', Tavistock, London.
CAIN, M. (1973), 'Society and the Policeman's Role', Routledge & Kegan Paul, London.
CICOUREL, A. (1968), 'The Social Organisation of Juvenile Justice', John Wiley & Sons, New York.
COHEN, S. (1973), 'Folk Devils and Moral Panics', Paladin, London.
DEMUTH, (1978), '"Sus": A Report on the Vagrancy Act 1824', Runnymeade Trust, London.
ERIKSON, K. (1962), Notes on the Sociology of Deviance, in H. Becker (ed.), 'The Other Side', Free Press, New York, pp. 9-21.
GILL, O. (1977), 'Luke Street-Housing Policy, Conflict and Creation of a Delinquent Area', Macmillan, London.
HALL, S. (1975), 'Mugging, the State and Law and Order', Working Paper, Centre for Contemporary Cultural Studies, University of Birmingham.
HERBERT, D. (1977), An Area and Ecological Analysis of Delinquency Residence: Cardiff 1966 and 1971, 'Journal of Economic and Social Geography', vol. 1, pp. xviii, 2.
LAMBERT, J. (1970), 'Crime, Police and Race Relations', Oxford University Press, London.
LEMERT, E. (1951), 'Social Pathology', McGraw-Hill, New York.
LEMERT, E. (1967), 'Human Deviance, Social Problems and Social Control', Prentice-Hall, Englewood Cliffs, NJ.
PARKER, H. (1974), 'Views from the Boy's, David and Charles, Newton Abbott, Devon.
SKOLNICK, J. (1966), 'Justice Without Trial', John Wiley & Sons, New York.
TRASLER, G. (1972), The Context of Social Learning, in J. Mays (ed.), 'Juvenile Delinquency, the Family and the Social Group, Longmans, London.
WESTLEY, W. (1970), 'Violence and the Police', Addison-Wesley, Reading, Mass.

YOUNG, J. (1971), The Role of the Police as Amplifiers of Deviancy, in S. Cohen (ed.), 'Images of Deviance', Penguin, Harmondsworth.

Chapter 7

PUNISHMENT AND SOCIAL ORGANIZATION

Peter Young

In recent years an analysis of punishment - indeed, of legal and penal control in general - has become an accepted part both of sociological and Marxist discourse (for example, Scull, 1977; Smith and Fried, 1974; Althusser, 1971; Pashukanis, 1978). In the former case, the significance given to punishment stems largely from a logic within the discipline which, in endeavouring to forge conceptual and empirical links between the phenomena of deviance, law, control and the notion of social order, has focused attention quite naturally upon the origins, nature and function of differing modes of penal control. In the case of the latter, however, interest in punishment has emerged from a general reassessment and rethinking of the status of 'superstructural' elements, particularly those involved in theorizing relationships between the state, law and processes of legitimation. Here penal control is perceived of both as an exemplar of bourgeois power - and thus as a salient instance by which to investigate the social formation as a whole (Foucault, 1977) - and as a fundament of the capitalist mode of production as it, purportedly, encapsulates that which is seen as constitutive of this form of production (Pashukanis, 1978).

One of the refreshing aspects of these developments is the sense of rigour and attention to theoretical protocol that has accompanied them. Rather than assuming punishment to be a natural, pre-given object that can become, unproblematically, an object of knowledge, both sociologists and Marxists, with varying degrees of system, have made serious efforts to determine its import for their respective disciplines. Far from it being simply thus another area ripe for colonization into a specialist discipline - another 'sociology of' or 'Marxist theory of' - this concern with penal control has led to the development of a form of reasoning characterized by a formalist/rationalist logic which, it is argued, fixes the concept, rather than the fact, of punishment into its requisite position. A sound explanation therefore is modelled more by its theoretical coherence or harmony than by its empirical coverage or precision.

While, undoubtedly, this development has benefited the predominantly incoherent - indeed, at times, inconsequential - state of social science, there are a number of tendencies and problems attendant upon it that should make the theorist cautious about too readily adopting it as a lexicon or standard for his future explanations. It will be the objectives of this paper to illuminate some of these problems and also to suggest a possible alternative which, though not totally foreign to this process of reasoning, does diverge significantly from it. More specifically, the paper will be concerned with three separate but related themes. First, some attempt will be made to identify the nature and explain the cause of my disenchantment with these developments in social science. This will be achieved by undertaking an examination of some recent Marxist versions of theorizing about law and penal control because it is within Marxism that these rationalist/formalist formulations are most systematic and predominant. Second, a brief attempt will be made to give an exegesis of an alternative sociological way of conceiving of penal control which, it will be contended, may avoid the problems previously outlined. Third, the concepts of punishment and treatment will be interpreted within this alternative.

MARXISM, LAW AND PENAL CONTROL: ALTHUSSER AND PASHUKANIS

The process for deciding whether penal control is an object of knowledge for Marxism involves the theorist in satisfying two conditions. First, it must be shown that the object in question can be assimilated into the general and abiding concepts of Marxism; that penal control can be accommodated within the concepts of class, class struggle, state, ideology etc. (Hirst, 1975). Second, it must be shown also that, in more concrete terms, the object can be described by the more specific theoretical formulations of Marxism; that the emergence, function and decline of methods of penal control are explicable by a combination of Marxist concepts. To put this in different terms, it is the particular way in which Marxism describes the conditions of existence of a social formation that in turn determines the answer given to the question of under what circumstances 'penal control', 'law' or 'crime' become its objects of knowledge (Bankowski, Mungham and Young, 1976).

Obviously, for one who adheres to rationalism then priority must be given to the first condition - that referring to the general concepts of Marxism. For, if some answer can be proposed upon this level it must follow that through deduction answers to the second condition can be found. Hence, it is to the logical position and the logical status of a concept within a general scheme that a rationalist Marxist would pay attention.

For example, for Althusser the significance of law and penal control within Marxism is decided by their inclusion into a model of the capitalist formation which is seen to be composed of a variety of instances or structures conditioned by the economy. Penal control finds its place within this totality as it expresses aspects of the political and state relationship of capitalism. In Althusser's terms, penal control is an element within the repressive and ideological state apparatuses (Althusser, 1971). More fully, Althusser reasons that if a capitalist formation is to reproduce itself then this must be achieved, in part, by the state producing those ideological and political conditions made necessary by the economy and the class struggle. The specific form and content of legality and penal methods will themselves be 'secured' by the demands of these higher order instances or structures. Although, according to Althusser, the repressive and ideological apparatuses may have a 'relative autonomy', the boundaries to this are severely limited through a 'determinism in the last instance' by the economic.

Althusser's work provides a fine example of rationalist/formalist logic within Marxism. His scheme is given mobility by posing a certain abstract model of a mode of production from which the detailed nature of more specific social processes are deduced. It is as if the structures or instances which invariably compose a mode of production have certain 'needs', the job of which it is specific forms of social practice to fulfil. As Hindess and Hirst (1976) have cogently argued, this form of reasoning contains an essential circularity; it has an implicit teleological structure which, in effect, closes off the system. The nature and content of the ideological and repressive apparatuses are established not by examining the material conditions under which they arise but by hypothesizing that all modes of production, if they are to reproduce themselves, have certain prerequisites which determine the functions that institutions must meet. Moreover, the inherent rationalism of Althusser's work - for he is claiming that the concrete is determined by the conceptual - comes dangerously near to removing Marxism from any reference to actual events and developments. What one finds here is a theory of the requirements of a capitalist formation stated more or less only in logical terms; what is missing is any theory of how these requirements are produced or of how specific social practices emerge to meet these requirements.

The second example, that of the work of Pashukanis (1978), provides a similar, although in detail different, illustration. The similarity with Althusser's work resides in the manner by which Pashukanis utilizes a pre-set conceptual scheme resplendent with a series of distinctions and determines the place given to penal control in terms of this. The difference from Althusser's work is that Pashukanis employs a more straightforward base-superstructure metaphor, gives hints as to its inadequacy (but remains ambiguous upon the point); and finally, his work can be differentiated as he relates it directly to struggles and events then current in Soviet Russia.

Pashukanis's basic thesis is as follows: (i) The true class nature of law and punishment is reflected not in its content but, more subtly, in its form (juridical form or relationship). (ii) Law and punishment are historically specific, being tied up with the emergence of generalized commodity production. The form of law both reflects the material interests contingent upon this form of production, and also (and this is where Pashukanis is ambiguous) constitutes part of the mechanism by which this production takes place. (iii) Criminal law and punishment represent, to the highest degree, those characteristics which are basic to the bourgeois form of law, namely, the emphasis upon equivalence and the constitution of all citizens as legal, right-bearing subjects. In breaking the law the individual thus intervenes into that which is basic to capitalism; and, further, the organization of sanctions, through the police and courts, make public those values implicit in the form of law.

As Korsch (1978) has commented, there exists a central and important tension in Pashukanis's work; while he starts from within Marxist orthodoxy - particularly in his use of the base superstructure metaphor - he finishes, ironically, by implicitly revising this metaphor through overworking its formal aspects. Pashukanis's emphasis upon the form of law and punishment produces - as in Althusser - a strangely abstract explanation. Indeed, the stress upon form is so exaggerated as either to complete a separation of form and content or, equally as problematically, to imply that the formal features of social practices should be given priority in analysis. Arguably, this formalism constitutes a break with Marxist tradition where it has been the very dialectical relationship between form and content that demarcated its special contribution to social study.

While in epistemological terms it must be conceded that rationalism does not play a crucial role in Pashukanis's work as it does in Althusser's, it is replaced by an equally contentious and remote formalism and abstractness. Even in his projected revision of the base-superstructure orthodoxy (in his suggestion that the legal defines not only the mechanism of exchange but possibly also that of production), Pashukanis never achieves a properly grounded dialectic. One consequence of this is that Pashukanis equivocates upon the specific relationships that hold between law and economy; the relationship is perceived neither within Marxist orthodoxy nor within some systematically worked out alternative. Rather, one is left with an implicit and attenuated critique of orthodox Marxist conceptions and some suggestive, but incomplete, reflections upon the ramifications of moving outside of these conceptions. Pashukanis's conception of the social formation thus portrays it as composed of a variety and number of different 'forms', some of which are 'economic' and others of which are not. The resultant is a rather weak conception of the legal and economic as two 'enigmatic' 'forms' which are grounded 'on the same basis' and within which the mode of production is exhibited 'simultaneously'. While the crudities of the base-superstructure metaphor thus becomes elided or, at least blurred, they are supplanted by a possibly neo-functionalist formulation in which each 'form' is attributed an equivalent causality or, better (to coin an Althusserian phrase), an equivalent 'effectivity'. Such a conception, while not constituting a problem for 'bourgeois' functionalism - that theory much derided by Marxists - amounts to a considerable lacunae for a Marxist. For in replacing the dialectical notion of causality essential to Marxism with the notion of 'interdependence', Pashukanis, as Korsch has noted, deviates 'decisively ... from the Marxist idea' (1978, p. 195).

There are, therefore, a number of severe problems that flow from the rationalist/formalist logic of these two theorists. In employing a pre-given scheme which is used to determine, in a purely conceptual manner, the status given to particular objects, both Althusser and Pashukanis end up by proffering arguments which appear decidedly non-Marxist in many respects. Furthermore, it should not be thought that the issues raised above vanish once one returns to a 'pure' form of Marxism. For both, Althusser and Pashukanis, simply take to an extreme tendencies which inhere in the very fundamentals of Marxism and specifically in the crucial role played by some versions of the base-superstructure metaphor. It is adherence to this metaphor - even in Pashukanis's ambiguous revision of it - that generates problems to which, for example, a movement to formalism or rationalism are but two solutions. The nub of the issue is this: once it is in employment, the base-superstructure metaphor works as a universal framework which legislates both the position assigned to a particular object in its hierarchy and the manner in which the theorist arrived at this conclusion. Not only does such a form of reasoning place beyond question the adequacy of the original universal scheme, but it also contains an implicit rationalism and formalism. If this metaphor - which, as Hall (1977) has argued, is at the heart of Marxism - is used, then the theorist has little choice but to follow a rationalist discourse as it is the concepts of the metaphor that 'fix' the ontological status of particular objects. This can be illustrated by examining, briefly, the distinction drawn by Marxists between the legal and the economic.

For Marxists some sort of distinction between the 'economic' and the 'legal' is crucial. Moreover, as this distinction is made in terms of the base-superstructure metaphor it must bear, of necessity, those ramifications (like notions of causality or relative autonomy) that accompany it. Thus, while the economic is attributed one sort of ontological status, the legal is assigned to another, usually subordinate, ontological realm. Law 'reflects', 'corresponds to' or can be 'reduced to', the economic. (Even Pashukanis's possible deviation from the commonly accepted notions of the relationship between law and economy initially admits of some distinction between the two.) However, upon what criteria and upon what grounds can such a distinction be drawn, and upon what basis is a relationship between law and economy established?

The response to this question is commonly to assert that such a distinction is demanded by Marxist orthodoxy and Marxist method. For example, Korsch's (1978) vitriolic criticism of Pashukanis essentially takes the form of castigating him for deviating from the 'Marxist idea', of threatening the tradition of Marxist thought. The 'proof' of this argument amounts to an archaeological resurrection of some snippet of text actually written by Marx (or Engels or Lenin) which purportedly establishes the standard from which the disciple has erred. Rather than being mounted on logical or empirical grounds the critique thus takes the form of an appeal to authority. And, as with other arguments by authority, this leaves the superordinate untouched, as beyond question.

Consequently, the grounds for drawing some distinction between the legal and the economic reside in an acceptance of tradition and orthodoxy. However, this elides a central logical problem. How can one validate the authenticity of an argument or of a distinction by referring to the very theoretical edifice whose adequacy is anyway in question? In the absence of any demonstration of grounds other than those of authority, the logic of such arguments become question-begging in the extreme.

This question becomes all the more acute if one contemplates the descriptions given of the role of law in capitalist society. Law is described variously as, in part, setting the conditions of existence of the productive process by effecting, through the law of contract, the labour market, or as structuring also the sphere of distribution by establishing the conditions which govern exchange (for example, Thompson, 1975; Cutler et al., 1976; Pashukanis, 1978). Moreover, the concept of private property inextricably involves a legal dimension, for unless one promulgates a most un-Marxist version of essentialism, there is no universal or natural concept of this phenomenon. Rather, private property always refers to a relationship, and it is in the regulation of this relationship that law enters. In short, legality is tied up with basic 'economic' categories. While one may not be able to understand the legal outwith the economic the reverse seems to be equally as true.

The problems raised above, while perhaps not amounting to reasons per se for abandoning the variants of Marxism outlined, do raise issues which, it is contended, go to the heart of this form of reasoning. Rationalist and formalist Marxism constitute unhappy solutions to two questions which reappear not only within their boundaries but also within other types of theorizing. These are, first, the tensions implicit in endeavouring to justify the construction of a particular object as an object of knowledge in terms of some general or universal scheme; second, the perennial issue of how best to describe causality between different social practices or levels. Marxism highlights these considerations by employing explanations that make reference to some notion of structure. Immediately a structural explanation is referred to, the questions of how to specify a particular object in terms of the structure and how different elements of the structure are connected become acute. Rationalism and formalism, although moving away from an admittedly illusive 'pure' Marxism, do not transcend these problems; rather, they exacerbate and thus focus attention all the more clearly upon them.

SOCIALITY AND SOCIAL ORGANIZATION: THE WORK OF G. GURVITCH

In this section, I propose to outline an alternative sociological framework for explaining penal control which, arguably, goes some way to satisfy the questions raised above. Although this alternative framework is not perceived as solving these problems it does supply a suitably different theoretical and methodological approach to at least extend an appreciation of the nature of the issues raised.

The alternative I wish to propound is founded within an extension of the work of G. Gurvitch (1947) and the tradition of French sociology of which he is one of the more important relatively recent practitioners. As I understand it, the basic contentions of this tradition are contained in two key propositions:

(i) that all 'societies can be viewed as differing forms of social organization (obviously this assumes 'organization' to be a sort of 'primitive' sociological a priori);

(ii) that each form of social organization is expressed most clearly in, and thus can be understood and explained in terms of, the forms of 'sociality' or 'sociability' that characterize them.

The thrust behind this mode of theorizing thus argues that the primary task of sociology is to explain what it is that constitutes the 'social' within the particular form of social organization in question. The notions of social organization and, in particular, that of sociality therefore are utilized as conceptual heuristics; they provide analytical devices with which to explain the nature of the social.

While it occupies an important position in Gurvitch's work, the exact meaning and definition of this concept of 'sociality' remains obscure. Rather like the Durkheimian notion of the collective conscience, that of sociality is deployed in such a manner that its meaning depends more upon illustration, general reference and example than on explicit and formal definition. Perhaps the nearest Gurvitch comes to offering a definition is in his stipulation of sociality as 'the ways of being linked to the whole and by the whole' (1947, p. 156). Breaking this down, sociality therefore would seem to have a dual aspect: first, it refers to the actual form and content of social relationships or 'bonds'; second, it refers to the manner in which these 'bonds' or relationships are held to the totality or form of social organization. Hence, to analyse a phenomenon in these terms would involve examining its effect both upon social relationships and upon the 'link' tween these relationships and the whole.

Several points of extension and qualification need to be made. In the way in which Gurvitch uses the notion of social relationships, he is referring not to a contingent instance of interaction between discrete individuals but to the bonds which supersede them and which, for analytical purposes, exist independently of them. Thus, although there is an inescapable phenomenological dimension to his work, Gurvitch places this under a series of controls which terminate its descent into a mindless relativism or subjectivity. Relationships are to be analyzed in a manner which, while rooting them in 'sensuous, human activity', also regards them as not explicable purely in terms of this activity. A further point follows from this: neither the concept of sociality nor that of social organization are regarded by Gurvitch as being fixed or transhistorical. Rather, both are perceived as historically and culturally specific. Indeed, one of the very purposes behind Gurvitch's work seems to be that of understanding change and impermanence; one of the very essences of the 'social' is its historical nature.

Law and penal control fit into this framework as they constitute one of the principal mechanisms of understanding and identifying change in the forms of sociality and organization. Their significance resides in two considerations: first, some form of penal control (not necessarily 'punishment') is an invariant part of all forms of sociality and organization; second, the concrete manifestations of penal control (like punishment and treatment) express that which is basic to the specific form of sociality. Penal control therefore is bound up with the very conditions of existence of social life. To conceive of 'society' thus involves regard to the form of penal control which is an inescapable element of it. An understanding of its concrete manifestations therefore will provide a vista into the manner in which a society both is regulated and reproduces itself. Or as Foucault recently put it, 'Penal punishment is therefore a generalised function, co-extensive with the function of the social body and with each of its elements' (1977, p. 90).

At its most general then, the sociological rationale for studying penal control is that it enables one to analyse and to capture in concrete as well as theoretical terms the very nature of social life, of sociality. Penal control is an object of sociological knowledge only inasmuch as it fulfils these ends. Not only does it example the form and content of social relationships; it of necessity also exemplifies the articulation between these and the whole.

Obviously, the nearest sociological analogue to Gurvitch's work is that of Durkheim. Not only does the notion of sociality sound suspiciously similar to that of the collective conscience, but it would seem that Gurvitch is claiming that law and penal control can be perceived as 'indices' of sociality and social organization. However, Gurvitch does distinguish his work from Durkheim's in a number of ways. Of most salience, Gurvitch argues that Durkheim's work on law and solidarity is vitiated by a failure to keep clearly distinguished the general concept of jural relationship, of legality, from that of the most recent expression of it; that Durkheim first identifies bourgeois law as the immutable expression of the jural relationship and then projects this conception back into time and through culture. Hence, argues Gurvitch, both Durkheim's theory of law and solidarity and, by implication, its specific derivative, the theory of penal evolution, are limited by an evolutionary progressivism; all is seen to converge, inexorably, upon the norm of modern, liberal society.

Against this, Gurvitch contends that bourgeois law is an historically specific form of control and that to understand its uniqueness one must search for specific causes. Among these Gurvitch identifies the emergence of a centralized power (the state) as an essential one, as it is this body which dispenses the coercive aspects of legality through punishment. However, for Gurvitch law is not tied up inevitably with the existence of the state; only one form of law and penal control is so dependent - that is, bourgeois law and control. Outside of this specific conjuncture one can still identify differing forms of legality and control. Legality thus is not historically confined to a state-dependent relationship, but exists as a necessary feature in all forms of social organization. While, undoubtedly, this conception indicates a movement to a degree of ab tractness and formalism - the concept of legality appears to be an empty conceptual formulation - Gurvitch endeavours to curtail this trend by stipulating the specificity of phenomena to particular conditions of existence. Legality and control can be explained only via their changing manifestations and examples. It is, therefore, the content of sociality that determines the form taken by forms of legality (the jural relationship) in particular settings.

Gurvitch's work avoids the problems raised in our discussion of Marxism in a number of ways. Both the concept of totality and the notions of how relationships between elements of the totality exist differ from Marxism.

Although Gurvitch's work does refer to some idea of structure within forms of social organization (what Gurvitch, in a most confusing fashion, calls the material substratum and the spiritual), it is a structure in which no hierarchy or causal relationship within a hierarchy are posited. All Gurvitch's work presumes is that all forms of social life imply some form of organization and that the nature of this organization can be discerned in the content of the social relationships of which they are composed. No a priori delineation of causality or priority between different aspects of the organization are specified; rather, this remains a question or issue soluable only by reference to particular conjunctures.

In more concrete terms the ramifications of these considerations are extensive. Not only does it remove the need to construct elaborate distinctions between law and economy; it also evaporates the problem of causality between them. Gurvitch's work would reject any pre-emptive endeavour to exhaust this question in abstract. Rather, the relationships that do hold between aspects of social organizations would be demarcated only after the nature of a particular conjuncture is understood. There is, therefore, no question or problem of needing to justify or make consistent with some universal or general scheme the particular object that one investigates. As no hierarchy can be presumed, then the issue becomes one of understanding and explaining the connection between forms of social relationships and forms of social organization, not one of determining the significance of one in terms of the other. At its most fundamental the only distinction one can draw between the legal and the economic is that they are both forms of social relationships recognizable by the effects they have. Attempts to do more than this remain problematic as they assume the very quality it should be the objective to explain.

PUNISHMENT AND TREATMENT

In this final section I intend to examine in a brief and schematic fashion the concepts of punishment and treatment within the framework outlined above. As this is undertaken more with the attempt to illustrate and demonstrate rather than to 'prove', the observations remain speculative and reflective rather than final and fully formed. It is more an attempt to ground the abstractions above than to propound a completed thesis.

One of the basic contentions of Gurvitch's work is that an appreciation of the nature of penal control enables the theorist to understand the content of the prevailing form of sociality, this in turn indicating the characteristics of the more general form of social organization. Furthermore, from the emphasis upon specificity, it follows that a distinction must be drawn between the propensity of all forms of social organization to have some type of penal control and the specific manifestation of this. Hence, both punishment and treatment should be regarded as historically unique and specific social practices. Thus, it is possible to reason - by integrating these considerations - that the emergence of these two social practices indicates changes in the form of sociality and their attendant forms of organization. While this may seem a rather trivial proposition it nevertheless contains an interesting analytical potential. For, in more concrete terms, it would imply that an investigation of the content of these social practices ought to clarify alterations within a social formation; that changes in penal control - for example, the shift from 'punishment' to 'treatment' - should indicate a wider shift in the mode by which the social organization is formed.

At its most general, the thesis I wish to argue suggests the following. First, that punishment, as a specific form of penal practice, is tied up with laissez-faire or competitive capitalism. Second, that the emergence of the concept of treatment as one of the purported aims of the penal system is bound up with the transition from competitive to monopoly capitalism. Third, that as modes of penal control both punishment and treatment can be perceived of as forms of unequal exchange in certain particular types of social relationship but that, whereas punishment is founded within the premis of equality or, to use Pashukanis's phrase, equivalence (the inequality being the effect of its practice), treatment is grounded in an assumption of inequality. Thus, while punishment assumes, theoretically, a symmetry between parties in the relationship, that treatment expressly presupposes an inequality. Fourth, that the particular types of social relationship to which these social practices refer are those consisting of the relationship between citizens and organized power; thus, punishment is expressive of one view of political obligation and treatment expressive of another.

The connection between punishment and competitive capitalism is most clear in regard to the relationship mentioned last: that referring to the modalities of power and authority. It is contended that a presupposition or condition of existence of punishment as a specific social practice is the articulation of an ideology which Franz Neumann (1964) has called 'jurical liberty', or what historians such as Lynd (1945) have named 'negative freedom'.

The basic tenet of this doctrine is a form of philosophical individualism - the idea that man holds only an attenuated and contractual relationship to the political system under which he lives. Each individual, it is argued, in his status as a citizen, possesses both certain 'rights' (like those of freedom or to private property) and also the 'right' to presume that these take priority over those of the state. This concept of freedom thus may be understood best as one in which freedom is an 'absence of restraint' (Neumann, 1964, p. 163).

The connection between punishment and this ideology is supplied by law. Part of this negative concept of freedom argues that law functions as the mechanism by which the 'rights' of the individual are defended and established. And in those circumstances, when the state endeavours to remove these 'rights', the onus of proof for justifiable intervention lies with it, rather than the reverse. 'Punishment' constitutes one of the principal methods by which this intervention operates, and, moreover, this intervention must work within the boundaries set by law. To punish an individual thus amounts to a removal or temporary suspension of certain rights imbued in him by law and his contractual relationship to political power. Significantly, the 'right' removed or suspended is that of freedom; and the demonstration that such intervention is justified resides in the proof - publically announced - that the individual by his own actions has violated or stepped outside of the tolerable bounds of freedom given him by law.

Inherent in this conception is the notion that all parties concerned in the relationship enter it as equals; than an essential equivalence holds between, on the one hand, the individual and, on the other hand, the state. Indeed, the state is perceived in this relationship not as an institution given a natural ascendency per se but more as a supra-individual who acts on behalf of the collective. Punishment thus presupposes an equality between those involved both in its dispensation and in its reception.

Historically, the outgrowth of this ideology can be discerned both in the writings of Hobbes, Locke, Montesqieu and Kant and also in the writings of such 'reformers' as Blackstone and Eden. Blackstone, for example, proposed that the infringement of man's right to liberty was limited by the extent to which he breached law, and such a conception, though justified in different terms, is contained even within the writings of Bentham. Punishment was to be limited by the proportion to which it violated the contractual relationship which was seen as the guarantee of freedom.

Furthermore, if a removal of the right to freedom could be justified as a punishment, then some institutional form of organizing this process is needed. Obviously, the growth of the prison can in part be traced to the emergence of these notions. While these ideological shifts can not alone account fully for the emergence of the prison, they do amount to necessary preconditions. It can only be argued that the removal of the right to freedom constitutes a punishment if, beforehand, there exists an ideology in which it is assumed that all individuals do have a right to this condition. If such an ideology does not prevail then an institution such as the prison lacks part of its requisite conditions of existence.

While punishment may originate in a premise of equality, its effect is to establish inequality. This inequality stems from a number of different though related sources. In the first place, the assumption of equality has a limited area of legislation. It operates only up to that point at which intervention is proven to be justified; beyond this, then both the organization of punishment and the ideologies utilized to justify it, establish and promote a rampant inequality. Indeed, the very removal of the right to freedom condones this, as it facilitates the perception of the individual as a non-citizen. And if this is the case, then regimes can be practised which otherwise would be problematic to 'civil society'.

Once deprived of citizenship the individual becomes victim to those forms of inequality current within a class society. As a non-citizen he becomes a recipient of practices focused towards entrenching his less-eligible status. The history of prison regimes, the organization of diet (for example, the Graham Diet), the organization of discipline and the organization of work all conjoin to extend the inequality transacted by the initial suspension of rights conceived of as otherwise to be inalienable. While the premise of punishment may be rooted in equality and carry with it overtones of liberal democracy, the actual organization and administration of punishment inverts these and supplants them with their opposite. As Foucault (1977) has argued, the organization of punishment constitutes a 'dark side' to democracy. It becomes a mirror image of those qualities held to be valuable and sacred in the foundations of a free and potentially equal civil society.

The justification and organization of punishment within capitalism, both in its early stages and more contemporaneously, express an essential contradiction. Punishment brings together two apparently incommensurable things - equality and inequality - and invites them to cohabit. And it is through this contradiction, underpinned as it is both with assumptions regarding political obligation and with practices often in opposition to this, that punishment expresses the form of sociality and form of organization. By bringing together clearly the espousal of formal equality undercut by substantive inequality, punishment exemplifies the conditions of social life inherent in competitive capitalism and the mode of their organization. In this sense, punishment may be regarded as a neglected but crucial modality within a specific form of social organization.

In an identical fashion 'treatment' expresses the conditions of social life, the form and content of sociality, associated with monopoly capitalism. And, as with competitive capitalism, the connection between sociality, organization and treatment is pronounced through the ideology of political obligation. As various historians (Lynd, 1945) have noted, the emergence of monopoly capitalism is characterized by a shift from the conception of 'negative freedom' outlined above to one of 'positive freedom'. Thus, rather than the state being regarded as an abiding danger to individual freedom, it is conceived of as an institution which can promote and establish this freedom. Rather than being an exception to the rule, state intervention can be perceived of as the norm, for if individual freedom is still to be regarded as the objective of the society, then organized power must both support and direct social life to ensure this end. Individual freedom, rather than being left to the vissitudes of an open market economy, can be guaranteed better by the intervention of a caring, beneficent state.

So conceived, the relationship between citizen and state must undergo a substantial transformation. The right to presume that the freedoms of the individual, of necessity, must be paramount is dissipated or at least challenged and replaced by the notion that the state has a right to intervene not only for the common good but also for the good of the individual. 'Rights', rather than being given and inalienable, thus become contingent and dependent upon an actual institution which previously was seen as endangering them.

It is within this context that treatment flourished as a particular manifestation of this transposition in political obligation. If 'rights' are invested in the state, then it is possible for them to be removed without it entailing that this be done under the rule of law, or that the manner in which an individual is treated, once under the tutelage of the state, be subject to any scrutiny whatsoever. For it is logically entailed in the notion of treatment that those who are to be treated should be regarded as inherently unequal. The very purported objective of 'treatment' is to change, 'rehabilitate' or 'correct' those who, for some definable cause, are perceived to be 'different'. The very context of treatment implies the existence of a super and subordinate, the super-ordinate being in possession of powers which substantiate, without question, his position. The actual renditions of what is this 'difference' can, and did, vary through time. It can be perceived as due to 'moral laxity' or biological defect. At the point at which intervention is justified such differences do not matter; both inherent moral turpitude or genetically determined defect compose criteria on which to assume an inequality between individuals so disposed and others. Moreover, doctrines that proclaim this inequality and difference have a common and significant function. By stressing inequality they both de-politicize and thus legitimate intervention by the state. For it is the caring, beneficent state which intervenes not to limit or curtail freedom, but in order, by treating those who are different and unequal, to raise them to a position wherein they can reap the fruits of freedom. Intervention and treatment thus operate under the auspices of an appeal to freedom. Treatment is done not simply to 'cure' crime or deviance, but also to ensure, for the criminal and deviance classes, a possible access to full citizenship. The state gives to these people 'rights' denied them by birth or uncontrollable circumstance.

The actual practice of treatment did not take, of course, the pure and logically encapsulated form that the above exposition may suggest. Rather, the notion of 'treatment' was introduced via a number of avenues, not always state-ruled, which blurred and compromised its logic. Police Court Missionaries, for example, operated not with a consistently worked out theory of corrections, but with an evangelically based, reformative ideology which was concerned more with saving souls than resurrecting capitalism. Moreover, the Gladstone Committee, often seen as the moment at which 'treatment' became an official part of the penal system, referred to 'reformation' rather than to the putatively scientific notion of corrections. While it is admitted that these and other examples introduce an empirical complexity not encompassed within this essay, they do not controvert its thesis. It has been argued elsewhere (Young, 1976) that Police Court Missionaries, for instance, were generated out of class relationships and that their actions had the consequence of enforcing a 'cultural dessication' on to working-class life. Rather than being an exception to the growing interventionist character of the society, they were important in extending it. Just as monopoly capitalism spread missionaries abroad in its expansion of the Empire, so too did it send missionaries into its cities. Its external colonialism thus was matched by an equally important, but often ignored, internal variety.

Ideologies of 'treatment' or 'corrections' therefore were important mechanisms by which the growing interventionist nature of the form of social organization was legitimated. They express and help to constitute changes in prevailing political relationships and, in consequence, were and are tied up with the very conditions of sociality and of social life.

CONCLUSIONS

While this essay should not be seen as providing grounds for the rejection of Marxism, it is argued that it has raised issues and problems which touch to the very core of it as a form of theorizing. The alternative offered, though not fully developed, does provide an example of how these problems can be avoided or transcended. In particular, in rejecting any sharp distinction between the legal and the economic the essay has sought to take further sociological thinking on this topic. Furthermore, some endeavour has been made to lay the basis from which a sociology of penal control could proceed. In relating penal control, the ideologies of punishment and treatment, to the organization of power and of social life in general, the essay has illustrated that a concern with these topics need be neither vacuous or insignificant.

BIBLIOGRAPHY

ALTHUSSER, L. (1971), Ideology and Ideological State Apparatuses, in Althusser, L., 'Lenin and Philosophy and other Essays', London, New Left Books.

BANKOWSKI, Z., MUNGHAM, G. and YOUNG, P.J. (1976), Radical Criminology or Radical Criminologist, 'Contemporary Crises', vol. 1, no. 1.

CUTLER, A., HUSSAIN, A., HINDESS, B. and HIRST, P. (1977), 'Marx's Capital and Capitalism Today', London, Routledge & Kegan Paul.

FOUCAULT, M. (1977), 'Discipline and Punish', London, Allen Lane.

GURVITCH, G. (1947), 'Sociology of Law', London, Kegan Paul.

HALL, S. (1977), Rethinking the Base and Superstructure Metaphor, in Bloomfield, J. (ed.), 'Class and Party', London, Lawrence & Wishart.

HINDESS, B. and HIRST, P. (1976), 'Pre-capitalist Modes of Production', London, Routledge & Kegan Paul.

HIRST, P. (1975), Marx and Engels on Law, Crime and Morality, in Taylor, I., Walton, P. and Young, J., 'Critical Criminology', London, Routledge & Kegan Paul.

KORSCH, K. (1978), Appendix, in Pashukanis, E.B., 'Law and Marxism', London, Links.

LYND, H.M. (1945), 'England in the Eighteen-Eighties', London, Oxford University Press.

NEUMANN, F. (1964), 'The Democratic and the Authoritarian State', London, Collier-Macmillan.

PASHUKANIS, E.B. (1978), 'Law and Marxism', London, Links.

SCULL, A.T. (1977), 'Decarceration', Englewood Cliffs, NJ. Prentice-Hall.

SMITH, J. and FRIED, W. (1974), 'The Uses of the American Prison', Lexington, Mass., Lexington Books, C.D. Heath.

THOMPSON, E.P. (1975), 'Whigs and Hunters', London, Allen & Unwin.

YOUNG, P. (1976), A Sociological Analysis of the Early History of Probation, 'British Journal of Law and Society', Professtional Books Ltd, vol. 3, no. 1, pp. 44-59.

Chapter 8

THE LAW CENTRE MOVEMENT: PROFESSIONALISM AND COMMUNITY CONTROL

Mike Stephens

Law centres are now firmly established within Britain as a permanent feature of legal services. They have brought to many inhabitants of inner-city or 'deprived' areas the opportunities to seek advice and, where necessary, subsequent action on a whole range of problems within the fields of welfare and housing law. During their past nine years of operation law centres have encountered many difficulties, notably those involving finance, high case loads and the granting of waivers. Many of these problems and difficulties have been satisfactorily resolved; a few have not. This essay will outline the major problem of high case loads, which has afflicted the majority of law centres, and it will discuss how law centres have often been so preoccupied with this difficulty that community development or education projects and group work have not received the resources they merit. Tracing the development of law centres within this country, I shall present four basic operational structures and then consider the potential of each to implement an effective system of community control. Community control, exercised through a management structure, is a central article of faith espoused by all law centres that are members of the Law Centres Working Group (LCWG). Unfortunately, it is a principle that has received very little empirical attention, and many law centres are still a long way from evolving a system of community control over policy. In this chapter I hope to point out not only the obstacles in the way of the implementation of an effective system of community control, but also to highlight some encouraging developments and to stress the important role that the LCWG can play in moving further forward.

The American experience with law centres could by no means be described as one of overall radical activity, but some legal services programmes adopted community action strategies or undertook important test cases sufficient to warrant inclusion as organisational combatants in the war on poverty. (1) In Britain, when the North Kensington Neighbourhood Law Centre (NLC) was opened in 1970 there were no outbursts of radical activity to parallel some of the events that had occurred in America. At the time the very opening and existence of a British law centre appeared to be a novel, even radical, departure in the context of our legal system. However, if the existence of North Kensington Law Centre was a novel one, then in most essentials of its operation it remained firmly traditional (North Kensington NLC, 1971, p. 4):

> The broad aim of the Centre is to provide a first-class solicitors' service for the people of the North Kensington community; a service which is easily accessible, not intimidating, to which they can turn for guidance as they would to their family doctor, or as someone who can afford it would turn to his family solicitor.

The emphasis upon a solicitors' service was enshrined in the centre's open-door policy, and although there was some intention to appoint a community worker during the centre's first year of operation a receptionist was appointed instead. So far as the appointment of a community worker was concerned Byles and Morris (1977) point out that some of the more senior legal members of the centre's management committee 'were wary of the implications of such an appointment' (p. 18). The legal personnel sitting on this committee along with representatives of the local Citizens' Advice Bureau (CAB) and other welfare agencies, adopted a rather cautious approach to the provision of legal services. In any event, local people themselves - the consumers of these legal services - were allotted only three representatives on the management committee. It was intended to create an advisory council composed of local people in order to keep the management committee informed of suggestions relating to the centre's policy. After a gap of two years the advisory council did come into existence, but instead of being composed of local people as intended originally, 'in practice it consisted almost exclusively of representatives of local voluntary welfare agencies' (Byles and Morris, 1977, p. 17). North Kensington Neighbourhood Law Centre itself reports that (1977, p. 2):

> Eventually, mainly through lack of meaningful involvement in the work of the Centre, the Advisory Council ceased to function altogether. In retrospect, it was felt that the approaches to date for involving local people had been incomplete and inherently unsatisfactory. Most of the policy discussions had remained with the staff, with the Advisory Council following, not leading, initiatives.

After six years of operation the Centre still had no effective system of community control, but it had now established three panels designed to exercise a policy-making role in the areas of housing, employment and crime. The centre reports that 'Membership of the panels is open to anyone living or working in the community who is able to contribute to them' (North Kensington NLC, 1977, p. 3). It is to be hoped that this experiment in community control fares better than previous ones attempted by the centre.

The lack of success in organising an effective management structure stems in part from the reactive mode of operation originally adopted by the North Kensington Law Centre. This mode of operation in its purest form consists of an open-door policy that generates high levels of individual case work. Cases need to be processed swiftly and efficiently so that, in the main, the client plays only a passive role in his relationship with his lawyer: it is the professional who dominates this relationship and who typically defines the manner in which the case is to be processed. In a largely reactive law centre the largest proportion of resources and personnel is concentrated upon individual legal case work, while community work projects and group work contribute only marginally to the centre's overall operation. This latter contribution might be termed the proactive aspect of law centre work. A largely proactive law centre reaches out into the community, either to make contact with existing local groups or to help organise individuals into groups so that they can act collectively to solve problems they have in common. The emphasis is upon self-help and upon acting as a legal and non-legal resource for community groups. The proactive method offers the encouraging prospect of being able to offer the 'meaningful involvement' which North Kensington was failing to provide.

North Kensington Law Centre was originally very much in the reactive mould. Many of its efforts - which might have been otherwise directed into more proactive work patterns and into the organisation of an effective system of community control - were spent trying to curb the excesses of case loads (North Kensington NLC, 1972, p. 3):

> The Centre opened with a full-time staff of three, a number which was totally inadequate to cope with the flood of cases which poured in. We have gradually expanded to the present complement of eight; but in spite of this, and in spite of the invaluable help of many volunteers, legal and non-legal, the pressure of work has never diminished.

Such a state of affairs, in which the legal expertise of the centre's lawyers continues to dominate the centre's activities, combined with an original management committee top-heavy in its numbers of various professionals, is not conducive to the establishment of a management structure composed of the consumers of the centre's services.

In 1973 the number of law centres in operation began to increase quite quickly, and by this time there were at least some partially successful examples of community-based management structures of which the new law centres could take note. The National Community Development Project advocated the establishment of local representation in and control over individual projects. Individual community development projects were involved not only in the reinforcement of existing structure of local groups, but also in the formation of new groups so that they might encourage the articulation of explicit demands and the abilities to solve problems experienced within the neighbourhood. (2) Community development projects also demonstrated that a social agency could be operated effectively through a management committee composed of representatives of the local populace. The author of a report on an information and opinion centre run by residents of a neighbourhood in Coventry finished his study with the following conclusions (Bond, 1972, pp. 14, 15):

> That poor working-class people from stigmatised areas, who may themselves be clients of other agencies, are able to administer and run a social agency which relevantly meets the needs of some of the most disadvantaged.
>
> That the local residents' informality, spontaneity and deter-

> mination to get things done, added to a way of appreciating others' problems as a result of being in a similar situation themselves, means that the services provided by such resident-run neighbourhood centres, and the style in which they are offered, are likely to be more relevant and more accessible to the community they serve and therefore more effective than the services provided by either statutory agencies or middle-class run voluntary agencies....
>
> There is a strong case for the Urban Aid Programme funding such resident controlled centres, and indeed other community controlled projects, direct, since freedom to develop a style of operation relevant to the local situation seems to be a clear pre-requisite of success.

Law centres, however, had other more powerful influences upon their styles of operation than the experiences of the community development projects. 'Justice for All' by the Society of Labour Lawyers was the embodiment of liberal professional concern for those people suffering from unmet need. It advocated the creation of law centres with salaried solicitors in which every effort was to be made 'to retain the personal solicitor-client relationship which is a main strength of the private legal system' (Society of Labour Lawyers, 1968, p. 39). Furthermore (1968, p. 39):

> The English tradition of the 'family solicitor', performing general advisory functions, should be incorporated into the working of the centres: for it is a professional man in such a position of trust who is best placed to assist the individual to deal with his problems, whether or not they are likely to lead to litigation.

The report carried an appendix highlighting the community action approach of some American law centres in which the participation of the 'poor' was actively encouraged. However, the recommendations of the Labour Lawyers were not influenced by such proactive phenomena: they were content to take the idea of a law centre employing salaried solicitors and to fit it into 'the English tradition'. To all intents and purposes this meant an open-door policy for law centres, a one-to-one professional-client relationship, and the minimum of group work and community development or action projects. North Kensington followed the format recommended in 'Justice for All' for the operation of a law centre quite closely, and other law centres were also to follow this reactive model. In 1973, speaking about the state of legal services in relation to the debate over the provision of law centres, Morris argued that 'the definition of unmet need currently being used is that of the lawyer' (Morris et al., 1973, p. 51). 'Justice for All' in its recommendations (3) and the actual operation of North Kensington Law Centre, established the overwhelming professional hegemony of the lawyer within law centres which was strongly to influence the operations of many of the law centres that came into being from 1973 onwards.

Just as North Kensington Law Centre had been inundated with cases, (4) the new open-door centres being set up also experienced severe difficulties in coping with the heavy influx of individual cases. (5) They soon began to look for ways in which they might restrict caseloads while retaining, in most instances, relatively free access to the centre by local people. These restrictions involved the reduction of catchment areas and the imposition of stricter eligibility criteria for clients; some categories of problems were no longer handled; increasing numbers of clients received advice only and/or were referred to other specialist agencies and to private solicitors; hours of opening were reduced; volunteer involvement in evening and weekend advice-giving sessions was increased; referral agencies were briefed to refer only cases falling within certain priority areas; do-it-yourself kits were instituted in order to encourage self-help activities by clients; in-service training became a feature within law centres as part of an attempt to make their services more efficient; internal reorganisation into units dealing with major problem areas occurred in several law centres; solicitors were encouraged to become self-servicing; and so it went on. In their various ways these and still other developments were designed not only to reduce or limit case load levels but also to free resources and personnel to be used on more proactive activities. Slowly, therefore, law centres tried to get to grips with the problems of individual case loads.

A few centres, however, had never encountered these problems to any great extent. Holloway, Newham and Brent came into operation as closed-door law centres. Naturally, they conducted their share of individual case work, but it did not dominate their operations. The reason for a closed-door policy is to be found in the desire of these three centres, and to a lesser extent of Adamsdown Law Centre too, to concentrate their efforts on a proactive approach. It was felt by these centres that merely responding to the flow of cases which came through the door was an inefficient use of limited resources. (6) Freed from the relentless pressure of individual cases and committed to a group work and community development and action approach, centres such as Brent, Newham, Holloway and Adamsdown were able to open and sustain a dialogue with various community groups which vitally influenced the tone and direction of their work, and which seems to offer real encouragement for the implementation of a system of community control.

The position today is that one can analytically identify four main types of law centre operation. Naturally enough, no actual law centre conforms wholly to all of the characteristics of each model; but I do not consider that a crippling disadvantage, for the models are only intended to be useful descriptions of the main trends within the law centre movement rather than to be exhaustive classifications.

The first model is the fully open or partially closed law centre. These centres attract large individual case loads which lead to subsequent attempts on the part of the staff to reduce them. Even when attempts to reduce or limit case loads meet with some success, reactive centres such as these still encounter difficulties in reorganising their work patterns in favour of a more proactive approach. However much there is a definite trend in such centres towards the implementation of more proactive projects, the overall dominating influence is still located in the belief in the hegemony of legal measures and legal processes and in the lawyer's domination of the one-to-one professional-client relationship. Such centres often justify their high proportion of individual casework by arguing that casework allows the staff to identify areas suitable for groupwork and community development activities. (7)

Second, there are the CAB-linked law centres in Paddington and Hackney. CAB workers act as a filter for cases subsequently taken on by the actual law centre. They are also highly orientated towards the individualisation of client problems. CABs themselves are not noted for having community-based management committees, which, on the contrary, tend to be dominated by various professionals and local councillors. Hackney Advice Bureau and Law Centre stated in its 1977 Annual Report that it lacked 'a properly established Management Committee with strong connections with the local community' (1977, p. 9). This in fact was the LCWG's strongest objection to Hackney Law Centre, which (LCWG, 1977, p. 23)

> was promoted not by community initiative but by CAB and local authority. This agency has now run into enormous difficulties in respect of the management of the centre which could have been avoided if the original initiative had come from the community.

Although the centre at Paddington did emerge as a result of community initiative and abides by the principle of community control over its policies, the LCWG feel that CAB-linked law centres are unsuitable as models for replication elsewhere. Their central objection (LCWG, 1977, p. 24)

> to the CAB method of operation is that no matter how it superficially adapts itself, i.e. in terms of accessibility and public presentation, it is an external initiative not subject to community-based control....

Third, there are specialist (largely closed-door) law centres that receive appropriate referrals from other local advice and aid-giving agencies. The law centre attempts to 'educate' referral agencies through courses, reports and personal contacts to refer only those cases which the centre considers itself adept in handling, and which fall within the priority areas decided upon by the staff. Training courses may be held for staff members at referral agencies such as CABs and housing aid centres so that they can themselves handle a wider range of routine problems. The danger in such a system is that the criteria for the referral and acceptance of cases may tend to be 'hard' legal ones. A management committee, even supposing it was composed of local people, may not feel it ought to interfere in the selection of these criteria - indeed, it may feel it is unable to do so. The adoption of a specialist 'back-up' approach would seem to court increasing levels of professionalisation in the operation of the centre, and accordingly would appear to do nothing to dispel the mysticism of the law. In short, if the referral of 'appropriate' cases really means specialist legal cases of important interest to the law centre staff, then the role and authority of the lawyer is likely to be extended at the expense of the opportunities for a community-based management committee to exercise its own control over the centre's policies.

Finally, within the whole law centre movement there are a few 'resource' centres (usually closed-door), whose style of operation tends towards the proactive end of the reactive-proactive continuum. They focus their efforts, in the main, upon various community action and education projects, and they liaise closely with a range of community groups offering them the use of a variety of legal and non-legal services. This type of approach is broadly similar to the one advocated by the LCWG in its Memorandum of Evidence to the Lord

Chancellor and his Advisory Committee. (8) In this document, however, there is a heavy emphasis upon law and legal skills even in the realm of community development work. (9) I am not suggesting that legal skills should play no part - they are a valuable addition to a person's range of competences - but professional interest in law should not come to dominate the more proactive side of law centre operations. There are other skills and other strategies which may be used instead of or in conjunction with a legal approach.

It is with the more proactive centres that I feel there are encouraging steps towards implementing a system of community control. Even here, there are some disappointing results. Holloway law centre has put its position thus (Pitt, 1972, p. 391):

> a neighbourhood law centre must be a politically sensitive community action-orientated body, with deep local roots, if it is ever going to do more than provide a free legal service for the poor.

The thrust of this argument is that law centres created by local council authorities tend to have on their management committees not only councillors and representatives of local advice-giving agencies, but also a heavy representation of lawyers which inhibit involvement and control by community representatives. Therefore, Pitt prefers (Pitt, 1973, p. 391)

> to see law centres evolve through community development programmes, with overwhelming local involvement from the start. A local law centre must be seen and felt to belong to local people, who must dominate its management committee. This is something that lawyers do not easily understand, which is unfortunate, since the drive for new centres seems to be coming mainly from the legal profession.

However, despite the fact that Holloway itself evolved as part of a tenants' movement, and despite its attempts to instil in the groups with which it has contact 'a practical philosophy of self-reliance' (10), for the first five years of its operation the centre had no formally structured management committee. The centre has relied upon 'a network of friendships and cooperative efforts' out of the totality of which policy decisions have emerged - in the manner in which leaders of the Tory Party used to 'emerge'. This state of affairs prompted the staff to state that they were 'worried by the lack of clear answerability' (Pitt, 1974, p. 237). The invisible process by which policy decisions emerged was clearly unsatisfactory and unsuitable for other centres with much larger staffs, who often exhibit their own internal divisions on policy, and who are unlikely to be as completely immersed in their own local community affairs as directly as were the staff at Holloway. Holloway has now created a management structure composed of volunteers who help run the centre's advice sessions or who are involved more generally in the centre's work.

At Newham Rights Centre there was a strong commitment to the setting up of a community-based management committee as well as to the choice of a community development and group work approach. (11) However, though the centre opened in January 1974 no management committee was set up until May 1976. The reason given for this delay was 'the need for the Centre to become established in the Borough first' (Newham Rights Centre, 1974-5, p. 67). The consequences of this delay meant that policy, priorities and work patterns had all been decided upon by the staff long before the management committee began to operate. The centre has gone some way towards rectifying this state of affairs. Newham Rights Centre is now a registered Industrial and Provident Society, whose membership elect from among themselves the management committee representatives. It is to be noted that (Newham Rights Centre, 1975-7, p. 3):

> Membership of the Centre is open to representatives of any organisation whose 'principal purposes ... include the improvement or protection of the working or living conditions of that organisation'.... The full membership have quarterly meetings to discuss the work and progress of the Centre, whilst the day to day running of the Centre is delegated to the elected Management Committee, which meets monthly.

A monthly meeting would hardly seem sufficient to control the centre's day-to-day affairs, a possibility recognised by the centre in its first annual report (Newham Rights Centre, 1974-5, pp. 70-1):

> By the very nature of the way in which a Law Centre works, it is inevitable that the day-to-day work of the Centre will be carried out by the staff.... Nevertheless it is essential that, if the Management Committee is to exercise real control over the policy of the Law Centre, as many decisions which relate to policy as possible should be referred to the Management Committee. Ratifications of decisions already taken must only be a last resort in the staff's effort to involve the Committee in the working of the Centre.
>
> Because of the power of the staff in taking decisions and communicating information about the work of the Centre to the Management Committee ... it is the staff who ultimately have the power to give real control to the Management Committee, or make it a sham. There is a great danger of Management Committees becoming mere tokens of community control. This must be avoided by the provision of full information to the Committees and reference to them of all important decisions.

The extent to which issues regarding policy are effectively decided at staff meetings with the management committee acting as a rubber-stamp is unknown, but Newham are right to warn of the dangers.

The position at Brent Law Centre may go some way towards avoiding these dangers. Brent Law Centre dates back originally to discussions in 1971 between representatives of tenants groups, trade union branches and solicitors and law students who were interested in running an advice session in the area. Brent's first annual report discloses that (Brent Community Law Centre, 1975, p. 4):

> It was at these meetings that the idea of a Law Centre in Brent developed and plans were made for setting one up.
>
> One of the most important points to arise out of the discussions was that the local groups and their representatives, rather than the staff, should determine what work the Centre would do, and, in particular, the basis on which this work should be selected. While this arrangement left to the staff full control over the manner in which they would conduct work for clients, it was intended by it to ensure that the work of the Centre - especially the lawyers - was in accordance with the aspirations of represen-

tatives of the sections of the community for whose benefit the Centre was intended - the 'consumers' of its services.

The law centre acts as a 'resource' for local groups and has a closed-door policy.

The centre has now incorporated itself as a company limited by guarantee. The membership of the company (some 200 people) is composed mainly of nominees of each trades union affiliated to the local Trades Council, and nominees of various tenants and residents associations in the area. Over thirty local groups of various kinds are involved in this manner. The members of the management committee, comprising six representatives from tenants associations, six from trades unions, and three of the centre's volunteers, are elected by the full membership at an AGM. The AGM, like the general meetings held four or more times a year, is usually well attended. Law centre staff, local councillors, local or national Law Society representatives and representatives of other welfare and advice-giving agencies in the locality are excluded from membership of the management committee. Law centre staff are on hand at management committee meetings to present issues and to answer any questions asked of them. As representatives of local groups the management committee members enjoy a wide range of first-hand experience relating to the various problems which afflict their own memberships, and the issues which are of vital importance to them. To this extent, they are often in a position to judge the quality and the comprehensiveness of the information that staff members put before them.

Law centre staff take all plans relating to intended major projects for decision to the management committee, which has the power of veto over any such project. In order to get off the ground, projects must have the backing and interest of thc majority of management committee members. In this way, it is essentially the community interests which decide upon priorities, and not staff interests. Decisions concerning projects are thoroughly discussed and other options are canvassed and their relative costs and benefits assessed by the management committee. And this discussion does not begin or end here: the kinds of priorities which might be of importance in the year ahead are discussed at general meetings.

The developments at Brent are encouraging; certainly there seems to be a commitment on the part of management committee members to act in the best interests of the community and to eschew purely sectional interests. Furthermore, many of the members are involved in the centre's work not only as management committee representatives but also as participants in some of the centre's actual projects. Brent Law Centre is certainly an experiment in community-based management that is worth further study, and some of the encouraging developments there have been borne out by the experiences of Adamsdown Law Centre.

Adamsdown Law Centre is a centre which has always sought to develop the more proactive aspects of its work, and has enjoyed considerable success in helping to set up a local housing association and in tackling the problem of disrepaired roads and pavements in the locality. (12) The law centre was encouraged by the fact that people in the area were slowly beginning to organise themselves and to articulate their views and needs. It reported that (Adamsdown Community and Advice Centre, 1975, p. 6):

In Adamsdown it was hoped that activities at the Centre could encourage this awakening of local democracy, and for this reason the Centre was placed under the control of local people, and managed by a Committee of residents elected at public meeting.

Given the sheer weight of material that passes through the Centre, the Committee's task is far from easy. None the less the Committee has grown increasingly capable of making informed decisions and setting policy objectives for the Centre staff.

Individual membership of the law centre is open to everyone living within the ward boundaries, but the centre would like to see more people becoming interested in the centre's work than has been the case so far. Notwithstanding this matter, the centre confidently stated that (1975, p. 7):

> Experience in Adamsdown demonstrates that when people are given the opportunity to play a constructive role, and so long as they are given support in terms of having the information necessary to make informed decisions, they will make good use of that opportunity. Local people can manage community facilities successfully, and they can participate in the formulation of alternative policies, ones which reflect their views and needs directly.

The important roles both of a management committee composed of local people and of non-legal staff employed within law centres were underlined by the findings of an empirical study into the operation of Adamsdown Law Centre. The study echoed many of the experiences at Brent Law Centre in respect of the selection of issues for subsequent action and noted how important were locally based management committees and non-legal staff 'in focusing and concentrating legal services resources to the greatest effect'. (13) Furthermore, the report helped to dispel any doubts about the management committee of local people being manipulated by the professional staff. In this respect the position resembles that at Brent Law Centre, where the staff are dependent upon the support and interest of their own community-based management committee if they are successfully to initiate a proposed project. At Adamsdown, the research study stated that (Adamsdown Community Trust, 1978, p. 61):

> There is no doubt that there have been occasions where staff have suggested issues to management committees as matters of concern - perhaps because there appear to be legal possibilities - but where in the event the issue fails for lack of a constituency. And if there is no constituency, it will always fail. In deprived communities there are so many issues potentially to take up that only those which touch a nerve of genuine concern can have any hope of a successful candidature for Law Centre resources. To operate in any other way is simply counter productive in terms of the alienation created amongst management and amongst the local community.

Finally, after an investigation of the centre's interventionist approach of making contact with local groups in order to make them more aware of their rights and of the possibilities for enforcing them, the report concluded that 'it is the non-legal staff, locally based management committees, and the contacts which have been developed in the community who are the key to successful intervention' (1978, p. 49).

The LCWG argue that a management committee composed of representatives from the local community (LCWG, 1977, p. 47)

> serves as a constant check that the law centre is remaining responsive to local need and not getting bogged down in rigid work-structures as professionals left to their own devices have an inclination to do. By imposing upon the lawyers a demand for constant explanation in terms that are comprehensible by a lay Management Committee, they fulfil the additional valuable function of preventing the lawyer from drifting back into a professional distance from the community and hiding in the shadows of professional or technical language and ideas.

The above statement only implicitly recognises the dangers presented by professionalism for the implementation of a system of community or communal control. The influence of professionalism is partly admitted by the LCWG (1977, p. 47) when it states that the creation of a community-based management structure has been

> something of a problem in the early days of the Law Centre movement. Funding agencies have invariably demanded the right to impose representatives upon the Management Committees, while at the same time universally accepting the principal of independence. There has been a general failure to recognise potential conflicts of interest, e.g. in the imposition of Law Society representatives. There is a tendency to include other professionals in Management Committees which seems to serve no useful purpose that could not be fulfilled in other, occasional ways as the need arises. The difficulty is that new Law Centres will usually turn to existing Law Centres for models, so that these tendencies perpetuate themselves. (14)

There is another source of professionalism besides those mentioned in the above quotation, namely the historical and continuing influence of those liberal lawyers who helped to fashion most of the early law centres in Britain into predominantly legal case work, open-door agencies. To be sure, law centre staffs are busily modifying this type of approach in the light of experience, and there is a trend towards greater involvement of local inhabitants in the work of law centres. None the less, many centres remain whose management committees still contain councillors, local and national Law Society representatives and various other professionals, and there is some evidence to suggest that the presence of these people inhibits the contributions made by community representatives. (15) This problem has still to be resolved, while the problem of the professionalism of law centre staff is rarely even discussed. Professionalism exists, in the opinion of Johnson, where 'the producer defines the needs of the consumer and the manner in which these needs are catered for' (Johnson, 1972, p. 45).

The LCWG proposes an evaluative study of a variety of aspects of law centre operation. It must turn its attention also to this problem of professionalism, and it must give active and practical consideration to the possibilities of implementing a system of community control 'in which the consumer defines his own needs and the manner in which they are to be met' (Johnson, 1972, p. 46). This issue is a political as well as a technical issue. The LCWG quite understandably wishes to avoid not only undue Law Society influence over law centre operations, but also any centralised code of practice and a uniform management structure which may be imposed with the possible advent of permanent government funding for law centres.

To reiterate that law centres are (or should be) controlled by local community representatives makes it more difficult for government or any other institution to arrogate control to itself, should such a choice be made. Law centres also make much of their individual ability to respond flexibly to local needs, but this should not blind them to the fact that there are also common problems of operation that need to be considered. These problems include the original impetus within the law centre movement to create what was essentially a solicitors' service immersed in traditional professional-client relationships that has subsequently posed many difficulties for law centres attempting to move towards a more proactive approach. There has been too, very little discussion of the dangers of professionalism undermining attempts to implement systems of community control, and a lack of an adequate understanding throughout the whole law centre movement as to how community control operates in practice.

At Brent and Adamsdown Law Centres the management committees essentially had the power of veto - the ability to halt proposed projects - but there was little evidence to suggest that they played a more innovative role. In order to promote such a role, which would give greater scope to the meaning and practice of community control, a way must be found of involving local people in the work of law centres. Holloway Law Centre, despite its commitment to proactive involvement with local groups, failed to attract local people to sit on its management committee, though this may have owed a good deal to the centre's severe lack of resources and personnel. At Brent and Adamsdown the picture is more hopeful, but there is nothing to suggest as yet that these management committees will progress beyond the 'veto stage' to a more innovative stage of development. In order to do so, law centres must have staffs prepared to encourage the development of communal control and must be prepared to respond to initiatives mooted by the community-based management committee. This could be partially achieved, perhaps, through the correct mix of community workers within law centres, though even here one can have professional domination within a community work set of activities. But where are the lawyers to come from who will be prepared to work this way? Who will train them? And how? Even if this form of communal control remains unfeasible there is still the problem of those management committees in which community representatives participate at a low level of commitment and who are reduced to ratifying dexisions taken elsewhere. How can these be improved?

The idea of community control is sometimes confused with the idea of flexibility and responsiveness to local needs. Local needs are identified by the flow of cases coming into many open-door law centres, the legal aspects of these problems being ultimately idenfied by lawyers. Other factors too influence the responsiveness of law centres, such as the incidence and type of local advice-giving agencies, the size and composition of a law centre's resources, the restrictions imposed on all law centres by the Law Society, the availability of agencies and private solicitors to which a law centre can refer some of its clients, and so on. (16) As inevitable as these factors may be, they are a long way removed from a community-based management committee determining the responsiveness of a law centre through the explicit articulation of needs and demands. Remaining responsive to local need must not be allowed to degenerate into the identification of problem categories by legal professionals. (17) At every opportunity law centres must encourage community groups and their representatives to articulate their own needs and demands, and it is the proactive approach which, I believe, offers the best hope for such a development.

A proactive approach means that the domination of law and legal processes, and the traditional professional-client relationships, no longer held sway. As Pitt has remarked (1974, p. 237),

> It simply is not possible to sit on the fence and try to provide a service, as a professional is trained to do, and at the same time try to inculcate a philosophy of self-reliance. This does not mean that a professional cannot make his particular expertise available; but there is a distinction here between the ethos of professionalism and making expertise available. Everyone has some sort of expertise - the problem is to utilise it communally in a liberating way. This is a dilemma which all socially conscious professionals, acting as professionals, must try to resolve.

If a system of community or communal control is to operate, then professionalist domination of lawyer-client relationships and of work patterns must give way to relationships and patterns of working in which knowledge and expertise is not only shared with community groups but is put at their disposal. This type of involvement in local groups, from which would come management committee representatives, can increase self-confidence and self-reliance among group members. A few British law centres have started out on this proactive road and have attempted to offer the clients/groups high levels of informed consent which include the options of legal and non-legal courses of action. In this manner, clients play a more active role in their relationship with the law centre and the dangers of dependency are therefore lessened. Only as law centre clients escape the dominating influences of professionalism can one expect to see the emergence of community-based management committees exercising effective control over the creation, direction and implementation of law centre policy.

This essay has highlighted many of the difficulties facing law centres, and I urge the LCWG in its forthcoming evaluative study to address these difficulties seriously if the concept of community control is not to remain a term of general convenience. Law centres have hitherto done a remarkable job in the context of the provision of legal services to those who otherwise would have gone without. But if they are not to ossify and to retreat into patterns of professionalist control they must ensure that they are truly accountable to their local communities. They must confront the notions of professionalism contained within much of their own activities, however painful this may prove to be.

NOTES

1 See Stumpf et al. (1971); also Finman (1971).
2 See The National Community Development Project (1973), p. 52.
3 'Justice for All' (Society of Labour Lawyers, 1968) recommended that a trained social worker be attached to a law centre as a receptionist (p. 62), the purpose of the receptionist being to sift the legal from the non-legal (p. 45):

> This would have the advantage of saving the lawyer listening to problems only to discover that they require a different expertise, while at the same time ensuring that the reputation of the office was primarily based on its provision of a legal service.

4 The problems of high case levels had also occurred in many American legal services programmes; specifically, see Sykes (1969).
5 The following are but a few examples of the difficulties faced by reactive law centres.
Balham Neighbourhood Law Centre, Annual Report, June 1974-March 1975, p. 5:

> The centre is one of many agencies that is in danger of being swamped by housing casework.

Islington Community Law Centre, Annual Report, 1975, p. 2:

> Certainly, we are trying to reduce our own work load; we are now rejecting small accident and consumer claims. But, whatever we do to reduce the load of appointments or eliminate certain types of cases, the pressure goes on.

Paddington Neighbourhood Advice Bureau and Law Centre, Annual Report, 1975, p. 11:

> Following a couple of relatively short periods when the staff became so overladen with work that they could only accept referrals which were emergencies, we decided, after much heart-searching, that as from the end of the year under review, the catchment area of the Law Centre would have to be restricted....

6 See Newham Rights Centre (1974-5), p. 8.
7 I would place in this category Camden, North Kensington and Islington Law Centres, to name just a few.
8 See LCWG (1974), p. 7.
9 LCWG (1974), p. 11, para 3.6, and p. 13, para 3.7 (111).
10 For a fuller outline of the approach of Holloway Law Centre see HNLC, Annual Report, 1974, pp. 2 and 14-15. See also Pitt (1974).
11 See generally Newham Rights Centre (1974-5), and especially pp. 52-71.
12 For a full account of this problem of disrepair and of the centre's imaginative use of the green form scheme see Adamsdown Community and Advice Centre (1976).
13 See Adamsdown Community Trust (1978), p. 35.
14 Not only the composition of management committees but also aspects of operational approach have been perpetuated. See, for instance, Garratt Lane Law Centre's First Annual Report (1977), which fully acknowledged the dangers of an open-door policy and yet decided to adopt this approach in the belief that

by remaining closed for a short period in the week the centre would escape a large flow of cases during the rest of it.

15 Byles and Morris (1977), p. 15, reported that non-legal members of the North Kensington law centre's management committee found themselves unable to communicate with committee members and some complained that the atmosphere was so formal that they were inhibited from making any contribution at all to the discussion. There was a suggestion that the lawyers seemed always to dominate the proceedings, a view also shared by some lay members of the committee itself, who expressed the view that they felt at a disadvantage when professional matters were being discussed.

16 See LCWG (1977), pp. 29 et seq.

17 At North Kensington, a reactive law centre, Byles and Morris (1977, p. 51) reported that several community groups were critical of the centre's overall case work approach and wanted to see the adoption of a more' aggressive' role involving the stimulation of community organisations. The centre did not adopt the suggested role.

BIBLIOGRAPHY

ADAMSDOWN COMMUNITY AND ADVICE CENTRE (1975), 'Annual Report to Members, 1974/75'.

ADAMSDOWN COMMUNITY AND ADVICE CENTRE (1976), 'Disrepaired Roads and Pavements'.

ADAMSDOWN COMMUNITY TRUST (1978), 'Community Need and Law Centre Practice. An Empirical Assessment'.

BOND, N. (1972), 'The Hillfields Information and Opinion Centre - The Evolution of a Social Agency Controlled by Local Residents', Coventry Community Development Project. Occasional Papers. No. 2.

BRENT COMMUNITY LAW CENTRE (1975), 'First Report'.

BYLES, A. and MORRIS, P. (1977), 'Unmet Neet. The Case of the Neighbourhood Law Centre', London: Routledge & Kegan Paul.

FINMAN, T. (1971), OEO Legal Service Programs and the Pursuit of Social Change: The Relationship between Program Ideology and Program Performance, 'Wisconsin Law Review', no. 4, pp. 1001-84.

HACKNEY ADVICE BUREAU AND LAW CENTRE (1977), 'Annual Report. May 1976-March 1977'.

HOLLOWAY NEIGHBOURHOOD LAW CENTRE (1974), 'Annual Report'.

JOHNSON, T.J. (1972), 'Professions and Power', London: Macmillan.

LAW CENTRES WORKING GROUP (LCWG) (1974), 'Towards Equal Justice', Memorandum of Evidence to the Lord Chancellor and his Advisory Committee.

LAW CENTRES WORKING GROUP (LCWG) (1977), 'Evidence to the Royal Commission on Legal Services'.

MORRIS, P. (1973), A Sociological Approach to Research in Legal Services, in Morris, P., White, R. and Lewis, P. (eds), 'Social Needs and Legal Action', London: Martin Robinson.

NATIONAL COMMUNITY DEVELOPMENT PROJECT (1973), 'Inter-Project Report', London: CDP (Information and Intelligence Unit).

NEWHAM RIGHTS CENTRE (1974-5), 'Report and Analysis of a Community Law Centre'.

NEWHAM RIGHTS CENTRE (1975-7), 'Two Years Work'.
NORTH KENSINGTON NEIGHBOURHOOD LAW CENTRE (1971), 'Annual Report'.
NORTH KENSINGTON NEIGHBOURHOOD LAW CENTRE (1972), 'Annual Report'.
NORTH KENSINGTON NEIGHBOURHOOD LAW CENTRE (1977), 'Annual Report'.
PITT, J. (1972), Neighbourhood Law Centres: A Community Resource, 'Race Today', vol. 4, no. 12, pp. 390-1.
PITT, J. (1974), A Culture of Silence, 'LAG Bulletin', October, pp. 236-7.
SOCIETY OF LABOUR LAWYERS (1968), Justice for All, 'Fabian Research Series: 273'.
STUMPF, H.P., SCHROERLUKE, H.P. and DILL, F.D. (1971), The Legal Profession and Legal Services: Explorations in Local Bar Politics, 'Law and Society Review', vol. 6, pp. 46-67.
SYKES, G.M. (1969), The Legal Needs of the Poor in the City of Denver, 'Law and Society Review', vol. 4, pp. 255-77.

Chapter 9

THE LEGAL WRONGS OF BATTERED WOMEN

Rhian Ellis

INTRODUCTION

'Battered women' is a term which has become firmly established in our vocabulary and wife-beating a phenomenon which has come recently to be elevated to the status of a 'social problem'. The 1970s have seen a steady widening of interest in, and much debate on, the nature and origins of this 'new' problem. Part of this discussion has focused on the effects of the law and its attendant institutions upon the social situation of battered women. The issues addressed have included the effectiveness of legal remedies available to women who have been battered, and proposals and suggestions for possible legal reforms. These issues form part of this paper, but are presented in a context which seeks to explore the assumptions of legislators, reformers and resisters alike, as well as trying to gauge the strength and weaknesses of specific pieces of legislation.

In order to better appreciate the ways in which the law impinges on marital and intra-family relationships we need to look first at the general legal position of women historically, mindful of the fact that women have always been (and still are, despite certain recent reforms considered in this article) unequal before the law.

A HISTORICAL PROFILE

The aim of this section is simply to sketch in the major legislative landmarks (if they can be called such, given their limited appeal and impact) and dominant attitudes and arguments concerning the character and causes of marital violence.

Women have traditionally been regarded as second-class citizens, through being assigned an inferior social and legal status to - and by - men. And as shall be seen later, even after the passing of sex discrimination legislation, women are still in no real sense equal before the law. Where wife abuse is concerned there has always been a popular opinion willing to give credence to the idea that it is acceptable and reasonable that a man should be able to beat is wife. Husbands once had the legal right to do so, and although this privilege no longer has any legal sanction there is still an unwillingness among some segments of opinion to condemn wife abuse. This ambivalence is in sharp contrast with the responses to other forms of intra-family violence such as child abuse or incest. Looked at historically, wife-beating has failed until quite recently to attract any sustained condemnation or to generate a movement for reform powerful enough to bring about any substantial change in the legal or social redress available to abused women. As Dobash and Dobash observe, 'violence against women has throughout time and across civilizations provoked little approbation' (1976a, p. 1). Certain religious beliefs have helped set a framework for such attitudes by advocating and supporting the subjugation of women. The Christian attitude towards women has its roots in the Adam and Eve story, which portrays the woman as weak, evil and open to all sorts of temptation and the man as the innocent victim of this weak and evil woman. Thus, God's curse on all women, which resulted from Eve's sinning, has made women the 'culturally legitimate objects of antagonism' (Steinmetz and Straus, 1974). To add to all this, St Paul - the great misogynist - had his own views on the rightful place of women: his argument was that woman was created for man, for him to do with as he wished. (1) St Paul's philosophy has undoubtedly had a severe and chronic effect on 'billions of husbands and Christian church leaders and lawmakers thereafter' (Davidson, 1977, p. 9). Christianity's prejudice and the sort of image of woman it perpetuates has, says Ruether, 'justified almost limitless violence against [women] wherever they cross the male will at home or in society' (1977, p. 13). Ours is a patriarchal history, by and large written for men, by men (and this includes its legal code), which serves to emphasise the paucity of respect or concern traditionally offered to the female half of the population. Thus the Christian ideology of equality, liberation and dignity never applied to women. Instead, the Church has usually preferred to countenance theories of woman's subjugation rather than liberation. (2)

Given these kinds of institutionalised and widely diffused attitudes and understandings it is hardly surprising that, as Rowbotham (1973) and others have pointed out, women have, in certain important respects, remained hidden from history. The patriarchal legacy - woman's peculiar subjugation - was an important dimension of legal and social history in nineteenth-century Britain. In the Victorian household, for instance, women and children were expected to show a true and unswerving deference to the father and were taught to fear and revere God alone above him. A woman's duty, as one commentator of the time put it, was 'to suffer and be still' (Ellis, 1845, p. 73); it was an ideology which could command widespread social and legal support.

Legally, the nineteenth-century wife was a nonentity. Marriage meant that her identity as an individual was suspended; she was merely part of her husband's property. English Common Law declared (Blackstone, 1770):

> By marriage the husband and wife are one person in law, that is, the very being or legal existence of the woman is suspended during marriage or at least incorporated and consolidated into that of the husband.

This legal ownership of his wife gave a man the legal right to beat her; as Blackstone (1770) pointed out:

> The husband ... might give his wife moderate correction. For as he is to answer for her misbehaviour, the law thought it reasonable to entrust him with this power of restraining her, by domestic chastisement in the same moderation that a man is allowed to correct his servants or children.

Although the right of chastisement had come under some attack even in the seventeenth century, (3) legal opinion remained steadfastly ambivalent. There were few, if any, legal precedents to support a wife. Rather, in 1782 it was ruled that a man could beat his wife provided that he used a stick that was no thicker than his thumb (May, 1978, p. 139). This sanction complemented popular belief of a man's right and duty, to correct his wife by physical force where necessary, and this belief was not challenged until 1891. That year, in the case of R. v. Jackson, this ancient right was finally made obsolete in law. (4)

Throughout the nineteenth century there was a significant absence of any social reform movements concerned with bettering the lot of battered women. Although no major moral crusade ever emerged during this period, there was some mention of the problem of wife-beating from time to time. After 1850 J.S. Mill struggled to publicise the bleak circumstances of working-class wives who were beaten by cruel husbands. His efforts were substantial; indeed Davidson (1977, p. 16) feels that Mill's 'Subjection of Women' stood as 'the first significant document to spark the raising of public consciousness about the plight of battered wives'.

Mill advocated the right of separation for wives from husbands found guilty of cruelty, as well as the termination of any marital obligation on the wife's part. His ideas were revolutionary, and the controversy fired by his writings led to some limited action being taken in 1853 in the form of a Bill which gave a wife the same protection as had been previously given to 'poodle dogs and donkey's ('Parliamentary Debates', 1853, cxxiv, 1418). The Act for the Better Prevention and Punishment of Aggravated Assaults upon Women and Children 1853 gave magistrates the power to imprison the offender for up to six months or to fine him up to a sum of £20 and, in addition, to counsel the offender to keep the peace for six months. The Act was, however, scarcely more than a token gesture to allay public concern and was little used by suffering wives.

In 1856 J.W. Kaye (5) followed Mill in drawing public attention to the legal impotence of the ill-treated wife. But Kaye was careful to draw a definite distinction between what he saw as the refined, verbal, emotional and usually private torture inflicted by bad middle-class husbands, and the physical cruelties meted out by violent husbands in the working classes (Kaye, 1856, pp. 235-6). (6) He suggested some practical action which could be taken by working-class wives to help alleviate the beatings they were subjected to. Kaye felt that, in many cases, the slovenliness of the wife, brought about by ignorance of household management, resulted in a poor home for her husband to return to. This imagined comfortless existence was supposed to lead to the discomforted seeking solace in the public house, only returning home after closing time to beat his feckless wife. Thus it was up to the woman to improve her domestic skills in order to please her husband if she wanted him to stop beating her. However much we may marvel at this Victorian attitude, it is not so far removed from some current notions about the causes of marital disharmony.

Although a Divorce Reform Act was passed in 1857, it made little or no impact upon the plight of an abused wife. This was not only because of the financial costs involved, but also because the wife had to be able to prove her husband's adultery, as well as his cruelty, in order to be able to sue for divorce. It was not until the 1870s, when feminist campaigning began to gain impetus, that concerted action was taken. In 1874 the government commissioned an inquiry to look at the law relating to brutal assaults and the resulting report contained detailed statistics on the cruelties inflicted on women and children. (7) Four years later Cobbe (1878) published an influential article on 'Wife Torture' and at the same time prepared a Bill which would protect wives who had been the victims of aggravated assaults by their husbands. The Bill became part of the Matrimonial Causes Act of 1878, which allowed a wife to bring a complaint in her own right before magistrates, so to enable her to be formally released from any obligation to live any longer with her husband. To succeed in this, the wife had to prove that her husband had committed an 'aggravated assault' upon her.

Although matrimonial law has changed since the nineteenth century, legal practice is still based on the concept of the sanctity of marriage and on the inferior place of women within marriage. Dobash and Dobash put it this way: '"Love, honour and obey", is the lot of women in marriage.... Implied in that vow is the threat of rightful control over those who fail to obey' (1977, p. 403).

It was not only the 'unenlightened' nineteenth century which practised legal discrimination against abused women. The implicit right of a man to punish his wife has been supported through case law on more than one occasion during the past fifty years. In 1946 it was held in Meacher v. Meacher (8) that a husband had a right to assault his wife because she visited her relations against his orders. In a further case, in 1959, it was held that a man could punish his wife as he would punish a naughty child and not be guilty or cruelty. Even in 1975, 'a sheriff in Scotland ... expressed his support for the ancient principle that "reasonable chastisement should be the duty of every husband if his wife misbehaves" (Freeman, 1977, pp. 211-12). These examples help to show that while there have clearly been some legal advances in the sphere of matrimonial legislation since the early twentieth century and although a husband has now largely lost the proprietary rights over his wife's person and property, nevertheless current legal, as well as popular, thought seems to regard a bad or violent marriage as better than a broken one. Thus, the sentiments and ideologies which have been cultivated over time have now become an institutionalised part of our social world.

The law supports and is supported by the patriarchal order. As such the legal position of women reflected and still reflects sexual inequality. More specifically, the legal remedies available to battered women have been slow in coming, are limited in scope and cumbersome to operate. The legal resoltuions which have been made available at various times have been constrained by a number of factors: the weak economic position of the women affected (and that of women in general), the reluctance of the police to become involved in marital disputes, the difficulty of enforcing and sometimes obtaining injunctions, the problems of providing protection against husbands or co-habiters seeking 'revenge', a lack of alternative accommodation, and assisting agencies (doctors, social service departments) who have tended to emphasise 'reconciliation' and 'compromise' rather than separation and divorce. The rest of this paper examines the ways in which these factors, singly or in combination, come to bear upon the situation of the battered woman.

UP AGAINST THE LAW

Battered women have been and still are a forgotten statistic; according to Dobash and Dobash (1977, p. 410):

> despite overwhelming evidence that crimes of violence occur disproportionately in the home there exists a considerable reluctance to define such acts as criminal, to legislate against such acts, and most of all, to enforce the laws which do exist.

The dearth of protective legislation is apparent once we remember only one significant piece of legislation concerned with the amelioration of the problems faced by battered women has so far been passed. (9) Dobash, Wilson and Cavanagh (1977) note how, even in the 1960s, a decade marked by the genesis of multiple forms of radical action, including the rebirth of feminist awareness, there was a failure to produce any agency or crusade to work on behalf of battered women, in the same way as there was a failure to legislate during the same period. Thus, 'the legislation of the 1960s is not important because of what it achieved but because of what it reveals about the low status of women in marriage and society' (Dobash, Wilson and Cavanagh, 1977, p. 1).

Before the Domestic Violence Act 1976 came into force a woman who had been the victim of domestic violence found it extremely difficult to obtain any protection from the law. Although the Home Office has declared that the law is the same for assaults between husband and wife as for any other assault, the reality is that the police are reluctant to intervene in domestic disputes and the legislators seem to feel that the woman is old enough to look after herself. The legal redress that was available seem to focus on section 42 of the Offences Against the Persons Act 1861, and the obtaining of an injunction. Section 42 deals with common assault, and proceedings under this section must be taken by the aggrieved person. Moreover, that person must lay information on her own behalf before the justices in a magistrates' court. The hearing could take anything from six to twelve weeks to come before the court, and unless a woman could find refuge for this time she would have to stay with the person who assaulted her. The punishment for an offence under this section is usually a fine or probation order which, where a battered woman is concerned, offers her no protection from future assault. Thus, the woman was caught in a cruel legal trap; if she did not take legal action she might be battered again, if she did she would probably be battered even more.

The process for obtaining injunctions was a complicated and lengthy affair. If a wife wanted to obtain an injunction to stop her husband assaulting her then she had to start proceedings for judicial separation or divorce first. A single woman had to go to the county court to start proceedings for claiming monetary compensation for any injury, either to person or property, that she had received. When an injunction was granted it was enforceable only by court bailiffs, which meant the police could not arrest a man for breach of an injunction order.

Such was the legal situation of battered women when, in 1975, a Select Committee of the House of Commons was set up to look at the problem of violence in marriage. (10) A good part of the pressure for the setting up of this committee came from feminists, whose campaign to alleviate the problems of battered women had begun in earnest in 1973. At the same time, a Labour MP, Jack Ashley, began to take an interest and this involvement helped to bring about a parliamentary discussion of the problem. Not surprisingly, the Select Committee reported that the relevant legal remedies were very weak and because of this recommended certain changes. Some of their recommendations have been incorporated in the Domestic Violence Act 1976 (DVA 1976). But bare legislative enactments in themselves and of themselves are limited in impact and go only part of the way towards assisting battered women. If a piece of legislation is to have any impact then it must be conscientiously and vigorously implemented. To this end the Select Committee further recommended that the legal machinery for the implementation of the law should be reassessed and improved.

The majority of the Committee's recommendations have, however, been either forgotten or ignored, and many of those so disregarded bear directly upon the implementation of the law. Where the police were concerned the Committee's recommendation (Report of the Select Committee on Violence, para. 44) was that

> Chief Constables should review their policies about the police approach to domestic violence.... [There is no] valid excuse for the police not being more effectively involved in dealing with the problem of marital violence

The Committee also argued that the police should be prepared to arrest a man when there is evidence of injury, then subsequently to detain him, charge him and keep him in custody either until his appearance in court or at least until his wife and children have been taken to a safe place (para. 44).

The well-known reluctance of the police to intervene in domestic violence 'reveals an understandable but unacceptable schizophrenia in their approach to violence' (Pizzey, 1974, p. 98). This 'schizophrenia' has its roots in the training the polic receive, in the policeman's conception of wife abuse and in cultural attitudes concerning women and their proper place and duties within the family. In his study of the police approach to domestic violence, Parnas found that 'the overall emphasis in training seems to be on the danger of handling domestic disturbances' (1967, p. 920). Thus, while policemen (like everybody else), undoubtedly carry around with them all sorts of lay theories about the nature of violence against women, and these theories will sometimes pre-dispose them to do nothing when they should perhaps do something, the demand for more intervention by the police is a demand that they adopt what Chatterton calls 'an even broader service role' (1976, p. 47). Although the police are the main twenty-four hour assisting agency for battered women, they see themselves as a law enforcement agency and not as what they define as a social work agency. Their use of discretionary powers concerning which laws to enforce and which to ignore, coupled with other prevalent attitudes concerning the privacy of the home and the place of a woman within that home, combine to the detriment of battered women, and often mean that the police are of little use as agents for treating domestic violence.

In a recent study carried out at Canterbury Women's Centre, Pahl found that 'there was more dissatisfaction with the police than with any other of the official agencies to which women turned' (1978, p. 40). Of the twenty-five women interviewed in the sample, only two felt that the police had been of some assistance by referring them to the Women's Aid refuge. These findings are supported in a study I made of a women's refuge (Ellis, 1976). Of fifteen women interviewed, only one was referred to the refuge by the police and the evidence given to me pointed to a widespread reluctance by the police to intervene on the behalf of battered women. Eleven of the women I talked to had called the police at some point; nine of these thought the police were not very helpful or sympathetic towards their problem; only two found the police to be quite helpful, one because the husband assaulted a police officer when he was called to the house.

Of course, it is not only the police who are responsible for implementing the law. Solicitors and the judiciary also have a responsibility in this area. As yet nothing of substance has been published which discusses the solicitors' and judiciary's interpretation and implementation of legislation governing domestic violence. By drawing from the experiences of women's aid groups, however, we can make a reasonable guess that the legal profession's response would be similar to that of other statutory assisting agencies. As Gregory has pointed out in discussing social workers' response to domestic violence, '[they] have generally wished to support the family and are often reluctant to assist a woman who wants to leave home. Their advice has frequently been to "try again".' This statement could apply equally well to those solicitors and judges who urge women to 'try again' rather than withdraw from situations of violence.

Although obviously we cannot say that all members and segments of the legal profession would react in this way, many solicitors are as yet reluctant to grant injunctions giving the power of arrest to an abused wife. A recent press report claimed that 'It seems that solicitors are reluctant to apply for power of arrest and judges unwilling to grant it' ('Western Mail', 24 November 1977).

Evidence given to the Select Committee pointed to a number of deficiencies in the way solicitors treat cases of domestic violence. Pizzey (1974) felt that women were given poor legal advice and accused solicitors of not knowing the law. She further commented that it was often difficult to find a solicitor to take on this sort of matrimonial work because it was not a lucrative source of income. The law is, to most laymen, a complicated area, and a battered woman, unless otherwise advised, will naturally tend to follow the recommendation of her solicitor without question. It seems, not only from evidence given to the Select Committee, but also from reports from women's aid groups, that battered women are not getting the advice and action which formal justice requires they should.

The judiciary, it seems, is inconsistent in its handling of the DVA 1976. This is in part due to the lack of guidance offered to judges on the application of the Act, and we can add to this the problems caused by the poor drafting of the Act. While there are judges, as well as some policemen and solicitors, who are concerned with protecting battered women, many are apt to look upon wife-beating as a normal part of working-class life and not as classless cruelty. Thus, many judges refuse to grant injunctions unless they are convinced that the woman has suffered serious physical violence. Where the power of arrest is concerned, only 27 per cent of the injunctions granted during the period June 1977-May 1978 had a power of arrest attached to them. Although these figures do not show how many requests for a power of arrest were refused, it would be fair to assume that either solicitors are not asking for this power to be added, or judges are not willing to grant it.

Inadequate enforcement of the law that offers protection to battered women is, then, one of the major problems which the victims face, all of which seems to confirm Podgorecki's point that 'the functioning of law cannot be separated from the institutions which execute it' (1974, p. 254). As such, the enforcers need educating, and this can be done only by challenging the existing customs and socialisation process of the police and legal profession.

THE DOMESTIC VIOLENCE ACT 1976

Perhaps a clearer idea of the sorts of problems faced by battered women when seeking legal redress will come to light if we look more closely at the content and effect of the DVA 1976. Moves to change the law came with the recommendations of the Select Committee on Violence in Marriage and through the agitation of the National Women's Aid Federation (NWAF). (11) The Select Committee recognised that the relevant law was weak, as did the NWAF, who worked to create publicity for changes in the law and often held legal workshops to discuss the ways and means through which these objectives might be realised.

The DVA was introduced as a private members' Bill by Jo Richardson and came into force on 1 June 1977 after a great deal of deliberation and some objections. As the Bill was passing through its various readings, the police put forward an objection (12) to clause 2 (13) of the Bill. Richardson responded by calling a meeting with the Police Federation and after discussion was able to win their agreement to the Bill's contents.

The Act itself has five sections, two of which relate to domestic violence. (14) The Act enables spouse or co-habitee to obtain an injunction from the high court or county court to prevent molestation by the other spouse or co-habitee without having to start separation proceedings for divorce, judicial separation or damages for assault. The courts are also able to exclude a spouse (the precedent set concerning co-habiters will be discussed later) even from his own home before any divorce case, or to regulate occupation of the matrimonial home. The Act also gives judges the power to add an Order of Arrest to the injunction whether over proceedings under the Act or in any other matrimonial proceedings.

However, NWAF and others claim that there are damaging loopholes in the new Act. The innovative provision empowering a power of arrest to be attached to an injunction is not as useful to battered women as it first seems. For instance, before a power of arrest can be attached to an injunction, the judge must be satisfied that the respondent has inflicted 'actual bodily harm' upon the applicant and, further, that he is likely to do so again. This requirement excludes not only many mentally battered women, but many physically battered ones. According to Melville, 'Many of the men concerned ... are skilful in inflicting an injury where it cannot easily be seen' (1977). In a recent Court of Appeal case (Lewis v. Lewis, 1978), Ormrod LJ felt that powers of arrest should be attached only 'in exceptional cases where men or women persistently disobey injunctions and make nuisances of themselves' (p. 646). Agreeing with Ormrod LJ, Roskitt LJ felt that the power of arrest 'is not there for general indiscriminate use' (p. 647). This attitude condemns women to more than one severe physical beating before she can be granted an injunction with a power of arrest attached. Such judgments, although not binding, may make judges loathe to attach the power of arrest to an injunction and seriously weaken the power of the Act.

Although the power of arrest might have been granted, it is still left to police discretion when to arrest, but the police's known reluctance to intervene in domestic matters means that they may also be unwilling to arrest. If the police do arrest a man he must be brought before a judge within twenty-four hours. Obviously, if the violence takes place on a weekend, as much of it does, (15) or on a public holiday, it may prove difficult to get hold of a judge within the twenty-four hours. If this is the case, then the man must be released.

Not only are there loopholes in the Act, but there are also major omissions. The NWAF were expecting wider powers in the Act, but they claim, 'every time we asked for anything we were told that if we did so the government might withdraw its support' (p. 397). Although the Select Committee noted that (Report from the Select Committee on Violence, 1975, para. 21)

> The most insistent evidence we have received has been that specialised refuge facilities should be available very readily and rapidly for women who have been battered.... We accept the urgency of this constant plea and endorse it as a strong recommendation.

The DVA 1976 has failed to provide any financial support for refuges and crisis centres, 'many of whom ... are in desperate need of money' (Melville, 1977, p. 397).

What the NWAF fears is that the government will feel that by passing this piece of legislation it will have done enough and can begin to forget about the problem. Without doubt the Act falls short of providing adequate protection for victims; as Melville puts it, 'The Act acknowledged the problem exists, but then seems to wash its hands of it' (1977, p. 397).

One of the major loopholes in the Act was the ambiguity concerning a mistress's rights. First, the Act applies only to 'a man and woman who are living with each other in the same household as husband and wife' (DVA, 1976, 52(2)). As such, a single or divorced woman who is assaulted by a man she does not live with cannot take action under the Act. A further problem is the question of how long two people have to cohabit in order to be 'living with each other ... as husband and wife'. Second, it seemed that divorcees or co-habiters would not, unless they owned their own homes, be able to get an injunction excluding the man from the house. Thus a large group of battered women are unprotected.

The second issue has been the subject of a recent test case which went through two appeal courts and then on to the House of Lords (Davis v. Johnson, 1978). The argument centred on the question of the man's property rights. The facts of the case were that Davis obtained an injunction under the Act against her co-habitee, Johnson, to exclude him from their council flat. Johnson appealed against the decision and won; Davis fled to a refuge and appealed against Johnson's appeal. They were joint tenants of the flat and the arguments seemed to hinge on whether the Act changed substantive law, i.e. that one joint tenant can oust another. The House of Lords ruled that, even if a woman has no legal right to occupy a home as owner or tenant, she can have a violent man temporarily evicted. The Lords argued that, although the Act did not alter existing property rights, it did nevertheless put people before property. However, the ultimate test will come in those cases where women have no property rights in the home, that is where the home is solely in the co-habitee's name. In such situations judges might follow the precedent set by Davis v. Johnson or differentiate because of the property rights. This final test, then, has yet to come.

FAMILY, PATRIARCHY AND THE LAW

So far I have looked at the legislative redress and its enforcement available to battered women in nineteenth-century and in contemporary Britain. I now turn to look at the relationship of these legal solutions to wider social attitudes, and conceptions towards women and their assigned status within the family.

Whatever our feelings about the family, and however much we argue the family to be a close, loving and protective institution, many of the popular myths are dispelled if we view the family as one of 'the most conflict-ridden institutions to which the great majority of people are ever likely to belong' (Dobash and Dobash, 1976b, p. 5). In reality force and aggression are among the main tools of the family's trade; they are used regularly against children and have come to be an accepted and acceptable form of control and influence. (16) Violence within the family setting has been rationalised and physical punishment defined, not as violent behaviour used by one person against another, but as a parental duty, where children are concerned and a husband's right where a wife is concerned.

Within the family unit, as in most other institutions in British society, there is a socially determined and accepted hierarchy. In social, economic and political terms the power and authority is now and always has been vested in the man; patriarchy, indeed, insists upon this. This power, Bonger suggests, 'is a consequence of man's economic preponderance' and 'It is certain that there will always be abuse of power on the part of a number of those whom social circumstances have clothed with certain authority' (1969, p. 58). This 'abuse of power' has been a cruel and harsh reality for many women, but patriarchal domination, economic dependence and a legal system constructed by powerful interests and classes controlled by men has meant not only that women are bound to their position because they cannot escape, but that they are conditioned not to want to escape. For many battered women a regular beating may be preferable to the numerous problems which single parenthood brings: financial deprivation and insecurity, isolation and poor housing are frequently all the divorced woman (particularly a working-class one) can command. Legal or social reformers are rarely prepared to think about any variation on the conventional nuclear family theme. Instead, they do their best to reform or patch up what they have, however inadequate or oppressive this might prove to be. Wilson (1977) argues that the welfare state has struggled to arrest the 'atomization and disintegration' (p. 187) of the modern family and suggests that society and the state should waste no more time and effort on attempting to salvage an institution laden with inadequacies; instead they should 'actively seek in the present to work for the kinds of social change that point towards a truly equal society, one in which women and children are truly equal with men' (p. 187).

The very fact that the family has held together as a viable unit despite its obvious inadequacies reflects its inherent resilience, a resilience which is strengthened by patriarchy. This is not the place to press for alternatives to the family, and indeed my point is not so much an attack on the nuclear family as such, as a comment on the deficiencies of patriarchy. In the end it is not the family which needs reforming. What needs to be looked at are the sorts of power relationships which make up the family as we know and experience it, and it is these, as Wilson says, which should be rethought.

Women are one of the casualties of a patriarchal society, and in discussing battered women we would be wise not to forget that women are battered not because of factors peculiar to the family, but because they are in some sense victims of a society in which sexual inequalities and sexism are deep-rooted and pervasive. Obviously many factors may affect a family's ability to function harmoniously, and we cannot ignore the various 'causation theories' that have been put forward to explain wife-battering. But women are not victims because of various structural and stress factors; they are battered because their subordinate status has made them the '"appropriate" victims of marital violence' (Dobash and Dobash, 1977, p. 1).

CONCLUSIONS

Women are still fighting for the equality with men that should be theirs by right, and they are still expected to settle for token gestures. Formal recognition of the pervasive and many-sided character of sexual inequality in British society was indeed given expression in the Equal Pay Act 1970 and Sex Discrimination Act 1975. And yet both pieces of legislation are notable more for the way they have been avoided or narrowly interpreted than for any substantial advances that they have achieved for women.

The law and its enforcement where battered women are concerned is plainly lacking. Yet even if the law becomes better known, more accessible and adequately enforced it will still cope with only one aspect of the problem and provides no really comprehensive remedy. One reason why this is so can be found in Coote and Gill's claim that 'The problem of battered women is a social one deeply rooted in the way men and women are brought up to regard themselves and each other.... The battering won't end until men and women change their attitudes [towards themselves and each other]' (1977, p. 232).

The essential background to the problem of battering is woman's domination and exploitation in society and more specifically within the family. As any historical analysis suggests, battering is not a problem of the 1970s, and yet there are those who still persist in trying to ignore it.

NOTES

1 See, for instance, I Corinthians 11: 8, 9.
2 The arguments used in recent controversy within the Church concerning the accepting of women priests hinged, in the end, on the inferiority of women in the eyes of the Church.
3 For a discussion of this see May (1978).
4 See R. v. Jackson (1891), IQB 671.
5 See Kaye (1856).
6 Kaye's discussion, although based on nineteenth-century class consciousness and certain ideas of behaviour within social classes, does more than hint at the seeds of a popular and powerful contemporary stereotype that the middle class torture only mentally while the working class do so physically.
7 See Report to the Secretary of State for the Home Department on the State of the Law Relating to Brutal Assaults (1875) (c. 1138), LXI.
8 See Meacher v. Meacher (1946), p. 416.
9 See The Domestic Violence and Matrimonial Proceedings Act 1976.
10 Report from the Select Committee on Violence in Marriage (1975).
11 The NWAF was formed in 1975 to collate the experiences of various women's aid groups throughout England and Wales and to help orchestrate various campaigns on behalf of battered women. It has so far set up approximately 150 refuges for women in England and Wales and acts as a feminist pressure group in trying to improve the lot of battered women.
12 The police put forward two main objections:
   (i) they felt that the present Criminal Law offered sufficient protection and there was no need for this Bill;
   (ii) the police force was hard pressed and would have no time to enforce injunctions.
13 Clause 2 gives the police the power to arrest a man who broke an injunction, if that injunction had a power of arrest clause attached to it.
14 Sections 1 and 2 relate directly to domestic violence.
15 See Bedfordshire Police (1976), which shows that violence takes place much more often at the weekend.
16 For a discussion of the use of punishment towards children in Victorian England and later, see Gibson (1978).

BIBLIOGRAPHY

Act for the better Prevention and Punishment of aggravated Assaults on Women and Children, 16 and 17 Vic., C. 30, 1853.
BEDFORDSHIRE POLICE (1976), 'Reports on Acts of Violence Committed in the County'.
BLACKSTONE, W. (1770), 'Commentaries on the Laws of England', 4 vols, Clarendon Press: Oxford.
BONGER, W.A. (1969), 'Criminality and Economic Conditions', Indiana University Press.
CHATTERTON, M. (1976), The Social Context of Violence, in Borland, M. (ed.), 'Violence in the Family', Manchester University Press.
COBBE, F. POWER (1878), Wife Torture in England, 'The Contemporary Review', vol. 32.
COOTE, A. and GILL, E. (1967), 'Women's Rights: A Practical Guide', Harmondsworth: Penguin.
DAVIDSON, T. (1977), Wifebeating: A Recurring Phenomenon Throughout History, in Roy, M. (ed.), 'Battered Women', Van Nostrand, Reinhold: Wokingham, Berks.
DAVIS v. JOHNSON (1978), 2 WLR, 182.
DOBASH R.E. and DOBASH, R. (1976a), Wife Beating Past and Present, unpublished paper, University of Stirling.
DOBASH, R.E. and DOBASH, R. (1976b), The Importance of Historical and Contemporary Contexts in Understanding Marital Violence, paper presented at the Annual Meeting of the American Sociological Association, New York, August 1976.
DOBASH, R.E. and DOBASH, R. (1977), Love, Honour and Obey: Institutional Ideologies and the Struggle for Battered Women, 'Contemporary Crises', vol. 1, pp. 403-15.
DOBASH, R.E., WILSON, M. and CAVANAGH, K. (1977), Violence Against Wives: The Legislation of the 1960s and the Policies of Indifference, paper presented at the National Deviancy Conference, Sheffield, April.
DOMESTIC VIOLENCE AND MATRIMONIAL PROCEEDINGS ACT 1976.
ELLIS, R.M. (1976), The Problem of the Legal Regulation of Violence in the Family (Battered Wives), unpublished dissertation, University College, Cardiff.
ELLIS, S.F. (1845), 'The Daughters of England', London.
FREEMAN, M.D.A. (1977), Le Vice Anglais? - Wife-Battering in English and American Law, 'Family Law Quarterly', vol. 11, no. 3.
GIBSON, J. (1978), 'The English Vice: Beating, Sex and Shame in Victorian England and After', Duckworth: London.
HECKER, E.A. (1910), 'A Short History of Women's Rights', Putnam and Sons: London.
KAYE, J.W. (1856), Outrages on Women, 'North British Review', vol. 25.
LEWIS v. LEWIS (1978), 2WLR, 644.
MAY, M. (1978), Violence in the Family: An Historical Perspective, in Martin, J.P. (ed.), 'Violence and the Family', John Wiley & Sons: Chichester.
MEACHER v. MEACHER (1946), p. 416.
MELVILLE, J. (1977), Hitting at Home, 'New Society', 26 May.
MILL, J.S. (1869), 'The Subjection of Women', London.
O'FOALIN and MARTINS (1974), 'Not in God's Image', Collins: Glasgow Glasgow.

PAHL, J. (1978), 'A Refuge for Battered Women', London: HMSO.
'Parliamentary Debates' (1853), vol. cxxiv, p. 1418.
PARNAS, R.I. (1967), The Police Response to the Domestic Disturbance, 'Wisconsin Law Review', vol. 914.
PIZZEY, E. (1974), 'Scream Quietly or the Neighbours Will Hear', Penguin: Harmondsworth.
PODGORECKI, A. (1974), 'Law in Society', London: Routledge & Kegan Paul.
R. v. JACKSON (1891), 1QB, 671.
'Report from the Select Committee on Violence in Marriage' (1975), vol. 1, HC 533-i.
'Report to the Secretary of State for the Home Department on the State of the Law Relating to Brutal Assaults' (1875) (C. 113), lxi.
ROWBOTHAM, S. (1973), 'Hidden from History', Pluto Press: London.
RUETHER, R.R. (1977), Is God a Wifebeater? The Western Religious Tradition and Violence Against Women in the Home, 'Movement', August.
STEINMETZ, S.K. and STRAUS, M.S. (1974), 'Violence in the Family', Dodd Mead & Co.: New York.
'Western Mail' (1977), 24 November.

Chapter 10

THE DISCOVERY OF THE COMPULSIVE GAMBLER*

Dave Dixon

INTRODUCTION

The study of pressure groups and their influence on legislation and public policy is currently a somewhat unfashionable exercise in the sociology of law, carrying with it as it does the taint of American pluralist social theory. The implication is unfortunate, for it seems evident that the activities of such groups will not be ignored by any adequate account of law-making: while they do not operate in the political and economic vacuum previously suggested, they can and do play significant roles in policy formulation. The aim should now be to incorporate them into a wider theoretical perspective, rather than to ignore them because of the inadequacies of previous studies.

This essay examines groups opposed to gambling in Britain from the 1890s to 1978, focusing specifically on one, the Churches' Council on Gambling (CCG), and its resistance to threats to the influential position attained by it because of its early specialization in a notoriously under-studied area (Downes et al., 1976, p. 11). Since Gusfield's work on Prohibition (1955, 1963), some considerable attention has been paid to the natural history of moral crusades (Galliher and Walker, 1976): the CCG offers an interesting example of a weakening movement abandoning its moralistic condemnation of gambling as the audience for such a message faded away, and attempting to replace it through the establishment of compulsive gambling as a serious social problem. It is argued that, against a backdrop of the 'monopoly over vocabularies of motive relating to deviant activities' enjoyed by behaviourists (Taylor, 1972, p. 27), the CCG formalized and developed culturally available (Herman, 1977, p. 93) but inchoate images, (1) and rudimentary medical definitions, of compulsive gambling (in particular, through the establishment of, and use of, examples from Gamblers Anonymous); that the bid for recognition of excessive gambling as a decisive consideration in policy formulation was authoritatively rejected by the Rothschild Report (Royal Commission, 1978); and that this Report confirms a significant shift in official attitudes to gambling and marks the obsolescence, in this area, of the type of quasi-moralistic pressure groups discussed here. The present concern, then, is with a pressure group in crisis because of changes in its environment, and with the group's attempt to resolve that crisis by lobbying for the reconstitution of legal and social policy around a new definition of the situation as promoted by it.

'A LEPROSY IS O'ER THE LAND'

At the end of the nineteenth century, medical phraseology was rampant in the literature of the National Anti-Gambling League (NAGL) - but then, the sickness was not in the individual, but in society. Gambling was described by the League's journal as a cancer, 'a leprosy of certain growth that is eating into the moral health of our populace' ('The Bulletin', November 1899, vol. 2, no. 19, p. 151). The anti-gamblers saw 'a nation impregnated with this deadly virus' ('The Bulletin', November 1899, p. 152) and stridently insisted that, without immediate action, 'the leprosy will have covered the still healthy flesh' within a short time ('The Bulletin', May 1901, vol. 2, no. 22, p. 217). The winner of a hymn composition competition organized by the League in 1905 was entitled 'A Leprosy is O'er the Land' ('The Bulletin', November 1905, vol. 3, no. 31, p. 122).

By a curious process of self-persuasion, the NAGL came to take their metaphors quite literally and made them a basis for a campaign. Infection was said to be spreading down from the head through the body of society because of the bad effect of upper-class gambling on 'the lower orders'. 'The virus of the betting plague [and] its corrupt influence taints deeply the highest ranks of society [while] the state of the lower classes from the disease can only be described as bordering on moral putrefaction' ('The Bulletin', November 1895, vol. 3, no. 11, p. 134). 'The poison has filtered down into the daily life of the middle and lower classes so that our whole populace is infected' ('The Bulletin', November 1899, vol. 2, no. 18, p. 151). There was concern that the disease could spread to another body, the Empire of which Britain was the head: England had 'responsibility at the head of civilization for setting the example of gambling to other English-speaking nations' ('The Bulletin', November 1909, vol. 4, no. 39, p. 47).

The consequences of the adoption by the League of this definition of the situation (the abortive assault upon upper-class gambling habits and the subsequent co-operation into a partial campaign for legislation to repress working-class gambling) are discussed elsewhere (Dixon, 1978). The moral uncertainties and sense of deflected purpose, even failure, clearly present in attempts to justify the NAGL's role in the passage of the Street Betting Act 1906, seemed to presage dissolution. Instead, the League was given a new lease of life through the intervention of the young industrialist and social investigator, Seebohm Rowntree (vice-president and a prominent member of the York branch). The collection of essays edited by him in 1905 (Rowntree, 1905) and the discussion of gambling in his other works (2) showed conclusively that gambling could not be considered in isolation from other social factors, and they imbued the anti-gambling movement with a new seriousness which was a major factor in its longevity. But Rowntree's attitude was ambivalent, for although he tried to keep his personal morality out of his writing, he was a Quaker, and (at this time (3)) completely opposed to gambling of any kind. This ambivalence was consistently evident in the NAGL - the attempt seriously to understand gambling (which gave the group status before the Rowlatt Commission and other inter-war committees (4)) went hand in hand with a deep-rooted moralistic antipathy to it (which inevitably interfered with this hope of understanding).

At each official investigation, a League officer or associate appeared to expound the familiar tale of the dire social effects of gambling. (5) Here a clear distinction was made between the gambling habits of different classes: upper-class gambling might not have been exactly respectable, and there were occasional scandals; but it was essentially the gambling of the working class that was considered a social, rather than an individual, financial problem. While short shrift was given to occasional attempts to turn discussion towards the morality of gambling, as long as anti-gambling witnesses stuck to 'environmental' arguments they were generally well received. After all, they were merely stating in explicit terms what many of their audience's class continued to believe about the effects of gambling - or about what was so often really at issue, alleged working-class idleness and profligacy. But as the League's leadership grew older, their proposals became increasingly unimaginative and conservative: Secretary John Gulland's evidence on street betting to the Rowlatt Commission exemplified this (Royal Commission, 1934, p. 205 qu. 2904). While admitting that the choice lay between 'this disorganized, illegal kind of betting and an organized and orderly kind of betting in shops and offices', he preferred the former. 'As I look at it, I feel that I would rather bear the ills we have than fly to others that we know not of.' (6)

The League collapsed after the Second World War in a somewhat farcical episode: in an attempt to divert London's youth from gambling, the NAGL organized a series of classical music concerts at the Methodist Central Hall. It was a curious choice of a carrot to replace the stick, and the incompetence of the newly appointed secretary, H.C. Lawton, made them a financial disaster. In March 1949, a disillusioned Seebohm Rowntree recommended the withdrawal of the support given by the Joseph Rowntree Charitable Trust on which the NAGL depended: after this, it sank without trace.

Rowntree's interest and money were transferred to the Churches' Council on Gambling which, although established in 1932, had only recently become effective and was getting good publicity through the Protestant Church network. The relevant JRCT memo (dated September 1948) noted that 'the main London dailies and the BBC now seek their comments on news items connected with gambling ... and give very fair space to [them].' The same year (1948) Rowntree wrote in a letter that the 'financial and operational failure on the part of the League coincided with a great expansion of activity and increase of effectiveness on the part of the Churches' Council'.

The CCG carried on in the style of the NAGL, but times were changing fast, and a markedly liberal Royal Commission report on gambling was produced three years later (Royal Commission, 1951); it was almost a premature child of 'the permissive society'. In a vital passage (Royal Commission, 1951, para. 186) the Commission stated that they had been led by the evidence

> to the conclusion that gambling as a factor in the economic life of the country or as a cause of crime is of little significance and that its effects on social behaviour, in so far as these are a suitable object for legislation, are in the majority of cases less important than has been suggested to us by some witnesses. The object of gambling legislation should be to interfere as little as possible with individual liberty, but to impose such restrictions as are desirable and practicable to discourage or prevent excess.

This was the sort of language that was to become familiar in the stock phrases of liberal morality in the later 1950s and 1960s.

Rowntree was completely out of sympathy with the Report - understandably so, given the jibe at the anti-gamblers' evidence in the quoted passage. 'He believed that it had understated the seriousness of the problems and failed to relate [gambling] to its moral background' (Briggs, 1961, p. 323). Considering that the Report had done great harm and that a counter-measure was needed, Rowntree planned a new book on gambling. But he realized the difficulties (handwritten notes on Lavers and Rowntree, n.d., n.p.):

> However satisfactory we may think the arguments hitherto produced against gambling, the fact is that people in general do not accept them ... a new book should attempt a restatement of the arguments ... it is no good resting our arguments on those that the community has been rejecting for decades and which it now seems further than ever from accepting.

But, perhaps more than he himself realized, Rowntree's attitudes were also moving with the times: in a speech in 1954, he admitted that (Rowntree, 1954, n.p.)

> one of the difficulties in dealing with the problem of gambling is that the overwhelming majority of reasonable people do not believe that every simple act of gambling is a sin. On the whole, I agree with this view.

When, in the draft of the book, his assistant G.R. Lavers planned to describe football pools as 'a national menace' - traditional NAGL and early CCG language - Rowntree demurred, commenting in the margin (Lavers and Rowntree, n.d., n.p.) 'I wonder whether you have not exaggerated the evil of the football pools ... I don't think we can call [them] a national menace, nor do I feel any great concern to speak out against them.' Rowntree was never able to reconcile himself to the change in attitudes: the book remained in draft form at his death in 1954. (7)

The CCG relapsed into quietude, increasingly out of sympathy with the moral drift of the 1950s and with no influential spokesman to replace Rowntree. Hopes of ultimate rejection of the Willink Commission's recommendations gradually slipped away as 'the post-war experience of full employment and the lack of any increase in gambling throughout the relatively prosperous 1950s took the edge away from (their) opposition' (Downes et al., 1976, p. 41). Further blows came in 1956 with the introduction of premium bonds and the (long-delayed (8)) acceptance by the government of the Commission's recommendations, with a commitment to the preparation of legislation ('Hansard', v. 549 (1955-6), c. 2487). Once again, the anti-gambling movement seemed about to fade away.

'A NATION OF GAMBLERS': ANTI-GAMBLING IN 'THE PERMISSIVE SOCIETY'

Instead, just as at the beginning of the century, a new personality emerged to give the body new life. The Reverend Gordon Moody, appointed secretary of the CCG in 1958, was a representative of a new generation of moralists who accepted betting and gambling as a fact of life in a way that Rowntree and his colleagues had never been able to do. (Moody can even admit to gambling occasionally himself, although he adds 'I am not a threat either to the bookmaker or to myself - I'm too mean' (Wilson and Steeples, 1972, p. 23).)

After the old, moralistic, condemnatory approach suffered its final defeat in 1960 (when the Betting and Gaming Act implemented many of the Willink Commission's recommendations, notably including the legalization of off-course cash betting in betting shops), Moody set about the reconstruction of the CCG: during the 1960s, he turned it into a centre for information on gambling, conducting surveys, reviewing legislation, publishing pamphlets, but consistently avoiding abstract moralizing. In part, this was a reaction to the Willink Commission's failure to identify serious social consequences of gambling. - As Cornish comments (1978a, p. 213),

> This stress on measurable consequences has tended to shift the debate from questions of the morality or aesthetic value of gambling as a leisure-pursuit, to a more detailed examination of particular types of gambling and their relationship with extent of participation and probability of tangibly harmful effects.

For a considerable time, the CCG was responsible for providing the data for this debate. The notorious dearth of information about gambling (because so much gambling had previously been illegal, the government had virtually no official or informed estimates (9)) and Moody's willingness to avoid moralistic posturing meant that the press and even government departments came to rely on the CCG as a source of facts and figures. As Cornish says (1978a, p. 253), until recently, it

> was the only body, without direct or indirect commercial interests in the matter, to produce detailed financial and economic information about the gambling industry. Apart from the more recent work of the Gaming Board (since 1969) it has remained the only one to provide interpretation of existing statistics, to show a longstanding and informed concern about the social implications of all forms of gambling, and to stress the importance of considering the relationship between gambling behaviour and commercial developments in the gambling industry.

By the mid-1970s the CCG had achieved an influential and accredited position: it was described as 'an extremely successful lobbyist-cum-advisor on legislation' (Berlins, 1978a). Even when academics began to fill what was described as 'a strange gap in sociological accounting' (Downes et al., 1976, p. 11), the CCG was involved, helping to finance the first comprehensive sociological study of British gambling. (10)

This increasingly pragmatic and empirical approach coincided with, and formed part of, more generally, the movement in the churches to modernize and increase the 'relevance' of their activities (for which the dirty word is secularization) and, specifically, the continuing decline of moral condemnation of gambling. More traditional evangelical spokesmen found it increasingly difficult to gain a hearing, and the utterances of the last bastions came to be greeted with little more than mild amusement (as in press treatment of the General Assembly of the Church of Scotland's reaffirmation of total opposition to all forms of gambling (11)). The 1960s saw the decline almost to extinction of gambling per se as a social problem: as in the 1950s, relative affluence made it increasingly unlikely that everyday betting would push the punter beneath the poverty line in the way that Rowntree had found to be all too common in York earlier in the century (Rowntree, 1901). Today, condemnation of such gambling tends to be heard only when other factors are involved, as in the elements of class and sexist bias in criticism of bingo, popularly (though not accurately (12)) presented as a 'stupid' game for middle-aged, working-class women, and also of course when the punter is unemployed (see, for example, Chapman, 1978).

Opponents of gambling are now more than ever forced to use instrumental or indirect rather than moralistic arguments to have a realistic chance of success. (13) For example, an application for a betting shop licence in 1977 was opposed by three clergymen in Seahouses, Northumberland: their objections were stated in strictly instrumental terms. While it was said the shop would be a 'social temptation' to young people, the weight of their case was put in environmental terms: the proposed shop was in a bad location and would cause 'traffic and pedestrian problems'; it would be noisy; it would hasten the process in which 'a lovely, little village like Seahouses ... is losing all its heritage'. Reverend Grice-Hutchinson added, 'We do not want to add to the facilities in this area which is completely overburdened' (Betting Shop 'Temptation' to Young, 'Northumberland Gazette', 11 November 1977). These clergymen had not previously been noted for their active interest in environmental matters: to achieve their aim, they had to constitute themselves as an unofficial planning board and translate their moral objections into environmental concerns. By so doing, they were initially successful, but the magistrates' refusal of a licence was later quashed on appeal by the Crown Court (Seahouses Betting Shop Appeal Succeeds at Crown Court Hearting, 'Berwick Advertiser', 23 March 1978) as the site had county council approval and planning permission: the amateur environmentalists had been outranked. (14)

So gambling can now resist direct attack, and indeed is thoroughly respectable. It is run by businesses with widely diversified interests within and beyond the leisure industry. Not satisfied with parliamentary consultants, bookmakers can suggest that they should have one of their own men stand for Parliament (Rolfe, 1977). Condemnation of famous individual gamblers from Stan Bowles to Lord Lucan, Sir Hugh Fraser and Jim Slater (15) comes only when others - wives or shareholders - get hurt: in the blanket press coverage in 1978 of court cases involving Kitty Milinaire, even adverse comment on gambling which led to losses of £3,000,000 in under three years was hardly to be found (see national newspapers for 26 January 1978). This movement is reflected, and likely to be accelerated, by the latest Royal Commission on Gambling (chaired ironically by a man whose family Queen Victoria had first refused to ennoble because they had made their fortune through gambling on the Stock Exchange: 'Pendennis', the 'Observer', 9 July 1978; Corti, 1928, p. 451.

Their report devotes a mere two-and-a-half pages to the discussion of religious views on gambling (Royal Commission, 1978, paras 51ff.) and goes on to recommend the reintroduction of state lotteries; even if not implemented, this recommendation is symbolically extremely significant, for anti-gamblers had traditionally used the dire effects of the old state lotteries as a conclusive argument against any suggestion of legalized gambling.

This is not to claim that what went with gambling - as distinguished from gambling itself - was not defined as a social problem: indeed, there was a moral panic in the media around 1964-5 on the theme that Britain had become 'a nation of gamblers'. The difference was that this time the concern was about the indirect effects of gambling. The change is best expressed in Davies's characterization of the shift in moral attitudes in the 1960s as being from moralism to causalism, from judgments based on ethical grounds to ones made on a calculation between good and bad effects, a cautious, short-term utilitarianism (Davies, 1975). So gambling was regarded as an undifferentiated part of the general 'permissiveness', with specific problems of commercialization and monopolization of the gambling industry - the development of the now familiar chains of betting shops and amusement arcades - and the infiltration of the casinos by organized crime. This panic originated in the proliferation of casinos which, having slipped through a loophole in the 1960 Act, were largely unregulated. The idea that the Mafia was getting a toehold in Britain by taking over casinos was (and continues to be) the accepted explanation of the Gaming Act 1968.

Two footnotes can be added to this. While the theory drew heavily on the myth of the American Mafia (Bell, 1960; Albini, 1971), it does seem to be the case that American organized crime was interested in the British (and particularly London) casinos (Clark, 1966a, b, c; Smith, 1970, pp. 24, 115-29). But the 'wide-open city' implied is false: standard accounts (see, for example, Levin, 1977, p. 14) leave out the existing structure of London's organized crime which had run respectable but illegal gambling clubs (most profitably after the war, when currency restrictions limited the traditional availability to the wealthy of continental casinos), and it was only natural that they should move into the legal casinos and organize protection rackets for betting shops and floating card games (Hebdige, 1974; Pearson, 1973, pp. 124-5). It was, of course, more simple and more dramatic to speak in terms of an 'American invasion'. (16) This characterization must be seen as part of a general tendency in the media to see British events as 'incipiently American in character' (Hall et al., 1978, p. 26) which leads to a 'continual search for parallels and prophecies' (p. 25) and a belief that, unless measures are taken, what the American press report as happening there will be repeated in Britain. (For a full discussion of this theme, see Hall et al., 1978, pp. 21-8.)

Second, the 1968 Act's removal of the control of gaming from police hands to the Gaming Board, the tradition of police complicity in illegal gambling going back to the time of the state lotteries (17) (i.e. predating an organized force), their inactivity against casinos in the 1960s which led to a writ of mandamus against them by Raymond Blackburn, and a 'Times' leader (2 January 1968) stating 'it is clear that the [earlier legislation] has failed to achieve its purpose not so much because it could not be enforced as because the police failed to do so', and, finally, the information now becoming available about Scotland Yard in this period (for example, Cox et al., 1977) - all at least suggest that concern about police integrity in the enforcement of anti-gaming laws played a significant part in the formulation of this Act. (18)

All this is something of a diversion: the essential point for present purposes is that the CCG could claim no special expertise on these secondary matters. Valuable as their provision of information was, the policy recommendations they made on the basis of it could be given no more, and possibly considerably less, weight than those of a host of other interested parties, such as the police, criminologists and 'state of the nation' publicists. This lesson was driven home by the limited influence of their vigorous campaign against casinos. (19)

So the CCG faced something of a dilemma: it was in danger of becoming an influential, well informed and well funded pressure group without a cause. The Council's sponsors could hardly be expected to go on funding research into something which the group itself had come to admit was inherently unproblematic; those working for it could not be expected to go on as an unofficial and underpaid Home Office research unit. Ironically, the CCG's sober provision of facts had speeded the decline of gambling's problem status. This decline has been confirmed by research showing that net expenditure on gambling 'represents less than one per cent of all personal disposable income. This figure has remained more-or-less constant since at least 1950' (Cornish, 1978b, p. 29). With everyday gambling now not only a morally neutral, but evidently also a socially harmless, activity, the very existence of a Churches' Council on Gambling could be seen as open to question, even superfluous: it was in this atmosphere of potential crisis that the compulsive gambler was discovered by Moody's CCG and Gamblers Anonymous was established in Britain.

'A GENUINELY SERIOUS COMPLEX OF PERSONAL, SOCIAL AND ECONOMIC PROBLEMS ...'

Gamblers Anonymous (GA) was originally based, and continues to rely heavily, on the American GA, which was 'the outgrowth of a chance meeting between two men during the month of January in 1957' as an attempt to do something about their shared experience of 'a truly baffling history of trouble and misery due to an obsession to gamble' (Gamblers Anonymous, n.d.I, p. 3). They in turn (like other American self-help groups) based themselves on Alcoholics Anonymous (AA), and in both countries GA has taken advantage of the public acceptance of AA (Herman, 1977, pp. 99-100). From his appointment, Moody defined his commission as being to investigate why people gamble, rather than to continue the analysis of the morality of gambling: this brought him into contact both with people with gambling problems, and the American GA literature. In 1964, he was quoted as saying: 'We are studying the American method and considering how it could be applied to this country. If we find it at all practical, we shall go ahead at once'

(Gamblers Anonymous, n.d. II, p. 1, originally from Bestic, 1964). The first group was actually established after a chance meeting between Moody and an American GA member on business here, a meeting described as 'either providentially planned, or an amazing sequence of events' by the promotional literature (Gamblers Anonymous n.d.II, p. 1). This implication of a 'greater power' bringing people together both in Britain and America is stressed in GA's accounts (Gamblers Anonymous, n.d.I, p. 3), rather than Moody's planning. Robinson and Henry (1977, p. 17) point out the consistent appearance of the 'ordained meeting' in self-help groups' own histories. These are often fabricated to suit self-help ideology: Robinson and Henry (pp. 26-7) show that AA did this, while the account (Gamblers Anonymous, 1964, pp. 1-3, 19-30) by a co-founder of GA in America tells how the 'chance meeting' came after he had been trying to establish GA for four years, and the other co-founder had heard of his efforts. Chance was no more involved than in Moody's deliberate planning in this country.

From the beginning, it was stated that 'there is no organic connection between the CCG and GA' (Gamblers Anonymous, n.d.II, p. 2). This was intended to allow GA to appear to be a non-sectarian, indeed non-religious, group, but in reality the connection remained strong. Moody was called 'founder-patron', and for the first seven years the groups shared a London address and telephone number. Above all, GA continued to be very important to the CCG as living proof that gambling was still a problem needing study - and indeed that the CCG was right in claiming as much against the prevailing wind of the 1950s.

The element of discovery is explicit in the literature. The press conference called to launch GA attracted a considerable number of phone calls to Moody's office: this, it was claimed, showed that 'the lid was off a large and complicated problem' (Gamblers Anonymous, n.d.II, p. 2). Where, one may ask, were all these compulsive gamblers before 1964? Moody explained: 'It is understandable that the facts should previously have been hidden because those affected managed to conceal the fact that gambling is at the root of their problem' (1972, p. 9). At the same time, he felt able to claim that 'the number both of hardcore and compulsive gamblers has at least doubled in the last ten years' (p. 8). The distinction between 'hardcore' and 'compulsive' gambling is not elucidated, but the disastrous effects of the slip from one to the other are: 'It is a fact that every one of them [hardcore gamblers] is in danger of stepping - or slipping - over the line into problem gambling where all control is lost' (p. 8). In addition, it was said that the average age of GA members dropped in the 1960s, and that 'Today many [young men] are involved to the extent that their lives are threatened before they have properly begun' (p. 8). Here we have the ingredients of the classic social problem, dragged into the light and tackled, but still a threat, on the increase, attacking vulnerable members of society, and into which any who dabble are in danger of falling irrevocably. When Moody wrote about the compulsive gambler his language was not far removed from that used by the NAGL about the 'social organism' at the beginning of the century. Now the individual, rather than society, is diseased but the results are the same - crime, suicide, bankruptcy and the break-up of the family. The compulsive gambler provided an outlet for the remnants of the evangelical indignation.

The issue was used (pp. 9, 45) to show that the Willink Commission was misguided in 1951, that their belief that 'there were no longer any serious consequences of gambling ... [had] been shown to be a misapprehension by the thousands who have applied for help to GA' (Moody, 1972, pp. 9, 45). The CCG had no tendency to modesty about its own role: in its evidence to the Rothschild Commission it stated that 'it is only through our Secretary's initiative in introducing GA ... to this country that it has been possible for any assessment to be made of the extent of the adverse social consequences of gambling' (CCG, 1976, para. 91).

From 1967, the CCG was involved in organizing conferences on compulsive gambling, designed not - as might be expected - for psychiatrists and psychologists to get together to increase existing knowledge, but rather mainly to spread what was already known among medical and social workers, probation and prison officers. In 1975 a 'Guide for the Helping Agencies' was produced (Dickerson, 1975, p. 2)

> to assist [them] to become more aware of the fact that gambling may be the source of a genuinely serious complex of personal, social and economic problems [and] to provide some practical advice so that the helping agencies may better assess whether or not a client has a 'gambling problem'.

This was described as 'an endeavour to shift the point of delivery away from institutions to any helping agencies in the community who might contact gamblers seeking help' (Dickerson, 1977, p. 3). Practically, it was suggested that the 'helping agencies' should include questions and observations in the routine of their assessment procedures, such as social enquiry reports (Dickerson, 1975, p. 4). It is not perhaps too cynical to comment that, if anything is likely to produce a wave of compulsive gamblers, providing available labels and definitions in such procedures is exactly it. The possible reaction can be seen in the report of the very first conference: it was noted (CCG, 1967, p. 29) that

> many who attended (20) said they now had a clearer idea of the nature of the problem and the symptoms for which they should be looking. It was recognized that medical and social workers are rarely taught to expect gambling to be the source of a problem situation, for which reason they are less likely to find it even when it is there.

The process of the provision of definitions could be seen developing in the inclusion of articles about compulsive gambling in social work house magazines (for example Simmons, 1977), and was taken further when such articles were regurgitated under sensational headlines in the popular press (Todd, 1977). The CCG's publicity campaign had more general success: journalists were provided with a ready-made story beginning 'it is not commonly realised that gambling can easily become compulsive' (Attwell, 1976), or 'for some time now it has been recognized that gambling can be as addictive as alcohol or heroin' (Coote, 1973). However perception of it is presented, compulsive gambling makes good copy. Features discussing it can be found in magazines all along the shelf, from 'Fiesta' to 'Family Circle' (for examples see Curtain, n.d.; Macdonald, 1977; O'Sullivan, 1977; Meysey-Thompson, 1978).

'THE MOST IMPORTANT MATTER THE COMMISSION HAS TO CONSIDER ...'

The CCG's campaign for recognition of the problem of compulsive gambling came to a head in 1976 with the submission of evidence to the Rothschild Commission: Sutherland (1950) noted the significance of the appointment of an official investigation in such circumstances. Here was the opportunity to have compulsive gambling established as a decisive factor in public policy formulation.

Moody, the principle author, wrote from the perspective of 'the new morality' and rejected the conservative opinion that society should disapprove of and limit strictly all gambling, and resist extension of legalization in principle. He claimed that: 'By contrast, liberal churchmen have rarely any substantial advice to give when gambling legislation is before Parliament', and that the CCG neither discussed, nor made any pronouncement upon 'the traditional ethical question' (CCG, 1976, paras f-g). They recognized that Parliament had to bring it within the law and had 'no hard and fast objectives' in respect of legislation, although whenever this was under consideration they endeavoured 'to advise and assist those concerned to do what is best for the nation'.

Almost throughout, there was a tone of scrupulous self-restraint and painstaking moderation: the appreciation that the clock could not be turned back was clear. A general reversal of the trend towards legalized gambling was regarded as neither desirable nor feasible; only in the case of gaming machines was prohibition recommended (CCG, 1976, para. 77). There was discussion of the issue of money for sport, lotteries and 'the practices and financial structure of the gambling industry' in a manner that gave the reader little justification for the churches' special interest in them. But when Moody turned to compulsive gambling, there was an echo of John Hawke and the early anti-gamblers in the establishment of the problem, the claim to knowledge of it and the insistence that measures should be taken to deal with it as a matter of public policy.

It was conceded (CCG, 1976, para. 42) that compulsive gambling was more difficult to recognize than alcoholism or drug addiction and that it was unknown exactly how many sufferers there were in Britain, but it was also stressed that this number was 'certainly more than the "tiny minority" to which reference is sometimes made', and that 'the casualties of high risk, high intensity betting represent a comparatively neglected aspect of the problem'. The CCG said that, when the state provided for 'dangerous activities', it usually took steps to deal with the consequences, and so the government should 'ensure that the Health and Social Services understand the nature of "compulsive" gambling, and are able to recognize and deal with it. That is nothing like the case at present' (CCG, 1976, para. 42). The need for reformulation of legal and social policy was made clear. Prison, probation and after-care service members had tried to estimate the amount of crime produced by gambling and to help those involved, 'but such endeavours should be a matter of policy. There is no point in either exaggerating or minimising the extent of such consequences of gambling.' Their existence was 'a fact of life which we hope the Commission will consider and make recommendations accordingly' (CCG, 1976, para. 42).

So while the CCG accepted liberal attitudes towards most gambling, it made clear that revisions of the law were necessary to deal with the new problem of compulsive gambling.

Compulsion was presented as a possible outcome of all kinds of gambling, but the CCG concentrated on that occurring in betting shops. There were several reasons for this: since Dostoyevsky, the compulsive gambler has been associated with the casino, but the CCG's claim to expertise on gambling had been usurped in that area by the Gaming Board; recommendations stand more chance of implementation if specific; and, linked to this, betting was one area in which something like scientific evidence could be called to show how compulsive gambling is produced.

The CCG were not alone in their interest in the idea of addiction to gambling: medical investigations were reflected in the appearance of several articles on the subject in professional journals in the 1960s. This was due in part simply to the dearth of studies of gambling, making it an invitingly virgin research area, and in part to the perceived increase in gambling (Dickerson, 1977, p. 1). More widely, interest in 'the addictions' must be seen in the context of the general trend towards medicalization of deviant activity. The most systematic of such research is Dickerson's study of gambling in Birmingham betting shops (Dickerson, 1974): in his evidence, Moody drew heavily on this source. If moderation had ousted moralizing from the CCG a replacement was needed: as in comparable areas, scientific validity was employed to fill the breach. While Moody was happy to use scientific findings, he was less careful about the caveats put on these. This was notably true of Dickerson's work: the qualifications imposed on his research (21) were ignored and his work somewhat crudely marshalled into support for the CCG's policy formulations.

Dickerson's major research objective was a behavioural analysis of betting shop gambling, working from the hypotheses that experiences of the betting shop environment are important determinants of gambling therein and that excessive gambling can be produced by reinforcement contingencies in this environment, with the 'blower' acting as an effective operant conditioner. His substantiation of these hypotheses was taken by Moody to show that betting shops are a harmful institution, that once again Parliament was wrong not to listen to the CCG's advice in 1960: as elsewhere, 'experience showed that parliament had not fully got to grips with its subject' (CCG, 1976, para, 36). It was claimed that 'this state of affairs arose directly from establishing one institution to provide for at least two quite distinct forms of gambling', the distinction being between simply 'having a bet' and 'getting into the action' through betting (CCG, 1976, para. 51): the latter is the type of continuous betting which Dickerson thought could be aggravated into compulsion by betting shop conditions.

In accord with the new liberal policy, Moody did not ask that betting shops should be banned because of this social threat - 'we believe that the wise course is for parliament to guide and contain the tendency to gamble and not to suppress it' (CCG, 1976, para. 48) - but rather that there should be a two-tier system, one of small, kiosk betting shops in which loitering and the 'blower' would be prohibited and which would pay out only after racing hours, and another with the 'blower', television and comfortable seats, but charging for entry or having a club membership, and so making them less accessible in order to contain the contagion of the compulsive gambler. The tone of the CCG was grave (1976, para. 65):

> We accept that if specially designed premises were set aside for 'action' betting, they would probably become gambling hells. We recoil from that prospect, but for some that is what betting offices now are. The degree of stimulation 'action' gamblers need, and the intensity of their response while gambling, is frightening for non-gamblers and mere punters to contemplate. Such arrangements should not be made without consideration of the casualties which would certainly follow and the preparation of arrangements adequate to deal with them on the part of the Social, Health, Probation and After-Care Services.

The reconstitution of the betting shops in order to provide for and deal with the compulsive gambler was the central point of the CCG's submissions of evidence: 'We believe this to be the most important matter the Commission has to consider' (CCG, 1976, para. 61). Acceptance of this promotion of the compulsive gambler's supposed interests would have meant a major reorientation of policy priorities: it would also have renewed the primacy of the CCG and confirmed the success of their new secularized message.

FAILURE OF A CAMPAIGN

The significance to the CCG of the Royal Commission's eventual findings increased as their deliberations stretched over two years, for the date of Moody's retirement was approaching with the Council unable to find a successor and facing declining financial support from the churches. When it was announced that the CCG was to be wound up at Moody's retirement in August 1978, the chairman mooted a new and better funded National Council on Gambling to carry on the CCG's work, and looked to the Royal Commission for encouragement (Bassett, 1978; Berlins, 1978a).

When it eventually appeared, the Report (Royal Commission, 1978) seemed promising at first. The almost statutory complaint about the dearth of information on gambling was made, with the Commission coming to the 'inescapable' conclusion that there was 'a serious shortage of reliable and accessible information about gambling in the United Kingdom' (Royal Commission, 1978, para. 4-5). This was notably true of excessive gambling: the Commission said that not enough work had been done to enable them 'to say with any certainty (or known degree of uncertainty) how many addictive or pathological gamblers there are in the country; nor even whether the number is large enough to cause national anxiety' (para. 1-7). Indeed, the Commission's very first recommendation was that it considered the establishment of a Gambling Research Unit 'to monitor and study the incidence, sociology and psychology of gambling' both essential and urgent (para. 4-5). This prominence given to the compulsive gambling issue by the Commission, their endorsement of the Willink Commission's policy of imposing or continuing 'such restrictions as are desirable and practicable to discourage socially damaging excesses' (para. 1-8) and their decision to abstain from lengthy comment on the psychology of gambling in favour of Cornish's study (1978a), with its broadly favourable treatment of behaviourist theories of compulsive gambling, implied congruence between the CCG and the Royal Commission. The implication was misleading: the substance of the Report revealed a depth of disagreement which fell little short of a total repudiation of the working assumptions of the CCG.

The respect in which Moody was held was indicated by the Commission's 'serious consideration' (Royal Commission, 1978, para. 7-46) of the CCG's proposed reform of the betting shops. But while they were 'sympathetic to the objects of the proposal' of a two-tier system, and paid tribute to Moody's 'moderation and ... great experience of the needs and weaknesses of gamblers' (para. 7-34), such compliments must have seemed little more than sugar on a bitter pill.

While some practical objections to the two-tier system were noted (upheaval and expense to owners of existing betting shops and the imposition of an unwelcome and heavy burden of supervision on the police: paras 7-35, 7-36), the fundamental disagreement was about the proper aims of a legal and social policy towards gambling. Although some internal dissent over the balance between 'paternalism' and 'libertarianism' was admitted (para. 1-10), it is indicative of the Commission's philosophy that they regarded the provision to the punter of information about the odds as a matter of priority (para. 1-8). To them, gambling is not only an accepted, but an acceptable, part of modern life, and the gambling industry no different from other 'leisure industries'. Their main concern was that it should be properly run and regulated, with the interests of its consumers protected: for the first time, the wishes of the ordinary punter were promoted as a decisive factor in public policy formulation. For the CCG, there was a sting in the tail of the call for more research into excessive gambling: until such time as proper evidence about compulsion becomes available, the supposed interests of the compulsive gambler rate only low priority. (22) Polite scepticism was displayed about drawing on research like Dickerson's: the Commission commented (Royal Commission, 1978, para. 7-39) that estimates of the number of heavy or 'hardcore' gamblers made on the basis of surveys of money spent on gambling and frequency of attendance at betting shops meant only that gambling formed a large part of the lives of such people. They went on to criticize the use of the term 'hardcore' as 'emotive': 'one might as well call people who spend all their evenings at concerts and opera "hard-core" music-lovers. It does not necessarily show that their gambling causes any social problems' (para. 7-39).

Dickerson's estimate of some 70,000 British betting shop punters being 'addicted in the sense that they would like to reduce their gambling if they could' was qualified by the Commission's observation that only 'wild guesswork' can suggest 'how many have developed their addiction for reasons which have nothing to do with the way in which betting shops are conducted' (para. 7-39). Add to this the assessment that 'the case for the conditioning theory is unproven' (para. 7-45) (as well as the implication that unfulfilled desire to reduce a habit is hardly useful as a definition of compulsion) and it is hardly surprising that the CCG's two-tier system was rejected.

The Commission commented that its disadvantages were 'plain and immediate', and that 'the particular addiction problem which it is designed to meet is of uncertain dimensions and its effectiveness in dealing with that problem is questionable' (para. 7-40).

To place the Rothschild Report in the context of a broader trend in public policy, it is useful to compare the remarks of the Erroll Committee on Liquor Licensing (quoted by Cornish, 1978a, pp. 213-14):

> With moderate social drinking such an established feature of the country's day to day life, it is difficult to accept the principle that changes in the law governing availability should be conditioned entirely either by the needs of those most vulnerable to its excessive use or by attitudes based on the social conditions prevailing at the turn of the century.

So it was indicative of a more general reordering of policy priorities that it was considered not only that the interests of the compulsive gambler were uncertain, but, more than this, that others took preference. Clear expression of this was found in the rejection of the proposed limitation on use of the 'blower'. Enforcement was not thought to be a problem here: instead the Commission weighted 'the obvious consequences of depriving a lot of people of enjoyment against the possible gains in reducing addiction to gambling' (Royal Commission, 1978, para. 7-46). In their opinion, too little was known about the latter to justify 'so drastic a step'. Refusal to accept proposals based on conditioning theories was followed by recommendations implicitly rejecting such theories: the drab, inhospitable conditions in betting shops required by regulations were dismissed as being unnecessary and unhelpful (para. 7-43). The Commission concluded (para. 7-41) that, although the existence of facilities conducive to continuous betting might in some way promote addiction to gambling, there was no practical way to prohibit continuous betting without losing many of the advantages gained by the legalization of betting shops: here the virtual freedom of betting from criminal interference was picked out as being particularly significant.

The length and detail of the Commission's discussion of the CCG's proposal for reorganization of betting shops indicates that much more was involved than the rejection of an isolated proposal: the Commission used this section to illustrate their views on what should be the basis of legal and social policy towards gambling. Unfortunately for the CCG, the major policy change recommended was a greater measure of what was called 'libertarianism' rather than a wholesale reconstruction to deal with the alleged threat of compulsive gambling, about which the Commission were at best unconvinced. The CCG's campaign had failed: it is hardly going too far to say that their new message found little more favour with the Commission than the moralism which it had replaced would have done.

The Rothschild Commission's allocation of priority to the interests of the ordinary punter is, in a sense, the other side of Davies's 'moral shift' noted above: a commitment to providing for the chosen pleasures of the majority may not satisfy critics of mass culture, but it was welcome in an area so long tainted by elitism and class bias. Gordon Moody graciously called the Report 'forward looking [and] recommended the Commission for laying the stress on the interests of the gambler' (Berlins, 1978b); however, it seems clear that the influence of the CCG's major recommendations was negligible. The medical and behaviourist theories which Moody had tried to transplant to replace the heart of the CCG's moral crusade were treated as being no more than unproven. It was not surprising that a psychologist should complain to 'The Times' that he found the Commission's treatment of 'the question of compulsive gambling ... more than a little disappointing' (Rankin, 1978). More generally, the press followed the lead given them: the tabloids which had made front page copy out of Kitty Milinaire again carried 'GAMBLING MAD' as banner headlines, (23) but this time the reference was to the normality and ubiquity of small-scale gambling reported by the Commission, not to the dangers of addiction. The 'quality' press mentioned compulsive gambling only to endorse the Commission's estimation of it. (24)

CONCLUSION

Presentation of the development of a group or organization in the way that has been attempted here is clearly in danger of being dismissed as teleological (cf. Dickson, 1968, p. 144), but some explanation is needed for the relative longevity of the CCG in the face of what were quite unsympathetic conditions. There is a useful contrast with American temperance groups which, in preserving their moralistic approach, resisted attempts to redefine alcohol problems as alcoholism in the 1930s (Gusfield, 1967); the result was that they have been in decline ever since (Gusfield, 1955). By embracing a medicalized conception of certain types of gambling, the CCG gained a new vitality in the later 1960s and 1970s.

While it is not claimed that the CCG was involved in the conscious and aggressive self-preservation identified by Dickson (1968) with the Bureau of Narcotics (Moody is no Harry Anslinger), the example of the CCG does seem usefully to add a case to the limited literature on the behaviour of declining 'value-oriented social movements' (Messinger, 1955, p. 3, n. 1). Becker suggested only two courses for the unsuccessful moral crusade (1963, pp. 153-4):

> On the one hand, it may simply give up its original mission and concentrate on preserving what remains of the organisation that has been built up.... Or the failing movement may adhere rigidly to an increasingly less popular mission.

While some opponents of gambling have chosen the latter course (Kerr, 1977), the CCG was able to find a compatible new mission. Messinger presumed this was possible, but thought it unlikely, although he also noted that (1955, p. 9)

> the organized arms [of value-oriented social movements] ... are not necessarily dissolved by the abatement of the forces initially conjoining to produce them. They may gain a certain degree of autonomy from their bases and continue to exist.

This the CCG was able to do for a time in the 1960s, during its period as a research and information unit; but it suffered the consequences of 'the abatement of the particular constellation of social forces giving rise to the movement' identified by Messinger (1955, pp. 9-10): competition for a declining support, financial threat and

> an increasing lack of public concern for the organizational mission ... reflected in the ending of public discussion of the issues which the organization represents or, perhaps better put, with [sic] these issues in the frame of reference that they are placed by organizational representatives.

The CCG's response to these challenges was to find itself a new social problem. To repeat, this is not to set up Moody as a manipulating, cynical entrepreneur. He, and the CCG, adapted with, rather than to, a changing environment (cf. Dickson, 1968, p. 145): the contemporary context of the increasing currency of medical and behaviouristic accounts, of action made the discovery of compulsive gambling quite intelligible and consequential.

It is more difficult to speculate on the ability of other groups to make this change of organizational objectives with any degree of success: few are likely to find a new mission as available and attractive as the CCG's. Equally, the possibilities of longer-term success are uncertain. Although it has been argued here that the Rothschild Report ended the CCG's crusade, this was not inevitable: the story might have had a different ending had a psychologist been appointed to the Commission. Again, while the group's particular campaign might have failed, its more diffuse influence in raising the issue is, as yet, difficult to assess. The almost unanimous praise of the Rothschild Report as being well above the usual Royal Commission standard should ensure that, despite Lord Rothschild's misgivings about their usefulness (Royal Commission's Value Questioned by Lord Rothschild, 'The Times', 30 June 1978), it will have considerable influence upon public policy. However, if the proposed Gambling Research Unit is established and psychological research into excessive gambling accorded priority, (25) it may be that, by the time of the next Royal Commission on Gambling, public policy will turn back to concern about the dangers of gambling.

Whatever happens in the future, and while the CCG may have helped to induce discussion about compulsive gambling, the significant factor for present purposes is that the philosophy which lay behind their campaign will play little part in future discussions. The group made a brave attempt to adapt to its changing environment, but more than the odds were against them. Moody's retirement and the demise of the CCG mark a firm conclusion to a history of organized opposition to gambling stretching back to the 1890s: within that history are traced vital outlines of social change in the reconstitution of the relationship between work and leisure and of the accompanying morality.

NOTES

* For help in collecting data used in this essay, thanks and acknowledgments are due to Mr Garth Waite of the Division of Social Responsibility of the Methodist Church; Reverend Gordon Moody; Dr Mark Dickerson, and Mr Trevor Jepson of the Joseph Rowntree Charitable Trust. Thanks also to Peter Conrad for the title.

1 See David Oldman's (1978) excellent discussion of perceptions of compulsive gambling.

2 For a full bibliography, see Briggs (1961), pp. 344-8.

3 See below.
4 See n. 5.
5 E.B. Perkins to Select Committee, 1918, p. 67ff. Perkins and John Gulland (Honorary Literary Secretary of the NAGL) to Select Committee, 1923, pp. 318ff. and 363ff. respectively. Gulland and several others to Royal Commission, 1932-3, pp. 185ff., 377ff., 425ff.
6 It should be noted that this conservatism was not out of time: the Commission's proposal of a modest form of betting office was ignored, and off-course cash betting was left outside the law until 1960.
7 Copies of the material quoted in this section are stored at the offices of the Joseph Rowntree Charitable Trust in York: see acknowledgments above.
8 Acceptance was so long delayed that the chairman was moved to write to 'The Times' expressing concern that the Report was being ignored (6 December 1955). See also Cartwright (1975), p. 204.
9 The only real exception to this being Kemsley and Ginsburg's survey (1951) which was prepared in connection with the Willink Commission and soon out of date. Cornish points out that even many of the more recently available statistics were collected not for the formulation of social policy 'but largely as the result of fiscal requirements. Because social considerations have played so little part in directing the collection of statistics, these are not always available in a form which makes their interpretation in social terms feasible' (1978a, p, 6).
10 This was Downes et al. (1976): the connection with Rowntrees continues, for the finance provided by the CCG came from the Rowntree trusts.
11 For example, Kerr (1977): ' a conscientious member of the Kirk in Scotland will have to quell any reckless urges to guess the weight of a cake or the number of peas in a jar at charitable bunfights.'
12 Downes et al. report from their findings (1976, pp. 174-5) that

> the alleged near-monopoly by women of bingo is not corroborated. Instead, proportionally just as many men as women play bingo, and this holds whether one looks at the regular or more occasional participation ... proportionately more of the young than middle-aged play bingo, and this is especially so for women.

The conventional wisdom is correct only in respect of class. Disappointingly, the Rothschild Commission ignored this evidence and repeated the old clichés: Royal Commission (1978), paras 20-6, 20-20.
13 The Rothschild Report noted that religious bodies offering specific recommendations 'concentrated on social issues, such as the measures needed to contain excessive gambling. Their reasons were given in social rather than religious or moral terms and none ... urged that the law or public policy should be determined by their religious views' (Royal Commission, 1978, para. 5-4).
14 The example is not as parochial as it may seem: a developing holiday village is one of the few areas where new betting shops are now opened in what is a saturated market.

15 Those questioning Slater's inclusion in this list would do well to look at his book, 'Return to Go' (Slater, 1977).

16 Charles Kray has dismissed the idea of a Mafia invasion. He admits to having met Angelo Bruno, the Mafia chief to whom, according to Smith (1970, pp. 115-29), Britain was allocated as a 'sphere of influence', but denies that there was any 'take-over'. Kray states (1977, pp. 166-7) that Bruno

> stopped off in London for a few days in the course of a tour of Europe. He showed a small interest in the gambling operation in the Metropolis, talked to many people in the business including the twins and myself, and went on his way. My impression was that he considered it very small beer in comparison with the American scene, as indeed it was.

As for the claim that the Mafia organized gambling 'junkets', Kray comments (pp. 166-7):

> I found nothing to suggest that the trips were anything more than a good idea thought up by a bunch of enterprising travel agents. Of course, it may be that the travel agents were members of the Mafia, but like most sensible persons I would like to have proof of that before I believed it.

Kray might not be thought a reliable witness, but those with better reputations would do well to heed his final remark. For a sensibly cautious comment, see Cornish (1978a), pp. 74-5.

17 See discussion in Committee ... (1808).

18 See the guarded comments of the Gaming Board on the background to their appointment: Gaming Board (1969) paras 20-8.

19 For a detailed account, see the report of the Churches' Council on Gambling Legislation, which was effectively the same as the CCG: CCGL (1968). See also CCG (1967, 1968).

20 This included six probation officers, seventeen voluntary welfare organization workers, nine professional welfare workers and three JPs, along with two psychiatrists and one psychologist CCG, 1967, p. 29).

21 See his undogmatic discussion of the status of compulsive gambling as an addiction, which concludes with the admission that 'perhaps to extend the concept of addiction to include "compulsive" gambling is not credible and would lead to a loss of the heuristic function of the concept of addiction' (Dickerson, 1977, p. 1).

22 For a clear statement of this, see Royal Commission (1978), para. 7-46. The 'Economist' noted the Commission's 'eagerness to establish gambling as a modern business rather than an ancient racket' and their belief that it should be 'straightened out and seen from both inside and out as a modern industry with a right to reasonable profits and a duty to give a fair deal to its customers' (Die Recast, the 'Economist', 15 July 1978, p. 21).

23 See the 'Daily Mirror' and the 'Daily Express' for 13 July 1978.

24 The 'Guardian''s leader stated that the number of compulsive gamblers was 'minute' (Rothschild's Odds-on Winner, 13 July 1978). The 'Daily Telegraph' concluded that 'there is not the least evidence at present to suggest that gambling is a major social evil in Britain today' (Gambling, 13 July 1978).

25 The Commission was vague about the Unit's intended role:

although first mentioned in connection with the psychology of gambling (Royal Commission, 1978, paras 4-1ff.), the Commission make clear that it should collect routine information about ordinary gambling; and, indeed, the only specific suggestion made is for a survey of outlay and expenditure on bingo (para. 20-19).

BIBLIOGRAPHY

ALBINI, J.L. (1971), 'The American Mafia: Genesis of a Legend', New York: Appleton-Century-Crofts.
ATTWELL, M. (1976), Are We Just a Nation of Losers?, 'Western Mail', 5 May.
BASSETT, T. (1978), Watchdog Body for Gambling Urged, the 'Guardian', 6 June.
BECKER, H.S. (1963), 'Outsiders: Studies in the Sociology of Deviance', New York: Free Press.
BELL, D. (1960), Crime as an American Way of Life, in 'The End of Ideology', New York: Free Press, pp. 127-50.
BERLINS, M. (1978a), Move to Set Up New Council on Gambling, 'The Times', 6 June.
BERLINS, M. (1978b), Royal Commission Urges National Lottery to Help Sports and Arts, 'The Times', 13 July.
BESTIC, A. (1964), Betting Bonanza, 'Tit-bits', 2 May.
BRIGGS, A. (1961), 'Social Thought and Social Action: A Study of the Work of Seebohm Rowntree', London: Longmans.
CARTWRIGHT, T.J. (1975), 'Royal Commissions and Departmental Committees in Britain', London: Hodder & Stoughton.
CCG (1967), 'Gambling: An Attempt to Estimate', Annual Review of the CCG, 1967.
CCG (1968), 'Gambling: A Bad Risk for Britain', Annual Review of the CCG, 1968.
CCG (1976), Submissions of Evidence to the Royal Commission on Gambling, mimeo, CCG.
CCGL (1968), 'The Gaming Act 1968: Views and Statements', London: CCGL.
CHAPMAN, R. (1978), Is this a Record asks Lazy Leslie?, 'News of the World', 22 January.
CLARK, E. (1966a), The Green Felt Gangsters, 'Observer Weekend Review', 18 September.
CLARK, E. (1966b), Gambling: How to Stop the Rot, 'Observer Weekend Review', 29 May.
CLARK, E. (1966c), Crime Wave Britain, 'Observer Weekend Review', 18 September.
COMMITTEE ... (1808), 'Reports from the Committee on the Laws Relating to Lotteries', pp. 182, 323.
COOTE, A. (1973), Woman's Guardian, the 'Guardian', 3 September.
CORNISH, D.B. (1978a), 'Gambling: A Review of the Literature and its Implications for Policy and Research', Home Office Research Study no. 42, London: HMSO.
CORNISH, D.B. (1978b), Surveying the Literature on Gambling, 'Home Office Research Unit Bulletin', no. 5, pp. 28-31.
CORTI, E.C. (1928), 'The Reign of the House of Rothschild', London: Gallancz.

COX, B. et al. (1977), 'The Fall of Scotland Yard', Harmondsworth: Penguin.
CURTAIN, C. (n.d.), Do You Really Want to Lose Your Shirt?, 'Fiesta', vol. 10, no. 5, pp. 52-5.
DAVIES, C. (1975), 'Permissive Britain: Social Change in the Sixties and Seventies', London: Pitman.
DICKERSON, M. (1974), The Effect of Betting Shop Experience on Gambling Behaviour, unpublished PhD thesis, University of Birmingham.
DICKERSON, M. (1975), 'Gambling: Associated Problems', London: Consultation on Compulsive Gambling.
DICKERSON, M. (1977), 'Compulsive' Gambling as an Addiction: Dilemmas, mimeo, Department of Clinical Psychology, the Royal Edinburgh Hospital.
DICKSON, D.T. (1968), Bureaucracy and Morality: an Organizational Perspective on a Moral Crusade, 'Social Problems', vol. 16, pp. 143-56.
DIXON, D. (1978), Class Law: the Street Betting Act 1906, unpublished paper, Department of Sociology, University College, Cardiff.
DOWNES, D.M. et al. (1976), 'Gambling, Work and Leisure', London: Routledge & Kegan Paul.
EDWARDS, D.L. (1974), Preface to Moody, G.E., 'Social Control of Gambling', London: CCG.
GALLIHER, J.F. and WALKER, A. (1976), The Puzzle of the Social Origins of the Marijuana Tax Act of 1937, 'Social Problems', vol. 24, pp. 367-76.
GAMBLERS ANONYMOUS (1964), 'Gamblers Anonymous', Los Angeles: GA Publishing Company.
GAMBLERS ANONYMOUS (n.d.I), Questions and Answers about the Problem of Compulsive Gambling and the GA Recovery Programme, GA pamphlet.
GAMBLERS ANONYMOUS (n.d.II), Formation of Gamblers Anonymous in Britain, GA pamphlet.
GAMING BOARD (1969), 'Report of the Gaming Board for Great Britain 1969', House of Commons 208, 1969-70.
GUSFIELD, J.R. (1955), Social Structure and Moral Reform: a Study of the Woman's Christian Temperance Union, 'American Journal of Sociology', vol. 61, pp. 221-32.
GUSFIELD, J.R. (1963), 'Symbolic Crusade: Status Politics and the American Temperance Movement', Urbana: University of Illinois Press.
GUSFIELD, J.R. (1967), Moral Passage: the Symbolic Process in Public Designations of Deviance, 'Social Problems', vol. 15, pp. 175-88.
HALL, S. et al. (1978), 'Policing the Crisis: Mugging, the State and Law and Order', London: Macmillan.
HEBDIGE, D. (1974), The Kray Twins: a Study of a System of Closure, Occasional Paper, Centre for Contemporary Cultural Studies, University of Birmingham.
HERMAN, R.D. (1977), 'Gamblers and Gambling: Motives, Institutions and Controls', Lexington, Mass.: Lexington Books.
KEMSLEY, W.F.F. and GINSBURG, D. (1951), 'Betting in Britain', Social Survey Report, n.s. 710/4, London: HMSO.
KERR, J. (1977), Kirk Still Firm Against Gambling, the 'Guardian', 31 May.

KRAY, C. (1977), 'Me and My Brothers', Tiptree: Anchor Press.
LAVERS, G.R. and ROWNTREE, G.S. (n.d.), unpublished draft of book on gambling.
LEVIN, B. (1977), 'The Pendulum Years: Britain and the Sixties', London: Pan.
MACDONALD, L. (1977), You Can Bet Your life, 'Woman's Realm', 1 October, pp. 12-15.
MESSINGER, S.L. (1955), Organizational Transformation: a Case Study of a Declining Social Movement, 'American Sociological Review', vol. 20, pp. 3-10.
MEYSEY-THOMPSON, S. (1978), The Shame of Women who Gamble, 'Family Circle', vol. 15, no. 3, March.
MOODY, G.E. (1972), 'The Facts about the Money Factories', London: CCG.
OLDMAN, D. (1978), Compulsive Gamblers, 'Sociological Review', vol. 26, pp. 349-71.
O'SULLIVAN, P. (1977), Wild Cards, 'Time Out', no. 393, 14 October, pp. 15-17.
PEARSON, J. (1973), 'The Profession of Violence', St Albans: Panther.
RANKIN, H. (1978), letter to 'The Times', 20 July.
ROBINSON, D. and HENRY, S. (1977), 'Self-Help and Health: Mutual Aid for Modern Problems', London: Martin Robertson.
ROLFE, M. (1977), A Bookie in the House?, 'Sporting Life', 18 August.
ROWNTREE, B.S. (1901), 'Poverty: A Study of Town Life', London: Macmillan.
ROWNTREE, B.S. (ed.) (1905), 'Betting and Gambling: A National Evil', London: Macmillan.
ROWNTREE, B.S. (1954), unpublished text of a speech on gambling.
ROYAL COMMISSION 1932-3 (1934), 'Final Report of the Royal Commission on Lotteries and Betting, 1932-3' (the Rowlatt Report), Cmd 4341, London: HMSO.
ROYAL COMMISSION 1949-51 (1951), 'Report of the Royal Commission on Betting, Lotteries and Gaming, 1949-51' (the Willink Report), Cmd 8190, London: HMSO.
ROYAL COMMISSION 1976-8 (1978), 'Final Report of the Royal Commission on Gambling 1976-8' (the Rothschild Report), cmnd 7200, London: HMSO.
SELECT COMMITTEE (1918), 'Report from the Select Committee on Premium Bonds 1917-18' (168).
SELECT COMMITTEE (1923), 'Report of the Select Committee on Betting Duty 1923' (139).
SIMMONS, G. (1977), This Deadly Game of Chance, 'Community Care', no. 188, 16 November.
SLATER, J. (1977), 'Return to Go', London: Weidenfeld & Nicolson.
SMITH, P.G. (1970), 'The Crime Explosion', London: Macdonald.
SUTHERLAND, E.W. (1950), The Diffusion of Sexual Psychopath Laws, 'American Journal of Sociology', vol. 56, pp. 142-8.
TAYLOR, L. (1972), The Significance and Interpretation of Replies to Motivational Questions: the Case of Sex Offenders, 'Sociology', vol. 6, pp. 23-39.
TODD, R. (1977), Lady Luck, You're So Sexy, 'Daily Mirror', 17 November.

WILSON, D. and STEEPLES, J. (1972), Gambling Mania, 'Observer Colour Magazine', 10 September, pp. 16-25.

Chapter 11

INDUSTRIAL RELATIONS AND THE LAW: FROM THE WEBBS TO CORPORATISM

Tom Keenoy

INTRODUCTION

The place of law, and in particular the courts of law, have typically been viewed with considerable mistrust by both practitioners and students of industrial relations. While those who see industrial relations as a matter of 'good administration' may view such suspicions as the product of ignorance and misunderstanding, these traditional objections to the law are grounded in both pragmatic and philosophical concerns which merit brief mention. Academic comment, while concerned to highlight the cumbersome ineptitude of legalistic regulation in the fine detail of daily indstrial relations, has laid primary emphasis on the social and philosophical desirability of preserving the fundamentally 'voluntaristic' character of industrial relations (Kahn-Freund, 1972; Flanders, 1970, 1974). Management, which in public has often pressed for legislation to control trade union behaviour (CBI, 1966), has, when given the opportunity to utilise such laws in private, invariably stepped back from any action which might seriously jeopardise existing relationships with shop stewards or trade unions (Weekes et al., 1975). Even 'good' law, it would seem, is no substitute for bad management. And workpeople and their representatives, the trade unions, have been similarly ambivalent in their approach to the law and its benefits. Their opposition to the law has been selective, primarily being confined to a rejection of any legal constraint on employer-trade union negotiation; and trade unionism has, for a very long time, (1) had pragmatic recourse to the law with regard to the provision of minimum standards in working conditions and social welfare provisions.

Despite the continued expression (2) of these deeply felt reservations, it is no longer realistic to analyse industrial relations in terms of the voluntaristic model. The extent of statutory regulation and state involvement has been increasing since the end of the last war (Panitch, 1976), and has expanded dramatically in the 1960s with incomes policy; in the deceptive afterglow of the Donovan Report (in 1968), there are now legislative provisions covering an unprecedented range of employment issues, trade union and individual rights. These include race discrimination, equal pay, trade union recognition, unfair dismissal, disciplinary, disputes and grievance procedures, disclosure of information, arbitration and conciliation - the recent White Paper on industrial democracy hints at more to come. (3) Alongside this fairly rapid construction of what can be described as a legal code of employment and trade union rights, the 1970s have also seen the virtual institutionalisation of incomes policy - which, despite the variety of labels since 1948, has always had the effect of limiting wages, salaries and occasionally dividends in the service of the national interest. The explanation of this qualitative change in the character of British industrial relations since 1945 is complex. It requires an analysis of changes in political ideologies and the economics of postwar reconstruction and malaise - the latter involving, in particular, some deferential genuflections in the direction of international trade and finance - together with a socioeconomic analysis of trade unionism.

Recently, in a number of studies it has been suggested that the explanation lies in the extent to which Britain is becoming a corporate state: a society which may be characterised as 'fascism with a human face' (Pahl and Winkler, 1974). In such a society, the behaviour of trade unions and employers would be severely constrained - either directly or indirectly - through state regulation. This paper is about one aspect of this controversial argument: the extent to which corporatist strategies are pre-figures in the development of industrial relations. After providing an outline of the corporatist argument, the Webbs' (1898) analysis of trade unionism will be examined in some detail in order to demonstrate the affinity between their 'collectivist vision' and what can be called the 'corporatist syndrome'. Finally, the significance of this correspondence - both for the study of law in industrial relations and for the whole corporatist thesis - will be considered.

THE CORPORATIST ARGUMENT

Put at its simplest, the corporatist argument states that British capitalism, while it displays many of the hallmarks of an economic system in deep crisis, and while it is clearly going through some process of institutional and structural transformation - a feature which is particularly evident in the area of economic and industrial policy - is not in the process of moving towards any form of socialist revolution. Capitalism may be dying but there remain viable alternatives to socialism. The emergent mode of economic domination - one which, according to Panitch (1976) can be identified in embryonic form as far back as 1945 - is one based on the continued existence of private ownership of the means of production. However, unlike traditional market capitalism, the institutional separation of the polity from the economy is replaced by a highly interventionist and, if necessary, coercive state. Its reliance on the use of law in the control and direction of the economy is legitimated by an ideological appeal to its role as identifier and protector of the 'national interest'. (The socialist revolution may yet still come - but in the meantime we have to await another 'final phase' of capitalism: the dictatorship of corporatism.) As an argument it comes in various forms and, while a thorough appraisal of the corporatist thesis seems as yet premature, it has understandably attracted its critics. (4)

The broadest elaboration of the argument to date is to be found in the series of articles by Pahl and Winkler (see note 4). They have specified what corporatism is, why it has emerged within the structure of capitalism, how it is being institutionalised and, somewhat more briefly, why it will be preferred to alternative strategies such as a return to any form of laissez-faire or a move to state socialism based on increased nationalisation. The paradigm model of corporatism is clearly differentiated from capitalism, socialism and syndicalism through the distinctive role played by the state in the 'control over the internal decision-making of privately-owned business. The State does not just attempt to influence decisions, it prescribes or limits the range of choice open to capitalist owners or managers' (Winkler, 1976, p. 104). It is this directive - as opposed to supportive or facilitative - activity which is the crucial theoretical distinction. The substantive character of corporate state intervention is guided by four principles, which not only provide for the legitimation of the state's action but also clearly indicate why the corporate state is likely, empirically, to be authoritarian if not coercive. The principles of unity, order, nationalism and success lay fundamental stress on the need for socioeconomic co-operation rather than interest group competition in the effort that all must make in the 'national enterprise' of preserving society from economic ruin. At the same time they mask such potential policies as the centralised direction and control of the economy, the 'rational' control of industrial conflict through the legal prohibition of strikes, a jingoistic return to economic protectionism in international trade and even, perhaps, a 'temporary' suspension of individual liberties in the interests of 'winning the war'. Hence, such institutions as the NEDC, the NBPI, the OME, the CIR, the NIRC, the Pay Board and the Prices Commission, and such statutes as those governing prices and incomes, the 1971 Industrial Relations Act, the Employment Protection Act, the Trade Union and Labour Relations Act and the 1975 Industry Act, are seen as elements in the growing corporatist scaffold.

All these themes are reflected, but by no means mirrored, in Crouch's contribution to the debate about corporatism. Significantly, one of the major reservations Winkler has about the progress of corporatism is the response of organised labour to the continuation of state controls over wages and industrial relations. For example, the failure of governments to maintain incomes policies and the demise of the Industrial Relations Act may be more than temporary hiccups down the road to national unity: they may reflect a deeply rooted independence in labour organisations which, despite their alleged subserviance to the integrative ideology of the Labour Party (Panitch, 1976), will require a degree of state coercion not seen in Britain since the Combination Acts of 1799 and 1800 if they are to be securely subordinated to a corporatist definition of the national interest.

Crouch (1977) addresses himself directly to the problems posed by trade unionism for the 'coming corporate state'. The fairly dramatic changes in British industrial relations between 1957 and

1976 are subjected to intensive and detailed analysis within a framework of five 'ideal-type' strategies available to the dominant interests in a class society. These are: (i) market individualism, which is the 'paradigm' case of classical laissez-faire economic organisation; (ii) liberal collectivism, or, as Crouch calls it, 'the Compromise', which refers to the character of British industrial relations between 1945 and 1964; (iii) statist corporatism, seen most coherently in the character of fascist Italy; (iv) voluntarist corporatism - the advocacy of reliance on productivity bargaining by the NBPI exemplifies this form; and (v) private corporatism, which is perhaps best illustrated by Dore's (1973) account of what is more usually called Japanese paternalism. These ideal types are differentiated according to the way in which they resolve certain strategic dilemmas faced by the dominant interest. Thus, corporatism is conceived as a series of dimensions stressing order and unity in employment relations, a legally coercive and economically active state, a collectivised but managerially oriented labour force and the application of equity as a moral criterion and rationality as a technical criterion in the administration and distribution of rewards. To the extent that the dominant interests in a (class) society operate with these strategies, that society may be characterised as corporatist. (5)

THE WEBBS AND CORPORATISM

The major issues in the contemporary debate about corporatism - the role of law in industrial relations, the degree and impact of state intervention in socioeconomic policy and the nature of the changes taking place in the character of capitalism - are all to be found at the centre of the often bitter dispute over the 'coming socialist state' which was conducted by the late Victorian intelligentsia. The bureaucratically oriented Fabians, led by the Webbs, were opposed by the democratically insistent Guild Socialists, an uneasy alliance of socialists, communists and genuine 'pink' liberals centred on G.D.H. Cole. The language and the labels were different - collectivism or guild socialism - but, in essence, their argument concentrated on the same issues. Significantly, differences of opinion over the role of the state in the 'new' society proved irreconcilible. In the event, it is the position of the Webbs which has prevailed in the test of time. Armed with utilitarianism, a sobering awareness of the need to provide a national minimum level of sanitation and a clearer perception of the changes imminent in the nature of economic and industrial organisation, the Webbs proved to be the more accurate in their predictions about the future of trade unionism.

In their analysis of trade unionism, the Webbs (1894, 1898) were concerned to identify what it was, where it had come from, where it was going and where it ought to be going - the latter two often becoming confused in their attempts to establish the pre-eminence of collectivism. And in these accounts there is a remarkable correspondence between their conclusions concerning where trade unionism was and ought to be going and the pattern of behaviour identified in the 'corporatist syndrome' provided by Winkler and Crouch. While the Webbs did not predict the corporate state, they certainly advocated trade union policies and changes in the institutional structure of industrial relations which could be comfortably accommodated within a corporatist structure. Indeed, there is now some evidence which suggests that they would have welcomed the undeniable authoritarianism of a corporatist 'national unity' (MacKenzie, 1978).

Given their traditional place in the historic rise of the Labour Movement, how is such an interpretation possible? In the analysis which follows an attempt has been made to use Crouch's conceptualisation of the four elements of the 'corporatist syndrome' as a set of guidelines.

(i) Order and unity in employment relations

The characteristic corporatist concern with order and unity in employment relations is identified by Crouch in terms of an emphasis on a unitary ideology (Fox, 1966) in the legitimation of a strictly hierarchical managerial authority. This is combined with an appeal to workers and trade unions to become involved in organisational decision-making and a tendency to identify and process industrial conflicts as issues of rights rather than confrontations over interests. This strategy is designed to highlight the community of interests within the factory (and the nation), the collective responsibilities of workers and management, and, as Winkler (1976) suggests, the fact that unity is derived from co-operation, not competition and conflict. Disputes are seen to be resolvable in terms of a predetermined framework of mutually agreed rules or laws: it is not simply a question of which actor has the capacity to impose a solution on the other.

The Webbs saw order and unity in employment relations as being contingent on the gradual emergence of the collectivist state which was to be fashioned by 'professional experts' operating through Parliament to ensure the complete overhaul of virtually all aspects of social policy, economic behaviour and administrative practice. From poverty to education, from local government reorganisation to nationalisation, nothing would remain untouched by the Royal Commissions, (6) which were to be the cutting edge of their strategy for social reform. (The trade unions were seen to have a distinctive role to play in the achievement of encroaching economic justice.) In this respect it must be said that the Webbs displayed an uncompromising naivety in their perception of the potential benevolence of the state as a neutral guardian of the national interest. The evil effects of 'unregulated competition' - poverty, disease, starvation wages and unemployment - were to be gradually banished through the education of employers and trade unionists in the economic benefits of the 'Doctrine of the Living Wage' (see below) and the increasing use of legislation to regulate the employment relationship.

An emphasis on order and unity pervades the Webbs' analysis and is best conceived as the managerial ideology underlying all their specific institutional reforms. The extent to which they were prepared to endorse 'legal-rational' solutions (Weber, 1964) is illustrated in their concluding speculations where they see the resolution of industrial conflict as a matter of establishing a 'floor of industrial rights'. In predicting an increasing trade union preoccupation with the establishment of a set of national minimum terms and conditions of employment, they assert that these will be deliberately enforced 'by an elaborate Labor Code' which will constitute 'a definite quota of education, sanitation, leisure and wages for every grade of worker in every industry' (Webb and Webb, 1898, p. 817). (7) Such a 'Labor Code' would clearly be much more extensive than the collective corporatist weight of all the various proposals produced by the Labour and Conservative governments of the 1960s and 1970s - a statutory incomes policy seems an indecently mild measure in comparison.

(ii) State regulation

The role of the state is the central pivot of corporatist structures. Crouch (1977, pp. 18-20) discusses the relationship between the 'polity and the industrial relations system' and is concerned with the extent to which the state regulates all aspects of the work relationship. Winkler is more concerned with the degree of state intervention in the whole range of socioeconomic activities and institutions. For the Webbs the state is to play the major role in the administration of social and economic justice, although there is absolutely no question of the state's activities being conceived as 'coercive' or operating to the advantage of any set of 'dominant interests'. Their image of the state is like that of Caesar's wife or Plato's philosopher-kings: above suspicion.

Throughout their analysis of trade unionism there is not only a continued advocacy of the role of law in industrial relations but also a persistent irritation at the failure of both employers and trade unions to appreciate its efficacy as a mode of regulation. It is the trade unionists' 'sturdy independence, naive self-complacency and extremely narrow outlook on affairs' which makes the Webbs 'despair of making any middle-class student realise the strength and persistency of this disinclination ... to call in outside counsel' (p. 267). And if trade unions or capitalists persist in their 'sturdy independence' there is always the law. The extent to which the Webbs were prepared to underwrite the role of law in socioeconomic affairs is illustrated by their position on three key issues: legally enforceable collective agreements, compulsory arbitration, and state direction of economic resources.

'Free collective bargaining' is the symbolic keystone of liberal collectivism. The legal enforceability of such agreements under contract law was, despite some qualifications, clearly favoured by the Webbs. They recognised the inflexibility of legal regulation compared with collective bargaining but nevertheless advocated legally binding agreements with the proviso that sanctions for breaking the agreement be included in the agreement itself. 'To this definitely restricted liability no Trade Union need object, provided that it were given ... the corresponding right to recover the penalty from its members in default, and provided that the Employers' Association were made reciprocally responsible to the Trade Union for the defaults of particular employers' (p. 535). (8)

This statement not only reflects their commitment to 'legal enactment' but, more importantly, illustrates the extent to which they saw social institutions such as trade unions and employers' associations as being disciplinary agents, operating, in effect, on behalf of the state. Both Winkler and Crouch lay emphasis on this corporatist strategy while the central thesis argued by Panitch (1977) is that the integrative ideological commitment of the British Labour Party has consistently operated to anaesthetise labour protest. Tactics designed to subordinate labour, whether ideological or legal-coercive, are central to the stability of corporatist structure.

However, the Webbs' commitment to legally enforceable collective bargaining is not entirely unequivocal, for they are doubtful that it can ensure economic justice and are concerned with the extent to which it can operate contrary to the general interests of society. They write of 'the half-conscious admission that neither employers nor employed are morally free to ignore the interest of the community as a whole' (p. 219). By the end of their analysis this 'half-conscious admission' had developed into an endorsement of coercive state intervention: in the event of a major dispute collective bargaining is to be superceded by 'some form of compulsory arbitration', for trade unions must accept that collective bargaining 'will become increasingly subject to the fundamental condition that the business of the community must not be interfered with' (p. 816). Not even the most legally coercive aspects of Barbara Castle's 'In Place of Strife' (1969) or those of the 1971 Industrial Relations Act went as far as this in subordinating collective bargaining to the law.

Indeed, the Webbs were prepared to go beyond the normal use of compulsory arbitration as a solution to deadlocked negotiations, for it was also viewed as a suitable addition to more conventional modes of rule-making. In Flanders's (1970) terms, they see it as another method of job regulation. Thus, in their discussion of how to overcome inflexibility of legalistic codes of behaviour, they suggest that 'there does not seem to be any impossibility in the rules being made and amended by the fiat of an executive department, a local authority or a compulsory arbitration court for the particular industry' (p. 799). Such rules are to have the force of law, and would retain 'the rigidity, impartiality and universality with which [the rule] is applied' (p. 806), while gaining in flexibility compared with the more conventional specific legal regulation. Such a proposal is clearly comparable to the device of the 'enabling act' which permits wide-ranging executive licence to act without recourse to Parliament. Their use, as Winkler (1975) has stressed, can lead to executive suppression of law, and they are a central weapon in the corporatist armoury. The Webbs' suggestion indicates the extent to which they are prepared to vest non-parliamentary representative institutions with such powers: their industrial democracy might amount to no more than a flexible, legal autocracy.

Finally, apart from legal regulation of trade unionism, in the broader field of economic and industrial policy the collectivists similarly seek 'a conscious adjustment of the resources of the community' in order to achieve the 'highest possible efficiency' (p. 599). Ten years ago this might have been taken as a covert reference to the nationalisation or municipalisation of industry, but now it bears close resemblance to what has been described as the state's directive role in industry (Winkler, 1976, p. 105).

There will be a clear-cut division of industrial authority based on conventional roles. Not only will trade unions continue to insist on the 'horizontal cleavage' in the occupational structure between workers and management and be vehemently opposed to both profit-sharing and any interference whatsoever in the wages system (pp. 550-2), but, furthermore, they will not be expected to play any part in the management of industry in a 'democratic state' (p. 818). The role of the trade unions is to determine and police the terms and conditions of employment, not to decide what is to be produced - a task allocated to consumers - and not to interfere with the 'directors of industry' who decide how to provide such goods and services. However, this model of pluralistic responsibility stops some way short of the voluntarism of 'liberal collectivism' (Crouch, 1977, p. 30). For above the trade unions, the consumers and the industrial and commercial moguls 'stands the community itself. To its elected representatives and trained civil service is entrusted the duty of perpetually considering the permanent interests of the State as a whole' (p. 822). This indicates the degree to which the independence and responsibilities of the actors in the collectivist society will be prescribed by the state. Indeed, it is not unlikely that the Webbs' institutional separation of roles would be regulated by law or, perhaps, by one of the numerous standing committees of trained civil servants designed to ensure administrative order and justice.

(iii) The nature of labour organisation

The third part of the 'corporatist syndrome' is the development of collectivised but managerially oriented labour organisations. According to Crouch, this manifests itself both in the encouragement of union organisation and in its establishment as a legal (rather than social) institution. But this legitimation of trade unionism by the dominant interests will be tolerated only so long as it remains ideologically supportive of managerial authority and values. In short, corporatist trade unionism is the functional equivalent of what is usually called 'company' or 'house' unionism.

The Webbs' ideal conception of trade unionism is clearly portrayed in the last chapter of 'Industrial Democracy' (pp. 807ff.): it will consist of occupational associations staffed by a civil service of technical, professional and administrative experts operating as a quasi-autonomous factory inspectorate. Until the full emergence of the collectivist state trade unions will continue to be engaged in negotiation, though in the main the latter will be conducted 'with the cordial cooperation of the secretary of the Employers' Association' (p. 825) rather than in the form of wasteful confrontations. Increasingly, trade unions will become preoccupied with occupational standards of competence, improving professional equipment, the education of 'masters', the provision of technical education, improving the status of members and giving advice on the wider aspects of social and economic policy affecting the working man. In order to fulfil these 'particular social functions in the best possible way' (p. 816) there will have to be contingent changes to the structure of trade unions. Foremost among these are a much greater professionalism and a considerable increase in the degree of centralisation of authority. In particular, local autonomy in 'trade matters' will have to be ceded to the national executive. 'The Trade Unionism of the future will, therefore, be co-extensive with its craft, national in its scope, centralised in its administration, and served by an expert official staff of its own' (p. 834).

The underlying rationale for these expectations lies in the Webbs' almost obsessive concern with efficiency in the expenditure of social energies. In industrial relations this could best be achieved by reducing industrial conflict to the 'administration' of the employer-employee relationship. Thus, the highly specialised cotton unions were held up as an example of 'good practice'. The Webbs admired their 'federalism' (different unions represented different occupations in the cotton industry, ensuring a clear articulation of interests), their acceptance of some managerial values, their pressure on employers to introduce new methods in order to increase productivity and their use of professional expertise in collective bargaining which, in cotton, 'approaches the ideal' (p. 204). (9) For the most part, however, collective bargaining is subject to continual criticism - the use of local 'non-commissioned officers' rather than a 'salaried civil service' (p. 182), and the failure to operate proper procedures (cf. Donovan, 1968) being singled out for particular attention. These, together with other deficiencies noted previously, mean that, generally, collective bargaining 'must be regarded as extremely imperfect' (p. 204). The significance of the employment of professionals to the collectivist, or for that matter to corporatist strategy, is highlighted in the Webbs' advocacy of the use of 'inexpensive experts' in the arbitration process: 'two professional men seldom find any difficulty in agreeing upon an identical award' (p. 236). Peace, it would seem, can be achieved through the subordination of interests to science.

The Webbs' emphasis on the need to centralise trade union authority is at the centre of their reform programme to ensure the 'managerial effectiveness' of trade union organisational structures. Thus, for example, they are opposed to the use of the referendum (except for the approval of strike action) as a decision-making process; they are highly critical of local branch autonomy since this only causes disputes and lockouts and undermines the credibility and authority of the national executives. This raises the question of how to facilitate trade union organisational control over the membership. One development praised by the Webbs is the centralisation of strike funds which has the effect of pre-empting localised action until approved by the central authorities. Another, more compelling, constraint is the closed shop. The Webbs' view is that, 'in its fullest development', collective bargaining implies 'compulsory Trades Unionism' (p. 534) and, provided there is due regard for individual liberty, such a development can only be beneficial, for 'the trade union must provide, in its constitution, some means of securing the obedience of all its members to the regulations decided upon by the majority' (p. 206). Such control becomes critical once collective agreements become legally enforceable and compulsory arbitration comes into regular use.

However, while trade unions are to have powers over their membership, their capacity for autonomous action is to be constrained. The Webbs' formal insistance in the countervailing power of trade unions is deceptive: the supremacy of the state at the level of policy-making and the central role accorded to law in the regulation of employment relationships would permit little scope for autonomous trade union action. In addition, the envisioned transformation of trade union protest into the technocratic servicing of uneconomic and inefficient industrial practice clearly eliminates any overtly political role for trade unionism. Indeed, the Webbs categorically deny that politics has any place in trade unionism. They claim that trade unionism had ceased to be influenced by any of the socialist ideas of Owen or Marx (p. 402) and therefore that socialist ideology will not be considered as an 'assumption' of trade unionism. And in their later remarks they complain, in what is possibly the most breath-taking passage of the whole book, that the 'weakness and inefficiency' of the contemporary trade union organisation and leadership springs 'not only from their extremely imperfect structure, but also from an entire misapprehension of their proper function' (p. 838). This astonishing assertion is based on the fact that any given trade union membership includes representatives of all shades of political opinion and that therefore trade union consideration of political questions - such as resolutions about economic or social policy - constitute a 'waste of time and a dissipation of energy over extraneous matters' (p. 839). While the dominant interests which orchestrate a corporatist strategy can be expected to minimise the political functions of trade unions, it seems likely that only in a fully developed dictatorship would the role of trade unions be as circumscribed as this. According to Winkler and Crouch, a corporate state could be ushered in without the degree of trade union subordination indicated by the Webbs' comments.

(iv) The criteria of income distribution and administration

Finally, to the last of the four elements of the corporatist strategy: the application of 'equity' as a moral criterion and of 'rationality' as a technical criterion in the administration of rewards and the distribution of national income. Crouch suggests that inequality of rewards is legitimated by reference to some notion of the 'just wage' rather than being explained in terms of the outcome of market forces and individual differences - in this respect, a corporatist wage policy is likely to intervene not only to curb the worst excesses of market forces, but also to establish the criteria upon which changes in the level of reward or the structure of inequality may be based. The critical feature which differentiates the corporatist from the 'socialist' strategy is the former's insistence on the maintenance of the structure of inequality: changes take place in the criteria governing this structure, but the structure itself remains.

The Webbs may be seen as endorsing the normative criteria which inform this corporatist conception of 'distributive justice'. The formal logic of their predictions concerning the gradual emergence of a collectivist 'national wages policy' rests on two empirical observations and the adoption of a particular strategy by trade unions in order to accommodate these expected empirical developments. The empirical observations are, first, the development of 'Great Industry' as the major producers in capitalist society, and, second, the emergence of the 'Doctrine of the Living Wage' to replace the 'Doctrine of Supply and Demand' as the 'fundamental assumption' of trade union wage policies (pp. 559ff.). The net effect of these developments will be an increasing preference on the part of trade unions to use the 'Method of Legal Enactment' rather than the 'Method of Collective Bargaining' as a means of enforcing terms and conditions of employment.

The development of large-scale organisation is seen by the Webbs as one which, while it follows the logic of economic effectiveness, has also been stimulated by trade union policies which insist on the establishment of 'Common Rules' throughout an industry or trade. Hence, the rise of 'Great Industry, with its bureaucratic hierarchy of salaried officials' (p. 558) is favoured by trade unionism because it eliminates the worst excesses of 'small masters' and recalcitrant employers. For trade unions, small is not beautiful; it simply means lower wages, poorer conditions and irresponsible management.

The second empirical observation is considerably more problematic. This is because it is never clear whether the Webbs themselves are convinced that a belief in the provision of a minimum standard of living for all workers has become the policy of trade unionism, or whether it is merely another of the many 'rhetorical aspects' (p. 145) of trade unionism. No matter; the Webbs certainly wanted to believe it was becoming the dominant trade union policy and conducted their analysis accordingly. They identify it as being 'definitely adopted' following the strikes by the match girls and the dockers in 1889 (pp. 584ff.) and claim that organised workers, 'deep down in their hearts', have always felt that 'wages must be so fixed' (p. 587) as to ensure a living wage for all workers. And, as if to emphasise that this is a demand for equity, not equality, they add that 'there is a growing feeling, not confined to trade unionists, that the best interests of the community can only be attained by deliberately securing, to each section of workers, those conditions which are necessary for the continuous and efficient fulfillment of its particular function in the social machine' (p. 590). (10) This passage implies far more than it says: it presupposes a rejection of both collective bargaining and free enterprise as well as an acceptance of direct state intervention and the maintenance of a hierarchy of income distribution.

The consequence of these two empirical observations is a predicted increase in the use of legal enactment. Since the maintenance of 'Common Rules' in the 'Great Industry' is dependant on the countervailing power of trade unionism, such terms can be ensured for the unorganised unskilled workers only with the aid of the state. Indeed, the belief in the need to establish a set of national minima, 'resting as it does upon the assumption that the conditions of employment require to be deliberately fixed, naturally puts the State in the position of arbitrator' (p. 596). (11) Thus the Webbs account for the ineluctable rise of 'corporatist' policies which are seemingly endorsed by the trade unions. (This is by no means an unfamiliar theme: both Carpenter (1976) and Panitch (1976) identify such leanings among the leadership of the TUC in the 1930s and 1940s.

However, despite this formal logic, there is a more fundamental and compelling theme which runs throughout the Webbs' predictions of a legally created system of national minima for all occupational groups: this is its efficacy as a method of ensuring the maximum utilization of resources. It is this theme which is central to their critique of collective bargaining, their advocacy of the criterion of equity in the 'Doctrine of the Living Wage' and their endorsement of inequality in the distribution of national income.

First, the rejection of collective bargaining is a natural corrollary of the Webbs' critique of laissez-faire forces. 'Wherever the economic conditions of the parties concerned are unequal, legal freedom of contract merely enables the superior in strategic strength to dictate the terms' (p. 217), and so long as this imbalance remains the only solution is the 'deliberate decision of the community expressed in legislative enactment' (p. 221). In addition, imbalances in power between different sections means that collective bargaining operates to the disadvantage of the lower paid and ill organised. It seems clear that the Webbs sought to eliminate what Crouch (1977, pp. 51-7) refers to as the opportunism and essential narrowness of collective bargaining in the allocation of wages. This inequity and irrationality of collective bargaining (12) also threatens the 'national interest', since the collective welfare of the community demands 'that no section of workers should be reduced to conditions which are positively inconsistent with industrial or civic efficiency' (p. 590).

This reference to 'efficiency' underlines the remarkably mechanistic criteria upon which the national minima were to be calculated. In practice, the lofty moral tenor of the 'Doctrine of the Living Wage' is translated, almost literally, into the provision of such food, clothing and housing as will ensure the maintenance of full physical and mental health for each trade. This is not without its difficulties, for 'there are practically no scientific data from which we can compute the needs of particular occupations', and it would, in any case, be extremely difficult to compare 'the muscular exhaustion of the steel-maker, plater or flint-glass maker, with the intensity of mental application of the cotton-spinner, engraver, or linotype operator' (p. 592). When the Webbs state that the 'Collectivist insists on the need for a conscious and deliberate organisation of society based, not on vested interests or the chances of the fight, but on the scientifically ascertained needs of each section of citizens' (p. 598), they mean precisely that: equity in the system of rewards requires that the social, mental and physiological resources contributed to the social machine by the individual be returned to him by the employer in order to ensure his continued performance. All this emphasis on the precise calculation of needs in relation to actual physical inputs suggests that the Webbs' philosophical sympathies lay uncomfortably close to the values of biological selection central to the work of their American contemporary, Frederick Winslow Taylor (1947). (13)

Such sympathies are also reflected in the Webbs' acceptance of the need to maintain a hierarchy of reward. First, 'there are sound reasons ... why the better-off sections should not forgo their superior incomes' (p. 593), for only thus can the necessary stimulus to improve productivity and ensure the optimum use of human resources be maintained. And second, as the Webbs are careful to point out, even in the collectivist utopia trade unionism does not 'furnish any complete scheme of distribution', since the 'owners of the material instruments of production must, under any system of society' (pp. 831-2) retain control over rent, land and capital. Property rights, together with the chance economic advantages of 'intellect or physical strength', seem to be the legitimate bases for differential income.

While the degree of technocratic lunacy in some of the Webbs' proposals has never surfaced in the concrete wage policies of the 1960s and 1970s, there are symptomatic parallels. The NBPI sought to institutionalise the productivity criterion, emphasised the legitimacy of income differentials based on differences in skill and responsibility, made frequent reference to low pay as a criterion of exemption from the prices and incomes policy, led the way in the popularisation of measured day work and job evaluation and, like the Webbs, was ambivalent about what to do with prices and profits (Crouch, 1977, pp. 84-128). Similarly, the pay policies of the 1970 Conservative administration sought to ensure 'equity' by stabilising the existing pattern of pay relations and rested precariously on the assumption that moral consensus and national harmony depended on all incomes (except profits) rising at the same rate. The 'heavy corporatism in this strategy' found its most coherent expression in the 'threshold agreements' (Crouch, 1977, pp. 136, 129-42). Despite the change of government in 1974 the attempt to ensure stability in the pyramid of income inequality continued almost unchanged with the provisions of the Social Contract. One significant change has been the attempt to eliminate the 'manifest inequity' of blanket threshold payments (which technically widened differentials) by the introduction of a combination of flat rate and percentage increases in earnings.

Although the objectives of such contemporary policies are concerned with economic survival rather than with the Webbs' collectivist future, the primal value which informs both strategies is that of economic efficiency. It is not the system which is in question but the viability of the prevailing socioeconomic arrangements and institutions as mechanisms for ensuring social justice. Throughout the Webbs' analysis there are detailed accounts of the worst effects of capitalist behaviour - such as 'sweating', 'parasitism' and the generalised exploitation of weaker groups. But capitalism itself, as a moral system which produces and indeed legitimates such forms of social injustice, is not condemned. And while the Webbs are convinced that society should guarantee a minimum standard of living for all its citizens, this conviction does not constitute an appeal to basic human rights. Theirs is an appeal to economic efficiency. Thus, 'the first necessity for obtaining the greatest possible efficiency of the community as a whole, is to so control the struggle for existence that no section is pushed by it into parasitism or degradation' (p. 789). What is wrong with capitalism is not that it produces such social evils, but that it is bad economics to do so. Capitalism, for the Webbs, is simply a wasteful and inappropriate means of organising the economy. And, similarly, what is right about the institutionalisation of the 'National Minimum' of health, leisure and wages is not simply that it eliminates social evils but that by so doing there is an increase in the effective use of economic resources. Their vision is not that of a humanistic welfare state in a sea of broken soil pipes and over-burdened poorhouses, but of a well oiled social machine monitored by bureaucrats and serviced by a metronomic trade union organisation. Collectivism, like corporatism, lays emphasis on ends, not means. Thus it is an appeal for the maximum utilisation of resources which provides the Webbs with the necessary logic for their use of the state as a major actor in all spheres of socioeconomic life; and it is the calculus of economic growth which condemns both collective bargaining and free enterprise - a constant theme in the pro-corporatist political programmes of the 1960s and 1970s. (14)

CORPORATISM OR COLLECTIVISM?

Clearly, there is a remarkable similarity between the so-called corporatist developments in the 1960s and 1970s with the proposals detailed by the Webbs in their 1898 account of the future of industrial relations and, by implication, of British capitalism. At one level, it is difficult to escape the prescience of their predictions - their collectivist vision differs only in detail from the general characterisation of corporatism as a system which 're-engages the policy with the economy and develops new forms of ideological legitimation' (Crouch, 1977, p. 34).

The two most striking similarities are: (i) the character of the institutional changes or reforms deemed to be necessary and appropriate, and (ii) the appeal to apparently neutral rational criteria as a guide to economic efficiency and social justice. The identification of this 'value consensus' in the underlying assumptions of both collectivist and corporatist stratagems is of central importance in accounting for the ambiguous political colouring of these modes of social organisation. Ostensibly, what differentiates collectivism from corporatism is their respective political labels. Collectivism represents the gradual institutionalisation of social and economic democracy; in contrast, corporatism represents the gradual institutionalisation of social and economic autocracy. At the level of ideology, they appear to offer alternative 'solutions' to the 'problems of capitalism'. However, at the level of policy, their strategies are remarkably similar: both pursue similar goals; both emphasise ends rather than means; and both utilise the state and the law to create and maintain similar economic and industrial relations institutions in their pursuit of the 'national' or 'community' interest.

Thus, we arrive at the paradox of the political alternatives offered by corporatism and collectivism: both in one sense can be seen as being fundamentally apolitical in character. (15) Philosophically, their only concern is with the grade of oil required to keep the machine running; running repairs can be carried out but there is no question of stopping to look which way the machine is actually going. The justification for such a statement is not hard to find.

First, there is what we might call the 'evidence of the advocates' regarding the nature of collectivism and corporatism. The Webbs are constantly seeking in their analysis to transcend 'mere' political considerations: trade unions are seen to be wasting their energies by becoming embroiled in political issues. And they see industrial conflicts - as Dahrendorf (1959) was later to argue - becoming increasingly separated from political conflicts in 'post-capitalist' society. The whole thrust of their argument is actively to translate what is manifestly a political issue - how do we organise society? - into a manageable administrative process. In consequence, the problem is not identified as a political problem, but as a technical problem. Thus, the central executive role accorded to the state does not trouble the Webbs - the state is obviously the most appropriate administrative organisation to 'manage' society. Similarly, the introduction of a (coercive) legal framework to regulate employment relations does not raise any questions about the political appropriateness of such controls, since they are addressing themselves to a technical problem. Collectivism was conceived not overtly as a political alternative to capitalism but as a logical rational-economic development which could and would 'administer' capitalism.

Similarly, in the work of both Winkler and Crouch, while corporatism is always portrayed as authoritarian, what remains unclear is the political tone of this authoritarianism. Winkler points out that corporatism is both anti-capitalist and anti-socialist and, in the earlier article with Pahl, suggested that the coming corporatism will be 'fascism with a human face'. The clarity of this image, however, is not reflected in Winkler's conceptualisation of corporatism where its distinctiveness rests too heavily on the directive role of the state in the economic affairs of a privately owned industrial structure. His four principles - order, unity, nationalism and success - despite careful elaboration cannot be seen as distinctive elements of a political ideology specific to corporatism. (16) But regardless of these difficulties, Winkler himself is concerned with the apolitical character of corporatism. As an empirical phenomenon, it is clear that he sees corporatist developments as the most likely pragmatic response to the continuing crises of British capitalism; in this respect he is almost at one with the Webbs in predicting that the structural changes taking place in British society are contingent on perceived economic necessities. It is the latter which he sees as constraining the choices available to political decision-makers to such an extent that the 'rule of law becomes threatened with the use of such devices as 'enabling acts': the latter become part of the 'technical equipment' used by a directive state in order to manage the economy. In the heady atmosphere of 'management by crisis' the objective consequences of such acts for the rule of law become justifiable costs in the search for economic survival.

Unlike Winkler, Crouch is not particularly concerned to single out corporatism as a specific mode of social and economic organisation: the fact that he identifies a series of possible corporatist structures graded in terms of increasing degrees of state control indicates the wide range of political structures in which it can be found. Thus, having explicitly acknowledged the importance of identifying increases in state intervention as being either 'right' or 'left' (Crouch, 1977, p. 13) he points out that, in the 1960s and 1970s, just as the Labour governments advocated corporatist strategies under the rhetoric of socialism, so the Conservatives adopted corporatist policies under the guise of market liberalism (p. 239).

In addition, Crouch also tends to see corporatist policies and institutions as pragmatic coping strategies developed by the dominant interests as responses to economic crises (pp. 34 and 255ff.). Consequently, despite the different 'types' Crouch identifies, the empirical character of corporatism - and, in particular, its political complexion - is contingent not on a coherent political programme or ideology but on the arbitrary conjunction of three variables: the specific requirements of a particular economic situation, i.e. the 'problem', the political party in power, and the circumstances in which that party comes into power. Corporatism can thus be seen as the ideological label used to characterise the political anomie of 'consensus politics' or 'group politics' (Beer, 1965).

Second, there is the fact that collectivism and corporatism share a commitment to the value of economic efficiency. This not only underlines the absence of any distinctive political values but also goes some way to explaining why this is necessarily the case. In both cases political choices are subordinated to what are seen to be economic necessities, and in consequence political debate is superceded by the discussion of administrative possibilities.

The significance of the apolitical character of collectivism and corporatism can now be put into context. The doctrines of capitalism and socialism insist, in their different ways, that man is the controller of his own destiny - in particular, that man can and should dominate economic organisation. In contrast, the logic of the Webbs' vision and that implicit in so-called corporatist solutions is that man should service the economic machine, not control it. The crude pragmatism that this engenders - whether we call it group politics, creeping corporatism or bureaucratic collectivism - means that the basic issues of social and political philosophy pale into insignificance compared with the problem of developing the most effective computer simulations for the allocation of capital and labour resources.

If this conclusion is accurate then it is necessary to re-examine the original question of how to characterise the changing nature of British capitalism. The collectivist structures predicted by the Webbs, in so far as they are empirically identifiable, can readily be seen as the outcome of corporatist strategies. Given this, it is difficult to resist the contention that the stress on the seemingly specious alternatives offered by collectivism and corporatism masks a more singular structural transformation; and that, as labels, they are part of the ideological cosmetics which invariably accompany any process of institutional change.

One solution is to return to the security of a Marxist interpretation and suggest that collectivism and corporatism are merely marginal and illusory deviations in the great circle of capitalist development and demise (Anderson et al., 1965; Westergaard, 1977). This, however, would be to minimise the significance of the distinctive ideological and institutional changes which have taken place and thereby to ignore the complexities of changes in industrial capitalism. The alternative is to opt for a sociological solution which, while it will certainly be narrower in scope, might well provide a more insightful account of what has been happening.

In his account of capitalism Weber (1964) stressed that the most pervasive feature of contemporary European development is the force of rationalisation - ultimately, barring charismatic accidents, he foresees this as the dominant social ethic which will characterise industrial society. It finds its clearest form in bureaucratic modes of organisation and its purest expression in the application of legal norms. This framework illuminates a number of issues in the collectivist-corporatist correspondence and provides a different logic to the changing character of British industrial relations.

First, the apparently antithetical political alternatives offered by collectivism and corporatism: this is explicable in terms of Weber's analysis of rationalisation, since (and this is part of his quarrel with Marx) it is a mistake to view socialism as an alternative to capitalism. On the contrary, socialism represents a higher level of development in the elimination of competition and the application of rational criteria in social organisation and the allocation of resources. Socialism will herald the triumph not only of democratic, egalitarian values but also of bureaucratic values, so that, 'far from being the antithesis of capitalism', it is 'instead its malign intensification' (Nisbet, 1967, p. 293). Rationalisation not only intrudes into all aspects of social life, but ultimately subordinates all values to technical, legal norms. Thus, while seemingly distinctive political ideologies may continue to be formulated, they are but hollow decorations on the bureaucratic rock cake. The Webbs, as has been shown, were fond of such confections and would have been delighted by such corporatist creations as incomes policy, the Trade Union and Labour Relations Act and the National Enterprise Board.

The second feature requiring explanation is why corporatist and collectivist strategies generate similar modes of institutional control over both management and labour. The reasoning offered above is that this reflects an underlying consensus on the priority accorded to the social value of 'economic efficiency'. This encourages the application of mechanistic and technical logics in the analysis of perceived socioeconomic needs and problems - the solutions, as both Crouch and Winkler indicate, pay less and less heed to the traditional political freedoms of liberal democracy.

This strain between the demand for democratic government and the demand for bureaucratic centralisation was, of course, one of the central dilemmas which occupied Weber's analysis. He saw it as being symptomatic of the double-edged character of the general process of rationalisation within industrial capitalism.

As what the Webbs called 'the Great Industry' emerges, so, according to Weber, its controllers are forced to decide between the maintenance of free market conditions and the administrative logic of centralised control: the modern corporation in its search for predictability and calculability seeks to minimise all elements of uncertainty, whether this be within capital, labour, raw material or consumer markets. Initially, such stabilisation is achieved through 'internal' bureaucratisation of procedures and processes and, where possible, of markets (cf. Galbraith, 1969). The move to reliance on state regulation is merely a logical progression in the process of institutionalising 'economic democracy'. The increasing control over 'free competition' upon which this 'uncertainty-reduction' is dependent is legitimated in terms of an appeal to 'economic efficiency' - as is the role of the state which is necessary, for example, to ensure that economic enterprise is not wasted in 'unregulated competition'. Hence any institutional change which increases the predictability (i.e. control) of socioeconomic behaviour will be welcomed by 'the Great Industry'. In this respect, the extent to which capitalism manages to eliminate competition becomes a measure of its success as a mode of economic organisation. Thus encroaching rationalisation can be seen to be accompanied by the elevation of the value of economic efficiency as a central theme within a unitary political ideology - and its institutionalisation, whether in a collectivist 'Labor Code' or a corporatist incomes policy, would seem to be indicative of a major, albeit insidious, advance of bureaucratisation.

The difficulties encountered by political opposition to this process are highlighted in Weber's concern with the potentially destructive impact of bureaucratic rationales on the democratic process itself. Weber and, of course, Michels (1959) were concerned with the fact that the effective mobilisation of opposition seemed to depend on the development of similar bureaucratic forms of organisation which, paradoxically, tended to pre-empt the pursuit of genuine alternative solutions. One of the conditions of 'success' for opposition movements, such as trade unions or Labour parties, is that they contain their demands within a framework which is acceptable to dominant elites. In practice this involves the recognition, if not the acceptance, of at least some of the values of the dominant elites: the trade unions and the Labour Party have long since embraced the value of economic efficiency (Panitch, 1976).

Third, the general significance of Weber's account is illustrated by the narrow context within which the collectivist-corporatist arguments have been developed: the Webb's vision and the latter-day corporatist prophecies are confined to British capitalism. (17) This has engendered an unwarranted emphasis on the significance of political ideology at the expense of social values and isolates the British experience from what is happening in Europe (cf. Fox, 1978). While the Webbs' anglophilia is understandable, the failure of the proponents of corporatism to consider the impact of the European Economic Community - which could easily be seen as Jean Monnet's monument to Weber's account of rationalisation in Western civilisation - prevents them from examining the wider social influences on the changing character of British industrial capitalism. It is the wider features clearly, which are germane to Weber's contentions.

INDUSTRIAL RELATIONS AND THE LAW

Some of the more important implications of the foregoing analysis can now be explored.

At the level of 'domestic industrial relations' it is no longer possible to view the role of law as one of providing a procedural framework within which the major actors, trade unions and employers, conduct their negotiations through the process of collective bargaining. Indeed, it seems likely that we have seen the end of collective bargaining as a major method of job regulation. In future developments - whether one sees them as collectivist or corporatist in character - the state's acknowledged role in national economic management will provide sufficient legitimation for whatever legal regulation seems appropriate. In a situation deemed to be one of continuing economic crisis, further encroachments by the state seem irresistible.

It could be argued that legislation relating, for example, to health and safety at work or new forms of incomes policy actually generate new items for the bargaining agenda, and that collective bargaining will not be eclipsed by legal regulation. This seems to be a delusion, for, more realistically, such developments would merely be indicative of the extent to which trade unions had become the policemen and enforcers of state welfare and incomes legislation. Winkler has argued that this is what is already happening and the Webbs suggested that it ought to happen.

The latter presupposes that trade union compliance with such developments is unproblematic. To what extent are trade unions prepared to accept such changes? In the Webbs' analysis it was recognised that the technocratic trade unionism they favoured was in part dependent on the emergence of a professional bureaucratic leadership operating with a non-conflictual social welfare model of trade union purpose. While trade union bureaucrats continue to be castigated in somewhat ritualistic terms (Lane, 1974), their social values have not yet been modified to the degree and direction required for the Webbs' expectations to be fulfilled. The evidence for such an assertion is circumstantial but none the less compelling: the trade unions' continued preference for traditional and charismatic forms of leadership - in itself a significant barrier to rationalisation - their reluctance to employ professional staff, and their patent refusal to leave the arena of politics to the politicians combine to underline the 'failure' of trade unionism to adopt the Webbian model of trade union purpose. This has obviously important consequences for future 'corporatist' developments which, in the absence of state coercion, depend upon similar accommodations.

However, demands for a return to collective bargaining cannot be viewed as anything more than a transitory appeal to traditional modes of operation by the more conservative trade unions: the potential for collective action to defend collective bargaining seems minimal. Both the white-collar sector - which is now of considerable significance - and, in particular, public employees seem to be increasingly committed to some form of incomes policy. All that the present character of trade union officialdom suggests is that the rationalisation of industrial relations is likely to be accompanied by considerable industrial and political conflict.

Second, concerning the role of law, it has been demonstrated, once again, that the social functions of law can be evaluated only in relation to the socio-political context within which it has been formulated. The Webbs' proposals were designed both to humanise capitalism - in that they sought to legislate against the destructive exploitation of employees - and at the same time to ensure the effective use of economic resources. The social 'cost' of such an exercise would have been a reduction in trade union and employer self-determination and, in all probability, the establishment of a legally enforceable national wage hierarchy.

That they did not consider the political implications of such developments to be of significance reflects their blind faith in the technical ethic of 'legal-rational' authority: the law cannot be seen merely as a technical or administrative aid available to those dispensing 'justice' since it invariably embodies social values and expectations relating to how citizens ought to behave. The Webbs' failure to recognise these covert moral imperatives prevents them seeing that their industrial democracy might amount, as suggested previously, to no more than legal autocracy. Similarly, as Winkler has shown, the perhaps necessary managerial flexibility inherent in enabling acts masks a potential threat to the rule of law itself.

Hence the resort to legal regulation in industrial relations as a solution to seemingly intractable economic problems could result in a transformation of the political character of society. This is not to say that the use of law in itself is the cause of such changes - legal regulation of employment relationships has long been with us - but rather that the social and political acceptability of legal solutions to major socioeconomic issues reflects significant changes in dominant social values. This predilection for legal-rational strategies underlines the potential encroachment of rationalisation as the dominant ethic in industrial relations. It can be illustrated by the 'low-pay dispute' of February 1979. The demand for a £60 minimum wage was not simply based on the notion of a 'living wage' but had been calculated as a proportion of the national average wage: in effect, the trade unions were saying that the state ought to recognise the socioeconomic status of the low paid hospital ancillary workers as two-thirds that of the 'national average employee' and ought to reward them accordingly. This is only a short step from accepting a national job evaluation scheme which could provide a 'rational' basis for institutionalised inequality. While such a development might meet with considerable resistance, it represents the logical objective of any strategy designed to control rewards which rests upon an appeal to 'legal-rational' criteria for its justification.

Finally, this directs attention to the longer-term implications of such legal regulation for the social character of the employment relationship. If the state becomes the dominant actor in the creation and enforcement of both the procedural and substantive rules governing industrial relations, then the traditional basis of industrial discipline and order will be undermined. Historically, the latter has been maintained through market power and legitimated with reference to 'managerial prerogatives' which in turn rest on the legitimacy of property rights.

In the process of marshalling support for its increasing role in economic management, the state has had to demonstrate its willingness to subordinate the 'freedoms' of both employers and employees. Thus the progressive limitation of trade union and employee bargaining activities has been ostenisbly balanced with increasing restrictions on the exercise of employer prerogatives: market 'freedom' is being rationalised into employment rights which are legitimated with reference to democratic-rational criteria. The statutes regulating redundancy, contracts of employment, various forms of discrimination, unfair dismissal and the range of trade union and trade unionists' rights constitute legal norms constraining, if not subverting, traditional employer rights.

It would be misleading to view such developments as merely the stirrings of an emergent legal paternalism. Indeed, such employment rights are likely to engender a greater dependency in the employment relationship than exists at present, for any challenge to the rules would become a challenge to the law and thus to the state as guarantor of economic justice and protector of the national interest. This, in combination with a legally institutionalised structure of income inequality, could provide the platform upon which the more insidious elements of the Webbs' economic democracy could be built. (18)

NOTES

I would like to thank Geoff Mungham and George Thomason for their helpful comments and advice in the preparation of this paper.

1 The Webbs note that Brentano (1870), in his classic history of the guilds, had argued that their fundamental purpose was the 'maintenance of the existing legal and customary regulations of the trade' (Webb and Webb, 1898, pp. 247ff.)

2 After the legal success of Grunwick Ltd in appealing against the ACAS recognition recommendation, there were parliamentary proposals to amend the Employment Protection Act in order to prevent the repetition of such appeals. Harry Urwin, chairman of the TUC Employment Policy and Organisation Committee, commenting on these proposals at the 1978 TUC in Brighton, issued a severe warning on the double-edged effect of calling for legal sanctions against recalcitrant employers: such proposals, he argued, would set a precedent for the government to make reciprocal demands for legal sanctions on recalcitrant trade unions or employees.

3 The major statutes relating to the employment relationship are:

Contracts of Employment Act 1963
Redundancy Payments Act 1965
Race Relations Acts 1965, 1968, 1976
Equal Pay Act 1970
Industrial Relations Act 1971
Trade Union and Labour Relations Act 1974
Health and Safety at Work Act 1974
Sex Discrimination Act 1975
Industry Act 1975
Employment Protection Act 1975

Trade Union and Labour Relations (Amendment) Act 1976

See also the Bullock Report (1977).

4 The corporatist thesis is contained in Pahl and Winkler (1974), Winkler (1975, 1976, 1977), Panitch (1976) and Crouch (1977). For comment, elaboration and criticism see Panitch (1977), Schmitter (1974, 1977), Drucker (1977), Cawson (1978), Carpenter (1976), Westergaard (1977) and Brown (1978).

5 See Crouch (1977, pp. 3-43). His framework is considerably more complex than the foregoing indicates: the four corporatist dimensions have been derived by combining elements of Winkler's analysis with the thirteen 'strategic dilemmas' which Crouch suggests are faced by dominant elites in a class society.

6 The use of Royal Commissions was to be the neutron bomb of Webbian Fabianism - Sydney had plans for a permanent secretariat to service them.

7 This and all subsequent page references are to 'Industrial Democracy" (1898).

8 It is therefore no surprise to find that Sydney Webb was opposed to the reform of the Taff Vale judgment which had made trade unions liable for damages in the event of strike action.

9 The Webbs fully endorsed the cotton-weavers' introduction of a competitive exam for the office of general secretary (p. 197) - it represented the beginnings of the professionalisation of trade union officialdom.

10 This passage, like many others in 'Industrial Democracy', is presented as an empirical observation. While the argument being presented is not a direct critique of the Webbs' analysis per se, it is worth noting that their evidence for such statements is often extremely thin and their 'scientific analysis' of trade unionism often far from convincing.

11 This passage is a good example of how the Webbs get from 'what is' to 'what ought to be': while the state may be the obvious institution which enacts and enforces such minimum standards, there seems no logical justification why it should also become the 'natural arbitrator'.

12 Such features have often been cited by Jim Callaghan in his attempts to legitimise incomes policy. For example, the inequity of collective bargaining was one of the central themes of his speech to the TUC in 1977. More recently (February 1977) he described it as 'collective vandalism'.

13 When discussing the benefits of the 'Common Rule' for example, the Webbs (1898, p. 733) state that 'what it does is perpetually stimulate the selection of the most efficient workmen, the best equipped employers, and the most advantageous form of industry'.

14 Even the Liberal Party, despite their influence, have consistently insisted on a statutory incomes policy.

15 This raises uncomfortable echos of Kerr et al.'s (1973) convergence thesis and Bell's (1962) argument about the end of ideology. Although there seem to be parallels, the present argument does not rest on the logic of technological change; the latter can be seen to play an important but not a major role in contemporary developments.

16 In his later accounts Winkler (1977) views corporatism as having

at least two forms: conservative and redistributive. This in itself is indicative of the different political ideologies which can inform the 'corporatist syndrome'.

17 And this in spite of the fact that both Winkler and Crouch place some stress on the role of international trade and finance in generating pressure for the adoption of corporatist strategies in Great Britain.

18 In a contemporary attack on the Webb's prescriptions Belloc (1912) developed his critique in precisely these terms: the title of his book, 'The Servile State', is indicative of the degree to which he identifies the Webbs' as advocates of what we now call corporatism.

BIBLIOGRAPHY

ANDERSON, P., et al. (1965), 'Towards Socialism', London, Panther.
BEER, S.H. (1965), 'Modern British Politics', London, Faber and Faber.
BELL, D. (1962), 'The End of Ideology', New York, Free Press.
BELLOC, H. (1912), 'The Servile State', London and Edinburgh, T.N. Foulis.
BRENTANO, L. (1969), 'History of the Guilds and Trade Unionism', New York, Burt Franklin (originally published 1870).
BROWN, R.K. (1978), From Donovan to where? Interpretations of industrial relations in Britain since 1968, 'British Journal of Sociology', vol. 29, no. 4.
Bullock Report (1977), Department of Trade, 'Report of the Committee of Inquiry on Industrial Democracy', London, HMSO, Cmnd 6706.
CARPENTER, L.P. (1976), Corporatism in Britain, 1930-45, 'Journal of Contemporary History', vol. 11.
CAWSON, Alan (1978), Pluralism, Corporatism and the Role of the State, 'Government and Opposition', vol. 13, no. 2.
CONFEDERATION OF BRITISH INDUSTRY (1966), 'Annual Report for 1965', London, CBI.
CROUCH, C. (1977), 'Class Conflict and the Industrial Relations Crisis', London, Heinemann.
DAHRENDORF, R. (1959), 'Class and Class Conflict in Industrial Society', London, Routledge & Kegan Paul.
DORE, R. (1973), 'British Factory-Japanese Factory', London, Allen & Unwin.
DONOVAN, Lord (1968), 'Report', Royal Commission on Trade Unions and Employers Associations, London, HMSO.
DRUCKER, J.M. (1977), Devolution and Corporatism, 'Government and Opposition', vol. 12.
FLANDERS, A. (1970), 'Management and Unions', London, Faber.
FLANDERS, A. (1974), The Tradition of Voluntarism, 'British Journal of Industrial Relations', vol. 12, no. 3.
FOX, A. (1966), 'Industrial Sociology and Industrial Relations', Royal Commission on Trade Unions and Employers' Associations, Research Paper 3, London, HMSO.
FOX, A. (1978), Corporatism and Industrial Democracy: The Social Origins of Present Form and Methods in Britain and Germany, in Social Science Research Council, 'Industrial Democracy International Views', London, SSRC.

GALBRAITH, J.K. (1969), 'The New Industrial State', Harmondsworth, Penguin.
HUNT, A., ed. (1977), 'Class and Class Structure', London, Lawrence & Wishart.
KAHN-FREUND, O. (1972), 'Labour and the Law', London, Stevens.
KERR, C., DUNLOP, J.T., HARBISON, F.H., MYERS, C.A. (1973), 'Industrialism and Industrial Man', Harmondsworth, Penguin.
LANE, Tony (1974), 'The Union Makes Us Strong', London, Arrow.
MACKENZIE, N. (1978), A New View of the Webb Partnership, 'Times Higher Education Supplement', 19 May 1978. See also 'The Times', 15 May 1978.
MICHELS, R. (1962), 'Political Parties', New York, Free Press.
NISBET, R.A. (1967), 'The Sociological Tradition', London, Heinemann.
PAHL, R.E. and WINKLER, J.T. (1974), The Coming Corporatism, 'New Society', 10 October.
PANITCH, L. (1976), 'Social Democracy and Industrial Militancy', Cambridge University Press.
PANITCH, L. (1977), The Development of Corporatism in Liberal Democracies, 'Comparative Political Studies', vol. 10, no. 1.
SCHMITTER, P.C. (1974), Still the Century of Corporatism, 'Review of Politics', vol. 36.
SCHMITTER, P.C. (1977), Modes of Interest, Intermediation and Models of Societal Change in Western Europe, 'Comparative Political Studies', vol. 10, no. 1.
TAYLOR, F.W. (1947), 'The Principles of Scientific Management', New York, Harper & Row.
WEBB, S. and WEBB, B. (1894), 'The History of Trade Unionism', London, Longmans Green.
WEBB, S. and WEBB, B. (1898), 'Industrial Democracy', London, Longmans Green.
WEBER, M. (1964), 'The Theory of Social and Economic Organisation', edited by Parsons, T. and Henderson, A.M., New York, Free Press.
WEEKES, B., MELLISH, M., DICKENS, L., and LLOYD, J. (1975), 'Industrial Relations and the Limits of Law', Oxford, Blackwell.
WESTERGAARD, J. (1977), Class, Inequality and Corporatism, in Hunt, ed. (1977).
WINKLER, J.T. (1975), Law, Society and Economy: The Industry Act 1975 in Context, 'British Journal of Law and Society', vol. 2.
WINKLER, J.T. (1976), Corporatism, 'Archives Européens de Sociologie', vol. 17.
WINKLER, J.T. (1977), The Corporate Economy: Theory and Administration, in Scase, R., ed., 'Industrial Society: Class, Cleavage and Control', London, Allen & Unwin.

INDEX